# FAMILY BUSINESS IN THE ERA OF INDUSTRIAL GROWTH

The International
Conference on
Business
History 10

# FAMILY BUSINESS IN THE ERA OF INDUSTRIAL GROWTH

## Its Ownership and Management

Proceedings of the Fuji Conference

edited by
AKIO OKOCHI
SHIGEAKI YASUOKA

UNIVERSITY OF TOKYO PRESS

658.045
F 1981

ISBN 4–13–047020–5 (UTP 47200)
ISBN 0–86008–346–2

## ORGANIZING COMMITTEE FOR THE SECOND SERIES INTERNATIONAL CONFERENCE ON BUSINESS HISTORY 1979–1983

Chairman:  Okochi, Akio          (University of Tokyo)
Treasurer:  Watanabe, Hisashi    (Kyoto University)
Secretary:  Yuzawa, Takeshi      (Gakushuin University)
            Daito, Eisuke        (University of Tokyo)
            Hara, Terushi        (Waseda University)
            Ishikawa, Kenjiro    (Doshisha University)
            Kita, Masami         (Soka University)
            Miyamoto, Matao      (Osaka University)
            Udagawa, Masaru      (Hosei University)
Advisory Board:
            Nakagawa, Keiichiro  (The International University of Japan)

            Kobayashi, Kesaji    (Ryukoku University)
            Morikawa, Hidemasa   (Hosei University)
            Yasuoka, Shigeaki    (Doshisha University)
            Yonekawa, Shin-ichi  (Hitotsubashi University)

**Participants**

Project Leader for the Fifth Meeting:
Yasuoka, Shigeaki (Doshisha University)

Asajima, Shoichi
(Senshu University)
Brockstedt, Jürgen
(Freie Universität Berlin)
Chimoto, Akiko
(Doshisha University)
Cusumano, Michael A.
(University of Tokyo)
Daito, Eisuke
(University of Tokyo)
Hara, Terushi
(Waseda University)
Hattori, Tamio
(Institute of Developing Economies)

Hiroyama, Kensuke
(Osaka University)
Ishikawa, Kenjiro
(Doshisha University)
Ito, Shoji
(Institute of Developing Economies)
Kawabe, Nobuo
(Hiroshima University)
Kita, Masami
(Soka University)
Lévy-Leboyer, Maurice
(University of Paris X-Nanterre)

vi

Mishima, Yasuo
(Konan University)
Miyamoto, Matao
(Osaka University)
Morikawa, Hidemasa
(Hosei University)
Nakagawa, Keiichiro
(The International University
of Japan)
Nakamura, Seishi
(Tokyo Keizai University)
Okochi, Akio
(University of Tokyo)

Payne, Peter L.
(University of Aberdeen)
Seoka, Makoto
(Kyoto Gakuen University)
Tucker, Barbara M.
(Rutgers University)
Udagawa, Masaru
(Hosei University)
Watanabe, Hisashi
(Kyoto University)
Yasuoka, Shigeaki
(Doshisha University)
Yuzawa, Takeshi
(Gakushuin University)

# CONTENTS

# PREFACE

The fifth and last meeting of the Second Series International Conference on Business History was held on January 5–8, 1983, at the Fuji Education Center, Shizuoka, Japan, under the auspices of Business History Society of Japan and supported by the Taniguchi Foundation.

The central theme for the fifth meeting was family business in the course of industrialization. No one denies the importance of family business in the business world even at present, its historical role in the course of industrialization of each nation, and the economic power of some families such as zaibatsu or the Rockefeller family, which managed the biggest business enterprises in their countries at one time or another.

Historians often write about family business without a clear definition of this term. However, the concept of family business in one country differs from that in others. When we try to compare the situation of family business within the different countries, and to get some mutual understanding upon the theme, some common yardstick for comparison first of all must be prepared. Because family business is a very broad, complex and historical concept rooted deeply in the social and cultural structure of each nation, hasty bridging or generalization of the concept between different nations will probably lead us into misunderstanding. Although we could forecast the difficulties of international comparison of such a concept as family business, at the same time, the theme seemed to be important and fitting for our project. Accordingly, the organizing committee asked Professor Shigeaki Yasuoka to take the part of project leader. Professor Yasuoka, in co-operation with the organizing committee, designed and organized the fifth meeting.

The following proceedings are a record of the meeting. On behalf of the organizing committee, I would like to express my sincere thanks to Professor Yasuoka for his effort in editing these proceedings and making the summary of the discussions. I would also like to thank the Taniguchi Foundation for its support of both the meetin and the publication of this volume. Lastly, I wish to express my appreciation to Ms. S. Schmidt and Mr. W. Izumi of the University of Tokyo Press for all their labors in producing this volume and preceding volumes. Without their patient labors, these ten volumes of the proceedings could not be published at all.

November 1983

Akio Okochi
General Editor and Chairman of
the Organizing Committee for
the International Conference on
Business History

# INTRODUCTION

The Fifth Meeting of the International Conference on Business History (Second Series) was held on January 5–8, 1983, in Susono, Shizuoka, Japan, under the theme "Family Business in the Formative Era of Big Business: Its Ownership and Management."

In Western society, large family enterprises are becoming a thing of the past. In Japan, the *zaibatsu*, one type of large family enterprise, were dismantled following the Second World War. However, since then attempts to reform them as conglomerates have led to the organization of giant industrial groups. While these groups are not family businesses and have no head office or holding company structure, the foundation for their amalgamation was laid at the time the *zaibatsu* were established.

In developing countries such as South Korea, Taiwan, the Philippines, Thailand, India, Brazil and Argentina, many of which have emerged from being colonies of the Western powers, industrial groups which resemble Japan's former *zaibatsu* have sprung up since the Second World War. Of course there are differences in the structure of society and the manner in which the owner exerts control over management. The manner of amalgamation also varies according to whether the banking system is under the control of government (as for example in South Korea) or not.

In spite of such differences, *zaibatsu*-like industrial groups have sprung up and exert considerable influence on the economy of their countries. But while such private industrial groups promote the economic development of their countries, at the same time they have a bad effect in that they invite an oligopolistic situation in several industrial fields.

In light of these developments, large family businesses are no longer the mainstay of the national economy in developed countries, while in developing countries they play a large and active part in supporting economic development. There is a corresponding substantial variation in research interest in family businesses between the West and the Third World. Interest in the subject among Western scholars has waned and turned instead towards middle-sized family businesses and the problem of estimating their role in the national economy.

In the developing world, where large family businesses are highly significant, research interest appears to center on the fundamental problem of whether or not they will continue to exist and if so under just what conditions. When one reads the various papers presented at this conference on "Family Business in the Formative Era of Big Business," this variation strikes one immediately. For example, in Japan the period in which family businesses were important falls between the latter part of the nineteenth century and the first part of the twentieth century, while in the developing countries it comes nearer the latter part of the twentieth century. Consequently papers treating quite different matters of concern were presented on the same theme, and discussions of certain economic or administrative phenomena are presented in different ways. This is of course precisely the reason why, in spite of the difficulty of effecting comparisons, international exchanges of studies are conducted. Participants at the conference were well aware of this. Nevertheless the conference turned out to be highly productive.

We were very pleased and honored to be able to invite Professor Peter L. Payne from the United Kingdom and Professor Maurice Lévy-Leboyer from France, both authorities in the field, as well as Dr. Jürgen Brockstedt from West Germany and Professor Barbara M. Tucker from the United States, two rising scholars. By also gaining the attendance of Messrs. Tamio Hattori and Shoji Ito and hearing their work on South Korea and India we were able to enrich previous research. Professor Matao Miyamoto's historical and statistical research on Japanese family business is perhaps the first such review. Professor Shoichi Asajima's paper on internal financing is the most up-to-date information available on this complex subject.

I would like to thank the members of the organizing committee and all the participants for making the conference so extremely successful.

Shigeaki Yasuoka

# FAMILY BUSINESS IN THE ERA OF INDUSTRIAL GROWTH

# Capital Ownership in Family Companies: Japanese Firms Compared with Those in Other Countries

Shigeaki Yasuoka
*Doshisha University*

## I. The Family Company in Japan

I would like to relate how the study of family business history is related to research on zaibatsu history.

Many people have come to believe that Japan's economy had been mainly controlled by zaibatsu (big business organizations peculiar to Japan) until the defeat suffered in World War II. At that time, 35.2% of total paid-up capital in Japan was that of the affiliated firms of the ten largest zaibatsu, which were controlled by a few families, the descendants of the zaibatsu founders. They were Mitsui, Mitsubishi (the Iwasakis), Sumitomo, Yasuda, Ayukawa (Nissan), Asano, Furukawa, Ohkura, Nakajima (Fuji Sangyo) and Nomura. It thus seemed that a few groups (zaibatsu families), who had control over the Japanese economy, had aided the war effort.

The Occupation Army, in parallel with the disarmament of the Japanese armed forces, also dissolved the zaibatsu and tried to democratize the Japanese economy. They also purged 56 members of zaibatsu families and 3668 executives of zaibatsu firms from economic and business activities.[1] The head offices of these zaibatsu were ordered to dissolve and the families were all forced to sell their shares in stock markets through the HCLC (Holding Company Liquidation Committee). Despite such severe treatment, within ten years after the War, various kinds of firms, including banks once under the same zaibatsu control, began to reunite again by means of intercorporate stock holdings, interlocking directorates and financ-

*1*

ing. The executive meetings of these companies began to be held regularly, too. These reunited groups of firms, which came to be called "business groups" (kigyo-shudan), soon became powerful and influential in both the Japanese and international economies.

It thus became necessary for economic and business historians to analyze the various kinds of conditions influencing the development and role of the zaibatsu. The study of zaibatsu has many aspects. For instance, the relationships between zaibatsu families (owners of capital) and their salaried managers, the decision-making of zaibatsu policies, the process of diversification of business, the relationship between zaibatsu and the government and the characteristics of zaibatsu compared with similar firms in other countries. An analysis of the characteristics of zaibatsu as family businesses is a considerably important problem worth taking up. Studies to date on family business in Japan have been roughly of the following types:

(1)   Historical study of merchant family relationships from the sociological point of view.[2]

(2)   Historical study of the shop system and merchant thought from the viewpoint of the history of commerce.[3]

(3)   Historical study of management and accounting from the viewpoint of business history.[4]

Now, some of the large merchant families in the Edo period were transformed into zaibatsu after the Meiji Era. Mitsui and Sumitomo were big ones while Kōnoike was a relatively small one. As was the case, historical study of merchant families came into contact with historical study of the zaibatsu. As most of the zaibatsu families, the owners, entrusted almost all management of their companies to *bantō* (head clerks) or salaried managers, historical study about entrepreneurs developed into research on the attitudes and performance of these salaried managers.[5]

As the evolution of capitalism and industrialization in Japan kept pace with the development of zaibatsu, we cannot overlook the contribution of zaibatsu to such industrialization. In spite of the modernization of the economy, zaibatsu as family businesses would not open their shares to the public, especially the zaibatsu head offices. This also requires a clear analysis of the relationship between owner-

TABLE 1   Family companies and size of capital (paid-up).

| Capital (million yen) | Legal person in activity | Family company levied on reserve fund | Family company of hidozoku | Non-Family company | |
|---|---|---|---|---|---|
| | A | B | C | D | D/A |
| under 1 | 211,619 | 207,427 | 1,012 | 3,180 | 1.5 (%) |
| over 1 | 320,342 | 314,961 | 2,115 | 3,266 | 1.0 |
| 2 | 429,619 | 418,875 | 4,347 | 6,397 | 1.5 |
| 5 | 237,674 | 227,637 | 4,379 | 5,658 | 2.3 |
| 10 | 136,360 | 125,250 | 6,564 | 4,546 | 3.3 |
| 20 | 80,040 | 64,802 | 9,047 | 6,191 | 7.7 |
| 50 | 17,547 | 11,020 | 4,168 | 2,359 | 13.4 |
| 100 | 12,240 | 4,590 | 5,213 | 2,437 | 19.9 |
| 500 | 1,826 | 248 | 899 | 679 | 37.2 |
| 1000 | 1,661 | 99 | 732 | 830 | 50.0 |
| 5000 | 325 | 5 | 90 | 230 | 70.1 |
| 10000 | 296 | 5 | 51 | 240 | 81.1 |
| Total | 1,449,549 | 1,374,919 | 38,617 | 36,013 | |
| | 100.0% | 94.7% | 2.7% | 2.5% | |

Source: "Showa 55 nendo Kokuzeicho Tokei Nenhokoku, Dai 106 kai" (Showa 55 (1980), 106th Yearly Report of the National Tax Administration Agency), Tokyo, 1982.

ship and management in zaibatsu. Of course, there were many family businesses besides zaibatsu. But it is clear that zaibatsu had some important characteristics of Japanese family business. As Table 1 shows, there are many family companies of medium and small size in present-day Japan. On the other hand, there are also some large family companies. However, we cannot help relying upon the public data in management records left by large merchant houses and zaibatsu if we try to make a detailed, historical investigation. In this paper I should like to delve into ownership and management of large family companies in Japan from the nineteenth century to the first half of the twentieth century. However, I would first like to address several points discussed by L. Hannah,[6] the organizer of the theme, "From Family Firm to Professional Management: Structure and Performance of Business Enterprise," at the Eighth International

Economic History Congress at Budapest, August 1982, in an attempt to elucidate recent trends in research about European and Japanese family business.

## II.　Summary of L. Hannah's Research

According to Hannah's paper, it is broadly acknowledged that the leaders of capitalism got their status through their talents. But there are two opposing opinions about the transfer of management control from the owner-family to the professional managers. Marxists say that at first glance there seemed to be so-called managerial control, but practically, it is the owners who control management; the basic class relationship is always unchanged. Amelioratists oversimplify the phenomenon by saying that managerial control has come to change property relations to authority relations. The divorce of ownership and control made progress gradually in the public sector of the Anglo-Saxon world, but this did not attract the attention of scholars. Early research placed too much emphasis on managerial control, but family majority shareholdings have been found to survive more widely than some early investigations suggested. In Europe there are some cases where owner control still survives despite the appearance of managerial control. The "managerial revolution" is a misnomer: the process is one of evolutionary change at a slow pace. It is not good to treat the problem as a simple dichotomy, owner control or managerial control. Some say it is very important to give considerable weight to control by banks or other financial institutions, but others argue that this had already greatly weakened by the twentieth century.

Recently, the significance of the ownership of pension funds has become very important. In the U.K., possession of ordinary shareholdings by financial institutions such as insurance companies and pension funds increased from 18% to more than 40% of the total between 1957 and 1973. The issue of shares has increased, but the inequality of wealth itself has never changed. The control of capital owners is not yet democratized, as the scholars supporting the theory of managerial control expected.

On the other hand, there is a theory that the growth and innovation of the family firm has been greatly disturbed by the third gener-ation's incompetence about profits and competition (the so-called Buddenbrook effect). Family firms were all eager to educate and train their successors. But even if the education and training were unsuccessful, the owners could influence management by some means. So it is necessary to further investigate the complicated situation of owner and managerial control.

In the United States, among the 500 largest firms, owner-controlled ones showed higher profits than managerially controlled ones, according to the investigation done by Arthur Francis between 1952 and 1963. There are also some studies in Europe which suggest that family firms have a good profit or growth record, although other studies are inconclusive or show the opposite. We should take notice also that different tax rates for the two kind of firms give rise to different rates of dividends and profits. It may be doubted that the different performance of managers comes not from different aims but from different information.

Why do family capitalists decide to make the transition to man-agerial ownership? And why do they sell shares openly: to keep control in their hands, or to get more funds? From the 1890s, in Britain and the U.S.A., it became increasingly common for family firms to sell out all or part of their capital interests to outside share-holders. Initially, such sales were often of fixed interest of other non-voting capital, but later the voting shares were sold off. Perhaps it was because professional managers behaved like owner-entrepre-neurs. Family owners can sell their shares, and by buying shares in other industries they hedge their risks safely. Knowing the motiva-tions for their changes would not guarantee a better understanding of the effect of the rise of manager-controlled firms, but it would help us to understand the dynamic forces in modern capitalist development.

The above is a summary of Hannah's studies of family firms.[6] Other papers have dealt with the same subject. R. A. Church[7] sur-veyed the transfer from family business to managerial enterprises in the automobile industry. F. Jequier and D. S. Landes,[8] trying to analyze the reasons for the decline of the watch industry in Switzer-land, could not clarify the correlation between the family firm and the watch industry. C. Baker and M. Lévy-Leboyer[9] pointed out the present-day significance of family firms and analyzed several stages in the historical development of family business.

H. Hanák's paper[10] treated the rise and fall of Hungarian family businesses. H. Keable[11] spoke about the appearance and recruitment of the so-called business elite in Germany and presented useful suggestions. H. Nussbaum[12] tried to compare the differences between British and German characteristics of monopolized organizations, such as cartels and syndicates which appeared during the transfer process from family business to large enterprise. H. Morikawa[13] pointed out that it was necessary to have technocrats in both family firms and joint-stock companies, analyzing three kinds of conditions attendant upon the appearance of salaried managers during Japan's industrialization.

Generally speaking, in former times, it was thought that most family firms declined when the joint-stock companies developed and became larger. It was also presumed that owing to their private character, family firms did not always harmonize with social progress. But some recent scholars think that although the influence of owner families over their large joint-stock companies declined, their power did not decline as much as was insisted upon by those who emphasized managerial revolution. Recent research conversely asserts that family firms provide the dynamic forces for such industries as retailing and "road haulage." I think these positive evaluations are very remarkable.

Such historical studies of family business are interesting to both Japanese and foreign scholars of business history. The plan to take up these family business problems at the Fuji Conference had already been made before the Budapest Congress. As the large families with much capital in the underdeveloped capitalist countries are very influential to their industries, the studies of family business in these countries are very realistic and vivid. Such aspects were not treated at the Budapest Congress. In many of the underdeveloped countries which gained independence after World War II, the governments, often making economic policy on the basis of the example of the industrialized countries, never entrusted important industries to private enterprises and tried to check the strong influence of large family businesses, substituting public enterprises in their place. Despite these efforts, family business groups became very powerful in the industrialization process in these developing countries.[14]

Even in Japan's automobile industry, such prominent companies as Toyota and Nissan built up their manufacturing bases by sub-contracting parts production to many small family businesses.[15] So then, even after the abolition of the zaibatsu, the study of family business is still an important academic theme.

## III. Ownership and Management of Family Business

### 1. A Hypothesis

Before analyzing the characteristics of the large family companies in Japan, I would like to present a hypothesis of comparison. Regarding the influence exerted by the nature of ownership upon management, I maintain that the more collectivistic business capital ownership becomes, the less professional is the function demanded of an owner; thus, the authority delegated to salaried managers becomes greater.

When ownership becomes increasingly collectivistic, there is a tendency for individual owners to pay more attention to the size of the dividend than to the working of capital (management), even though the working of the joint asset determines the dividend. The founders and their cooperators who amassed a great fortune had the experience and competence to convert small capital into something big. However, those who succeed to great assets accumulated in this manner usually will be less capable than the founders, because naturally they were given less chance to be trained than the founders. Nevertheless, because strong collectivistic restrictions are placed upon the assets in order to prevent them from being divided and diffused, the successors as individuals do not have the opportunity to nurture their capabilities as managers. It is actually safer to rely upon loyal and competent hired managers; thus it appears that the successors' interest is directed more towards securing a large dividend.

On the other hand, when a group whose members are regarded as highly competent submits its own assets for investment, the members' attitude is that they should be in charge of the corporate management. The group thereby adopts a system in which the investment share and management right either pass or are transferred to a motivated and competent member from among themselves. Such an individual is required to make an effort to improve his capabilities as a manager. Under these circumstances, the family members would also try to nurture a suitable successor and eliminate an inappropriate candidate. In this sense, the business capital becomes more of a co-owned capital which can be transferred and divided even though it is restricted by the ownership within the family. It is presumed that the capital ownership pursued by Du Pont and Rothschild, excluding the earlier stages, falls into this category. Even when the corporate size becomes gigantic, the owners of these families would, in principle, maintain their corporate functions. Should they delegate responsibility to hired managers, the delegation of responsibility would be limited to a specific function.

When investors are not necessarily required to be those who possess corporate functions, the delegation of management would actually tend to be unlimited delegation in which the entire management is entrusted, even though it may not appear so formally. The nine cases to be described later seem to fit this explanation.

## 2. Japanese Cases

Before observing the characteristics of large family companies, let us have a survey look at ownership and management of merchant houses in the Edo period (1603–1867). Large Edo period merchant houses were founded during the second half of the seventeenth century and the families became powerful merchants by the beginning of the eighteenth century. They were Mitsui, Kōnoike and Sumitomo. Next to them, second-class large merchants appeared during the middle of the eighteenth century, such as Shimomura (now Daimaru Department Store) and Nakai (an Ōmi merchant). Most of them started their careers with small capital and became successful after several decades.

Founders themselves, and the sons who assisted them, were in most cases talented managers. Kōnoike and Sumitomo both had excellent restorers in the third generatons. But in ordinary cases, when a lull ensured, the heirs of merchant families lost the talents for management from the third generation on, and trusted their tasks to the employed *bantō* (head clerks). They were severely trained from their apprenticeship and served their masters just like the vessals of feudal lords. They managed the business and house-hold daily with the delegation of their masters. Although they had to get their masters' approval when deciding important matters, they were virtually top managers.[16] There is an old proverb in Japa-nese: "The fortune made through the hard work of the first genera-tion is all lost by the easygoing third." Given the incompetent master of the third generation, the large merchant families would have been easily ruined if it had not been for the talented *bantō*. But in the case of most large merchant families, the method of selecting talented managers was firmly established. So, whether the present master was competent or not, the business continued successfully.

It is generally believed that the Japanese merchant houses hired their men on a lifetime basis, but this is not wholly true. The most competent men finally became top managers, but in rising up the ladder, they were carefully selected at each stage. From 1696 to 1730, the Kyoto headquarters of Echigoya drapers (Mitsui) hired 239 apprentices, but only thirteen (5%) of them could be live-out clerks (not live-in employees).[17] They seem to correspond to today's com-pany directors. These directors gathered at meetings of management, decided policies and controlled the business. Old merchant families which continued for a century or two most often adopted such a system of control. Masters also took responsibility for retired employ-ees with good records. This type of treatment might be considered a kind of paternalism or labor-management policy with a long-term perspective.

The owners of capital of these family businesses were, for the most part, the masters and family members. In some cases, however, *bekke* (branch family with no blood relation) and *tedai* (clerk) were allowed to be investors, but of course they were not on an equal investment footing with their masters. The capital inherited by the masters and their families was always succeeded to as a whole, so the family members, including the master, could not request division of their purparty. Each owner could only receive a dividend on profits.

Thus, we cannot call this type of capital ownership co-ownership (*Miteigentum*). This is almost a kind of *Gesamteigentum*, or other *Eigentum*. This may be a kind of *Familienfideikommisse* or trust property. The master (heir to the property) is only the nominal owner, not the real one. The real owner would be the family group or house (*ie*). Some scholars refer to this *ie* as "*tate no hōjin*," that is, historical legal person vertically continued.[18] The capital of merchant families took such a form of undividable collectivity. The strong factor of the family system (*ie* system) in Japanese society is closely related to the form of property ownership, but we have to prove this phenomenon more clearly.

How did these large-scale family firms change after the Meiji Restoration, the turning point from a feudal society to a modern one? In the Edo period, most enterprises were family businesses; only a few were run as partnerships of intimate friends.

From the beginning of the Meiji era, the government tried to propagate joint-stock companies that did not rely on investment by one family only. But its popularization was very slow, because most merchants of the time had hardly any experience with co-investment. By special government legislation, joint-stock company banks (*kokuritsu ginkō*) were established in the 1870s and within several years the number of banks increased to 153. The situation was the same in the railway industry.

Almost all the family businesses continued to exist, and even after the enforcement of the new Commercial Law in 1893, they maintained their traditional form of enterprise. At the same time, however, large family firms began to adopt the systems of unlimited and limited partnership. The investors in such ventures were limited only to masters and family members. The investment of hired managers was only nominal and was virtually excluded from real investment. This was because the owners of family businesses tried to keep the investment pure. In the Edo period, the right of employees' investment was weaker than that of the masters'. As both kinds of investment had to be treated equally after the enforcement of the Commercial Law in 1893 and Civil Law in 1898, the masters' side wanted to exclude employees' investment. Then, even if large family businesses had adopted the modern form of a joint-stock company, substance would not have changed very much.

In cases of limited or unlimited partnership, the sums of investment by each family member were indicated clearly in the terms of the contracts, but all participants could not ask to take back their own investments. Their shares only entitled them to receive the allotment of profit produced from the capital. The absoluteness of the individual property right given by the Civil and Commercial Laws was stripped of most of its substance by the strength of the traditional ownership system of property in Japan. In other words, the Civil and Commercial Laws were enforced owing to the influence from the West but were quite unsuitable to the customary system of ownership. Capital was under *"Gesamteigentum"* by the family members and not personal proprietorship, despite efforts to adopt a company system befitting the legal system. So the ownership of capital by family members was buried under collective proprietorship.

In the Meiji period, Japanese had no system like *Familienfideikommisse* in Germany and family trust in France, England and India (see Payne, Lévy-Leboyer and Ito's papers). Owing to the lack of such a system, the real substance of property ownership of large merchant houses and zaibatsu deviated from the texts of the Civil and Commercial Laws in Japan. But in 1886, hereditary property ownership by peers was permitted by law (Kazoku Seshūzaisan-hō).

In the case of unlimited partnership with family capital, sometimes the wives and children of masters became the investors (viz. partners), but they were *Anteilkapitalisten* substantially, as they usually did not have the function to manage enterprises, although they were legally functional capitalists (the ones who actually manage business). Given this situation, control of management rested in their masters only or, in old family businesses, in hired managers. This is the special "managerial control" established by custom in the Edo period; it did not appear with the dispersion of stock ownership, as was been asserted by Berle and Means. Such "managerial control" controlled the management of family businesses, which later became the gigantic zaibatsu, and the decision-making on policies. From the formulary point of view, the ownership of capital of Japanese zaibatsu is under *Gesamteigentum* or *Eigentum zur gesamten Hand* by zaibatsu family members; administration was conducted by managerial control delegated by the owners. To maintain such systems, large family companies[19] regulated the activities of each family member under family codes. Let us have a look at some examples.[20]

### 1. Mitsui Family Code (1900)[21]

The Mitsui family possessed family properties held by eleven families and business assets which were jointly managed by the eleven families; the following was stipulated with regard to business assets:

> Article 92.     Irrespective of the investment account, the purparty over the family assets other than the individual family properties shall be based upon the following proportion:
> Head family (1 family)      23/100
> Main family (5 families) each      11.5/100
> Collateral family (5 families) each      3.9/100
> Should there be a member of the family who retires or is expelled from each of the business offices and causes a decrease in the purparty held by each member of the family [the purparty] due in the foregoing paragraph shall naturally be changed in accordance with the situation.

Despite the fact that business assets were formally co-owned, in actuality it can be considered that they were collectively owned, since none of the members of the eleven families was able to retire the purparty entitled to his family at will. Although *Sōchiku Isho* (the predecessor of the Mitsui family code) of the Edo period stipulated the allotment rules of business offices and the purparty in the Mitsui family code, the ownership was de facto collective because allotment was never pursued. With regard to the behavior of the family members, the following was stated:

> Article 12.     The family shall be prohibited from engaging in the following:
> 1.   to join any political party or become publicly involved in any politics
> 2.   to create debts
> 3.   to become a guarantor of others' debts.
> The necessary rules for the enforcement of this article shall be established separately.

Article 13.    The family shall be prohibited from engaging in the following without the approval of the family council:
1.  to operate a commerce and industry privately
2.  to become a shareholder of a company or a financier of commerce and industry privately
3.  to become an executive or an employee of a company or a union other than that of each of the Mitsui business offices
4.  to be engaged in government or public office
5.  to be engaged in any other item which stipulates that it should receive the permission of the family council.

As seen above, no member of the Mitsui family was allowed to engage in political or economic activities which make a self-sufficient modern man.

## 2.  *Code of the Yasuda Family Corporation (1887)*[22]

Article 35.    The clique [a clan of ten Yasuda families] members are strictly prohibited from becoming guarantors of monetary debts and various deeds of contract upon requests made by their kith and kin, let alone non-family members; neither can they sign a paper of personal guarantee vouching for an employee. However, should the above be necessary within a legal framework, the matter must be discussed mutually by the clique. Moreover, only when a signature is required for business pertaining to the Yasuda Bank is a member permitted to sign upon receiving a permit from the general director.

Article 41.    The present assets of one million yen held by the Yasuda family are totally rendered in order to fix the capital of the Yasuda Bank at one million yen, which is to be in the divided custody as follows:

| Names | Number of Shares | Amount |
|---|---|---|
| In the name of the Family Corporation, | | |
| General Director | 5,000 | ¥500,000 |
| Main Family, Zenjiro Yasuda | 700 | ¥ 70,000 |
| Main Family, Zenshiro Yasuda | 700 | ¥ 70,000 |
| Main Family, Zennosuke Yasuda | 700 | ¥ 70,000 |
| Main Family, Shinnosuke Yasuda | 500 | ¥ 50,000 |
| Main Family, Saburohiko Yasuda | 500 | ¥ 50,000 |
| Main Family, Chūbei Yasuda | 500 | ¥ 50,000 |

| Names | Number of Shares | Amount |
|-------|------------------|--------|
| Branch Family, Fumiko Yasuda | 400 | ¥ 40,000 |
| Branch Family, Zensuke Yasuda | 400 | ¥ 40,000 |
| Related Family, Yagoro Ōta | 300 | ¥ 30,000 |
| Related Family, Sodeko Fujita | 300 | ¥ 30,000 |

Article 42.    It is prohibited to pawn, transfer or sell, etc., these Yasuda Bank shares to outsiders other than to clique members. Therefore, without the issuance of share certificates, a share account book should be created. Upon inscribing the number of shares held by each member in this book, the signatures and seals of the managing director and the auditor of the Yasuda Bank must be affixed, and the book must be kept in the safe of the main office.

Article 43.    The sum of 500,000 yen in the form of family corporation shares must be kept in custody by the six households of the main family as a deposit bestowed upon them by the ancestor who brought prosperity to the family. Thus, it must never be partitioned under any circumstances. Nevertheless, the representative must be set in the name of the general director to the clique members, and the certificate must be kept in the executive office of the Yasuda Bank.

Article 64.    The clique members are prohibited from managing business independently. If a member violates this rule and manages a business in secrecy which subsequently incurs debts due to business failure or some accident and becomes bankrupt, none of the relatives must render any help.

As seen above, as long as the approval of the general director and other directors was required, it is definite that the family assets and domestic affairs could not be "generally and totally controlled" by the family head.

On the basis of the above excerpt, it can be seen that the Yasuda family code is very similar to that of the Mitsui family. Thus, among the investors of the Mitsui Bank from 1876 to 1893, an organ that was in charge of the custody of the jointly owned Mitsui family property called Ohmotokata ["the head office"] invested one million yen (later 500,000 yen). In like manner, the investment of 500,000 yen in the name of the general director of the Hozensha family corporation appears to be of the same nature.

In view of Articles 42 and 43, it is evident that the clan of ten families did not have the disposal right regarding property (shares) held in divided custody. Article 35 and 64 reveal that the family heads of the clan of ten families were not recognized as self-sufficient individual economic persons because of the numerous restrictions placed upon them. The 500,000 yen of the shares in the name of the Hozensha family corporation that had to be kept by the six main families as "a deposit bestowed by the ancestor [Zenjiro Yasuda] who brought prosperity to the family" reveals that this property was collectively owned by the clan.

### 3. *Kōnoike Family Code (1889)*[23]

Article 12.    All the family assets are made to be managed by the elders of employees, and no family head should gain control over them.

Article 13.    A sum of money representing the family head's personal expenses should be determined and paid every month.

Article 14.    Such expenses as the construction and repair of houses and gardens which entail family funds should be discussed by the elders of employees, and a family head must not undertake these at will when approval is not granted by the elders.

Article 15.    When a descendant wishes to establish a branch family, his proportion must be dealt with in accordance with the rules of apportionment established by Master Sōsei in the Kyōho era.

As seen above, a family head was not given the power to dispose of his property, and the establishment of a branch family by the descendants had to be done in accordance with the rules of January 1723 (Kyōho 8). Sōsei (another name for the third-generation Zenemon Munetoshi) is noted for his competent leadership, for he brought prosperity to the Kōnoike family. The inheritance rules established in the Kyōho era by him survived for another 150 years and were perpetuated even after 1889. According to the above articles, it should be considered that the family assets did not belong to a family head who held the ownership right, but belonged to all the family members who abided by the family code.

### 4. Sumitomo Family

Although many family precepts and shop rules are also left by the Sumitomo family, no inheritance rule stipulating the continuity of the family is publicized. In this regard, the Sumitomo family rules lacking the inheritance rule were anomalous, and I have presented a tentative argument on the basis of the Sumitomo family precepts and shop rules deciphered thus far.[24]

#### Sumitomo Family Code (1891)[25]

Article 7.    Upon consulting with the general director and directors, the family head should accumulate some capital and personnel other than business capital and establish a means of custody so that he can be prepared to solidify the way of the family.

Article 11.    Even matters occurring within an individual family should be dealt with, if they are serious matters, by consulting with the general director and directors.

Article 14.    The family head must not dare to increase, decrease, or alter the articles in the family code and the family rules without obtaining a consensus from the general director and other directors.

### 5. Iwasaki Family

Upon the death of Yatarō Iwasaki, the founder of Mitsubishi Trading Company and Mitsubishi Mailing and Shipping Company, in February 1885, his younger brother, Yanosuke Iwasaki, succeeded to the president's post. Yanosuke branched off from the head family of Yatarō's eldest son, Hisaya, in 1891. It is said that the property given to Yanosuke at the time of establishing his branch family did not even come up to a quarter of the wealth owned by the head family.[26] Because Yanosuke's effort after the death of Yatarō was so instrumental in the maintenance of Mitsubishi wealth, it is presumed that the status of Yanosuke's branch family vis-à-vis the head family was considerably higher than that of ordinary branch families. Consequently, when Mitsubishi Goshigaisha (a limited partnership) was established in December 1893 with capital of 5 million yen, the amount invested by Hisaya and Yanosuke was an equal amount of 2.5 million yen each. The investment by both families fluctuated later and the radio of investment changed. This fact is interpreted to mean that the investment by both Iwasaki families was not collectively owned, but co-owned with possibilities of partition. However, the pattern of ownership inside the respective families is unknown. Although it was stipulated that the partners of this company should be the heads of both families or their heirs, Yanosuke's eldest son, Koyata, was added on as an investing partner in February 1907, and the capital of the company became 15 million yen. A breakdown of the investment was as follows: Hisaya—12.5 million yen; Yanosuke—1.5 million yen; Koyata—1 million yen. The investment ratio between Yatarō's line and Yanosuke's line was five to one. As seen above, although the restriction upon investors was somewhat lenient in Mitsubishi Goshigaisha, the "Company Contract"[27] revised in 1907 stipulated the following:

> Article 16.    A partner cannot voluntarily resign from this company while it is in existence. Should a partner die, the heir to the family headship is to succeed to the position. A partner shall never resign from the company because of lack of competence.

The competence of investing partners was thus not questioned, indicating that they became investors as the representatives of each family. In addition, it seems to suggest that the investment did not belong to individual partners. In other words, incompetent partners were granted neither the disposal right nor the apportionment right over an investment.

### 6.  Conclusion

As seen above, regarding the relationship between the several heads of the zaibatsu or the zaibatsu investors (families) and the investment, various restrictions had to be accepted as a result of becoming investors. In consequence, the following points can be ascertained (excluding the circumstances regarding the **Iwasaki** family):

1.  Because of the strong restrictions imposed upon the investments made for family businesses or corporations by the family group, it was impossible for each investor to withdraw the portion of investment in his name voluntarily. (This point also applies to Mitsubishi Goshigaisha.)

2. There were such rigid restrictions over the political and economic behavior of zaibatsu family members that they were not able to act at their discretion as independent individuals. When zaibatsu family members wished to be engaged in economic or managerial activities, they were restricted to their family business or their own corporation in which they were protected and supervised by hired employees (hired executives or managers). (Hozensha rules also contained this regulation in Article 39.)

3. We may presume that the common characteristics of zaibatsu and large merchant families are clearly revealed in the abovementioned five examples. For instance, the Yasuda is like the Mitsui, the Sumitomo is like the Kōnoike, and the Iwasaki is different from them all, which is rare in Japan.

## 3.  The Internal Relations of Family Business

Now let us look at the form of enterprise and the practice of business adopted by large family companies in Japan. In many family companies of unlimited partnership, masters, wives and children of minority participated as partners (like Mitsui, Kōnoike and Yasuda). In some cases of limited partnership, partners were restricted to roles as functional capitalists only (Mitsubishi, viz., the Iwasakis). We also can find other examples in Sumitomo, whose partners included masters' children of minority. In such cases, they were not treated as operating executive members. In this respect only, they observed the item of the law. Of course the money invested by these people was not drawn out, and their investment would be only nominal, not substantial.

In the case of Mitsubishi Limited Partnership, established in 1893, Hisaya Iwasaki and Yanosuke Iwasaki were both functional capitalists who could execute practical business. From this fact, we can say they should have adopted the form of partnership, not limited partnership. But they did not do so for some reason. They could have only limited liability, provided they did not use the family name of the owners as the name of the company, according to the Commercial Law of 1893. Various kinds of publications issued from Mitsubishi and the Iwasakis tried to explain the reasons for this, but unfortunately I do not find them persuasive.

One might doubt why family firms had adopted the company system. We might presume there were three advantages in adopting the company system, even if there might be considerable gaps between the form of the company and actual ownership and management:

1. Within the family, the shares of each member could be decided officially, although in reality each member could not request to receive his share.

2. By adopting the company system, the company itself could be the owner of assets and subsidiary companies. Both types of partnership in Japan were legal persons. Family councils, the organizations of family members, were not legal persons, so they could not be the owners of property.

3. According to the Income Tax Act of 1887, a person whose yearly income was over 3,000 yen must be levied at a ratio of 2.5% of income. The income ratio for individual income was from 3% to 5.5% and was progressive when over 10,000 yen, though the tax for individual income below 10,000 yen was not so high. Most owners of large companies had yearly incomes of over 100,000 yen, and the rate for them was 5.5%.

Perhaps for these reasons they decided to adopt the company system instead of customary forms of ownership and management. It is not so clear why they did not transform their *honsha* (head offices) into joint-stock companies. To be sure, they did not like to make the financial condition of their companies public as required by the regulations for joint-stock companies. Therefore, the head offices of zaibatsu had for a few decades been unlimited or limited partnerships, and as holding companies they held the majority shares of their subsidiary joint-stock companies which the head offices founded. Thus, most zaibatsu constructed pyramidal *Konzerns* from about 1909 to 1921.

In the 1930s, when the head offices of zaibatsu wanted to get more capital, they reorganized themselves as joint-stock companies (in 1937, Sumitomo and Mitsubishi; in 1940, Mitsui). Large zaibatsu were asked to invest in the munitions industries, and for that they had to raise much more funds. They then made their *honsha* joint-stock companies and partly offered public shares. Needless to say, however, they tried to keep their closed character by letting persons and companies related to them have the shares.

From the situations mentioned above, we might say that the company system born in Europe was not fixed firmly in the Japanese industrial world. One of the largest gaps might be the system of property ownership and the public character of joint-stock companies.

We mentioned the contradiction between the aims and regulations of the company system and its real practice. In spite of these facts, we cannot deny the contribution of this system to the Japanese economy.

### 4. Foreign Cases

Next, in order to make a comparison with the Japanese cases, I would like to make an observation on the ownership and management of the large family business in Europe, the U.S.A. and India. Although it is not well backed up by sufficient instances, it will clarify their differences to a certain extent.

What were the characteristics of ownership of property and of business capital in various foreign family corporations, in contrast with the cases of Japanese zaibatsu seen thus far? For this purpose, the cases of Du Pont, Rothschild, Krupp and Tata will be studied. A general prospect is that the business capital held by Du Pont and Rothschild is more a case of co-ownership while that of Krupp became collectively owned from a certain period onward; the Tatas' business capital is considered to have been jointly owned.[28]

### 1. Rothschild[29]

Meyer Amschel Rothschild (1744–1812) was a Jewish merchant who resided in Frankfurt. He started out in 1764 as an old coin and antique dealer. He subsequently became a world-renowned plutocrat as he became involved in the financial affairs and politics of various royal families and many governments while engaged in business. He sent four of his sons (excluding the eldest) to London, Paris, Vienna and Naples and had them establish branch offices there. He amassed a great fortune from the fluctuation of public bonds and exchange.

In 1810, the founder concluded a contract of partnership with his sons. The contract stipulated that the capital (800,000 florin) of Rothschild and Company in Frankfurt be partitioned so that the founder held 48%, the eldest son, Anselm, 24%, the second son, Solomon, 24%, and the fourth and fifth sons, Karl and James, 2% each. The profit and loss were thus distributed in accordance with these proportions. It is said that the founder's proportion contained the purparty of 24% held by the third son, Nathan (living in London), whose tie was discontinued due to the Napoleonic war at that time. Although the proportions held by the fourth and fifth sons were small, it was decided that the inheritance should be equally divided among the five sons so that each would receive one-fifth. Daughters and sons-in-law were given neither the right to speak up concerning the company management nor the right to look into the account books. Moreover, it was stipulated that family members could not create lawsuits over problems in the family. (A stipulation which prohibited a lawsuit was also seen in the Mitsui family code as well as in the Hozensha rules, and thus there is a similarity among them.)

Shortly before his death in 1812, Meyer Amschel evaluated his portion of the assets at 190,000 gulden and sold it to his sons. The money obtained from this sale was distributed to his wife (70,000 gulden) and five daughters (120,000 gulden). This differs clearly from the Mitsui and Yasuda families, in which sons-in-law were adopted into the family.

While Rothschild's enterprises managed in London by his third son and Paris by his fifth son were given independent positions from an early stage, the enterprises managed in Vienna by his second son and Naples by his fourth son remained as branches of the Frankfurt head office until 1848. Even though the enterprises in London and Paris were relatively independent, the capital was again invested jointly by the brothers and the profit was apportioned in accordance with each share. By 1818, James, who took charge of the Paris operation, also had a one-eighth share of the London office and a three-sixteenths share each of the Frankfurt and Paris offices. Nathan, head of the London office, had the largest purparty among the brothers, because he held a four-eighths share of the Paris office and a four-sixteenths share of the Frankfurt office.

Despite the father's wishing for equal inheritance by the five

sons, soon great gaps began to emerge between their portions, and
the Frankfurt head office later closed. Consequently, dependent on
the capability of each brother, the wealth of the partners fluctuated
in absolute terms as well as in relative terms. Each brother's management of his investment was highly individualistic, and thus it is
considered that the investment was based more upon co-ownership
which could be added and subtracted. Furthermore, although it is
said that there was strong unity among the five brothers and their
descendants, the investment possessed by the founders of each family
(five brothers) and their descendants was not totally submerged in
the relationship of collectivistic ownership.

Among the merchant families and the zaibatsu in Japan, the investment proportion held by the families fluctuated prior to the establishment of a family system. However, upon the establishment
of the family system, restrictions that strongly controlled the investors
and their families were created so that portions would not fluctuate
in accordance with the competence or incompetence of the heirs.
In the Rothschild family, it was possible for a younger brother to
surpass the older brothers and become prosperous. By the same
token, even the eldest son's family could go bankrupt and be abandoned. For the Mitsui families, the status of individual families was
so rigidly defined that no family was permitted to go bankrupt due
to individual circumstances.

### 2.   Du Pont

The Du Pont family emigrated to North America in 1799 during
The du Pont family emigrated to North America in 1799 during
the time of the French Revolution and started gunpowder manufacturing. The family firm later developed into a gigantic gunpowder
trust. Du Pont Company is now well known in the United States as
a rigid family corporation that has tried to have one of its family
members elected president of the company throughout the history
of the corporation.

Du Pont Company was founded by the capital of outsiders but
subsequently became a strong cooperative enterprise managed by
the children of the founder.

Upon the death of the founder, Éleuthére Irénée Du Pont (1771-

1834), the management of the company was succeeded to by the eldest daughter's husband, Antoine Bidermann. Although the eldest son, Alfred, was 36 years old at thid time and had experience making gunpowder for 16 years, he was not suited for the position of manager. The second son, Henry, aged 22, had resigned from his army commission and joined the company but had been with the company for only five months. The third son, Alexis, had just turned 18 and, although he was recognized as a powdersmith, he was too young to be entrusted with the company.

Bidermann had the experience of working with Irénée for twenty years. He paid off the investors as well as all debts within three years after Irénée's death, and the company became wholly family-owned. It is said that Bidermann reorganized the company in April 1837 and established a family partnership which consisted of three brothers and four sisters.[30] On the other hand, there is a description which indicates that the partnership was made up of only three males.[31] Judging from the manner in which investment shares were transacted later, the partnership appears to have shifted to the males. Duke wrote as follows:

> The seven signatures under Alfred's writing should solemnize the new ownership of the mills. No shares, except through Sophie's marriage to Sam Francis, would go to Victor's side of the family; even Sophie had agreed with Antoine that only Irénée's children deserved an interest in the company. The seven elected no officers. Theirs would be a simple partnership, with each of the brothers and sisters to draw an equal part of the profits at the end of each year; not even Alfred would receive a salary. What had to be bought for them or their homes, the company would buy. Personally, they would own nothing, not the furniture in their parlors, not the china they ate off, not even a carriage or horse. Should they need transportation, they merely had to inform Henry, and a buggy and driver would be dispatched.
>
> As a final touch to the agreement, a stroke of genius that would keep the company intact for generations and insure that business would be conducted as the partners intended, the shares were allotted to the seven brothers and sisters only for their lifetimes: when they died their children would not inherit their stake in the powder company. Instead, the remaining partners would choose a new partner from among the many younger du Ponts who worked in the mills.[32]

The new partners chose the eldest son, Alfred, as the second president because he was the oldest. Alfred, who was well aware of his own shortcomings, insisted on a triumvirate with Henry and Alexis. Thus, a management form in which a president is chosen from among the operating partners was decided upon, and this form existed for three-quarters of a century. Henry became the third president in 1850, and Eugene, Alexis's eldest son, became the fourth president in 1889. Although he attempted some reform, it was not a fundamental reform. At this time, although young family members— namely, Alfred I. (second president Alfred's grandson) and Charles I. III (Irénée's brother Victor's great-grandson)—were given fairly responsible positions, they were not included among the partners. Dissatisfied, they demanded a share and received the 20% share of the partnership which belonged to William (Henry's youngest son). This proportion was divided between them, as William returned his share because of personal reasons.

On October 23, 1899, Du Pont De Nemours and Company was inaugurated under the new General Corporation Law of the State of Delaware. Eugene became president. Francis G. (Eugene's younger brother) and Colonel Henry A. (third president Henry's eldest son) became vice-presidents, and Charles III was in charge of secretarial affairs and accounting. The first four were each allotted a 20% share of the company and Charles and Alfred were given 10% each.

Only those family members who were able to participate in management could invest in the company. The principle whereby family members who were qualified to be operating partners were also in charge of management was identical to Rothschild's case. Among the operating investors, Charles III was a descendant of Victor, who was the founder's brother, and not a direct descendant of Irénée.

Although Du Pont Company was a family corporation with strong unity, in the process of a member's succession to the investment shares, individual capabilities were questioned. Unlike the Japanese zaibatsu, it seems that a Du Pont partner was not provided with the status of partnership irrespective of his capability and function.

In Japanese cases, once a family was designated to have the

qualification of producing a partner, the partner's right was inherited by a successor (heir) irrespective of his capability, and his status, in principle, could not be taken by anyone else. While an individual's responsibility and authority were clearly defined in the case of Du Pont and Rothschild, the Japanese case is patterned so that a partner's responsibility and authority must be assumed by someone else. Therefore, in Japan a system developed of having hired executives or salaried managers who could indefinitely assume the duties of a partner (either an investor or a master).

### 3. *Krupp*

Unlike the cases of Du Pont and Rothschild, the Krupp case has many similarities to the Japanese zaibatsu.

Alfred Friedrich Krupp (1812–1887), the head of the Krupp family in the middle of the nineteenth century, stipulated in his will two points regarding the management and control of the plant.

First, to avoid the division of property, the eldest child must own the steel-casting plant, including all its appurtenances, and run it comprehensively. Second, the eldest child must utilize a part of the surplus profit for the innovation and improvement of the facilities in order to prevent the hazard of deterioration and stagnation.

These two points became necessary policies for the firm's maintenance and expansion on a corporate scale due to the circumstances of severe competition owing to the development of capitalism. Alfred's son, Friedrich "Fritz" Alfred Krupp (1854–1902), pursued these principles faithfully. Fritz, however, had only two daughters. When Fritz died, his wife, Margarette, submitted the following notice to the board of directors of Krupp and Company:

> I hereby notify that upon the death of my husband, the ownership of the entire plant including all outside offices as well as annexed facilities was transferred to my eldest daughter, Bertha Krupp, in accordance with the stipulation made in the will of my husband's father, the late Alfred Krupp, and that I will execute her authority until she reaches adulthood. . . .

The Krupp works in 1903 became a joint-stock company with a capital of 180 million marks in accordance with the will of Friedrich

Alfred Krupp. In 1906, Bertha married Gustav von Bohlen und Halbach (1870–1950), who became the successor to the enterprise. Subsequently, Hitler took the measure in 1943 to approve Krupp's inheritance method under a special law entitled the Krupp Law, and Krupp reverted back to a private company.[33] After World War II, Gustav's son Alfred (head of the firm at the time) died in 1967 right in the midst of a crisis for the company. His only son Arund (then 29 years old) abandoned the inheritance right, and thus the Krupp family's ownership of the Krupp works ended.

The system of primogeniture pursued by the Krupp family from the end of the nineteenth century to the latter half of the twentieth century emerged because of the social and economic conditions of that time. The other aspect of single inheritance by the eldest implies that the portions of the other children are indirectly included in the inheritance, and thus it must be said that the property held by the eldest was not owned solely by the individual. This was the same as under the Meiji Civil Code which stipulated that the head of a household, as the heir to the family fortune, had to assume the obligation of supporting his brothers and sisters. This fact seems to imply that a phenomenon similar to the Japanese *ie* (family) system also emerged under certain conditions in European society.

The first reason for Krupp's crisis in the 1960s was that the administration by Alfred and general manager Beitz could not appropriately cope with diversified operation. As the second reason, it is said that the crisis worsened because Krupp was stipulated by the family code to be a private corporation that could not be reorganized into a joint-stock company, which would have decreased the burden. Furthermore, Alfred's continuing faith in general manager Beitz, despite recommendations by the bank authorities that he be demoted, is said to have been one of the causes of the crisis.[34] It is likely that the relationship between them may have been closer than the delegated one between the zaibatsu head in Japan and his salaried managers.

### 4. Tata[35]

The Tatas, the largest financial clique in India, are Parsees. Nusserwanji gave up the priesthood and entered business. It is said that he came to Bombay destitute. He later acquired some funds through the procurement of military goods and ventured into the China trade in 1859. Nusserwanji's eldest son, Jamsetji, was then working in a lawyer's office, having graduated from university. He was 19 years old. The Tata families were gradually being united at this time, and unification appeared in the form of participation in Nusserwanji and Company. Because the greatest difficulty in trade with China at that time was the exchange of appropriate information, the Tatas tried to overcome this problem through reliance upon kinship relations. In addition, family-oriented values predominated in India at that time.

In the case of the Parsees, it is said that a child reaching a certain age was given the freedom to choose whether or not to join the family business as a functional partner, or to start a new business with an outside partner. The eldest son, Jamsetji, however, began to organize the family, thereby preventing a division of the family assets. By the 1880s, the Central Indian Mill Company Limited, which had been started by Jamsetji, was very successful.

Upon the death of Nusserwanji in 1886, Jamsetji decided to establish a head office (managing agency) in order to unify and control the family enterprise, and founded Tata and Sons in the following year, 1887, with a capital of 21,000 rupees. It is assumed that management was based upon private partnership. The partners comprised Jamsetji, his eldest son, Dorabji, and his cousin, R. D. Tata. The second son, Ratanji, was to join the partnership later. Soon after the founding of Tata and Sons, Jamsetji established a family trust to secure the livelihood of the members who constituted the family. Certain proceeds from Tata and Sons were established as trust funds for the family members so that each member could receive a dividend on the interest. What could be inherited was the right to receive the dividend, and restrictions were placed on any request for a division of the trust funds.

The family trust established by Jamsetji appears to have been modeled after the practices of the Hindu joint family which established co-owned properties in order to overcome the contradiction between the principle of equal inheritance prevalent in India and the prevention of family assets becoming diffused. However, while co-owned property of the joint family could, in principle, be divided into individual portions, the Tata family trust was indivisible from the beginning because of its objective of pursuing jointly owned assets in perpetuity. Isamu Hirota, who is studying this subject, concludes that the union of the Tata family which permitted the existence of the family trust contained the same factor as those found in the  union of the *ie* system in Japan.

Tata and Sons was transformed into an unlimited partnership with a capital of 15 million rupees in 1907 when the Tata Steel Mill was established. The family trust was dissolved at that time because the eldest son, Drab, and the second son, Ratan, held 80% of the shares, and the cousin R. D. Tata 20%. It appears that the independence of ownership by each partner was somewhat increased. Hirota presumes that the transfer of a family business to an enterprise in Indian society[36] requires an intermediate stage—namely, an *ie* type of union as seen in the case of the Tata family.

Among the foreign cases, Rothschild and Du Pont took special measures for the maintenance of business capital held by the family. Those members of the family who had occupational functions invested in the company and became partners, whereupon they obtained shares as functional capitalists with occupational function.

On the other hand, the Krupp family followed primogeniture over its business capital for three-quarters of a century starting from the end of the nineteenth century; thus, the proceeds from the business presumably contained portions to which the siblings of the heir were entitled. The same phenomenon concerning inheritance was observable among merchant families and the zaibatsu in Japan.

The Tata financial clique also tried to maintain the joint prosperity of the entire family through the establishment of the family trust in a period starting from the end of the nineteenth century to the beginning of the twentieth century.

## IV. Summary

As seen above, whether in Japan or abroad, the joint ownership of capital by family corporations was a commonly observable phenomenon. The content of joint ownership, however, was different. The most collectivistic ownership was seen in the form of collective ownership pursued by Mitsui, Yasuda, Sumitomo and Kōnoike. Krupp's ownership pattern is considered to be similar. The holding of Tata's trust funds by the family trust is also regarded as being close to collective ownership.

An examination of such differences was made because the nature of ownership greatly influences business management.

It is necessary to study the details further concerning the management pursued by the owners of the Rothschild Corporation and the Du Pont Company, both of which had business capital based on co-ownership. However, these companies are known for having a management controlled by family members. They differ greatly from the Japanese zaibatsu whose business capital was collectively owned. Is the difference derived from the co-owners with more independence showing a keener interest in management? In the case of the Mitsubishi zaibatsu in Japan, the business capital was co-owned by two Iwasaki families. Three of four presidents of Mitsubishi had been active and competent. Although research is still insufficient, is it not possible to make progress in an international comparison of ownership and management through an examination which correlates the comparison of ownership to the comparison of management, as shown thus far? In addition, could this not shine an objective light on the nature of various corporations in modern times?

I could not give sufficient space to the comparison of the method of management of family business in this paper. I simply explained the hypothesis that the forms of ownership greatly influenced the ways of management delegation. I would like to wait for another chance to make a comparison of the method of management.

### NOTES

1. E. M. Hadley, *Antitrust in Japan* (Princeton University Press, 1970), trans. into Japanese by Ohara and Aruga, p. 117.
2. Takashi Nakano, *Shōka Dozokudan no Kenkyū* (Studies of Merchant Extended Families), Tokyo, 1963.
3. Mataji Miyamoto, *Kinsei Shōgyō Keiei no Kenkyū* (Studies in Management of Merchants in the Edo period), *Miyamoto Mataji Chosakushū*,

Vol. II, 1977.

4. Eiichiro Ogura, *Goshū Nakaike Chōai no Hō* (The Method of Book-keeping of the Nakais in Omi District in the Edo Period), Kyoto, 1962. N. Nishikawa, *Kigyō Katsudō no Shiteki Tenkai* (Book-keeping of the Mitsui Partnership in the Edo Period), S. Yonekawa and M. Hirata, ed., *Kigyō Katsudō no Riron to Rekishi* (Theory and History of Business Activities), Tokyo, 1982. S. Takatera and S. Daigo, *Daikigyo Kaikeishi no Kenkyū* (Studies in the History of Big Business), Tokyo, 1979. Johannes Hirchschmeier and Tsunehiko Yui, *The Development of Japanese Business*, George Allen and Unwin, Harvard University Press, 1975.

5. H. Morikawa, *Nihongata Keiei no Genryū* (The Origin of Japanese Management), Tokyo, 1973. H. Morikawa, *Nihongata Keiei no Tenkai* (The Development of Japanese Management), Tokyo, 1980.

6. L. Hannah, Introduction to "From Family Firm to Professional Management," Adadémiai Kiadó, Budapest, 1982.

7. R. A. Church, *The Transition from Family Firm to Managerial Enterprise in the Motor Industry, an International Comparison.*

8. F. Jequier and D. S. Landes, *Swiss Watch Supremacy under Challenge: A Case Study in Enterpreneurial Response.*

9. T. C. Baker and M. Lévy-Leboyer, *An Inquiry into the Buddenbrook Effect in Europe.*

10. H. Hanák, *The Relationship between Family Enterprise and Managerial Enterprise.*

11. H. Keable, *From the Family Enterprise to the Professional Manager: The German Case.*

12. H. Nussbaum, *Cartels and Syndicates in the Process of Transition from Family to Large-scale Enterprise: Germany and Britain.*

13. H. Morikawa, *The Development of Management by Salaried Top Executives in Modern Japan 1868 to 1930.*

14. Shin'ichi Yonekawa, *Sekai no Zaibatsu Keiei* (Management of Zaibatsu in the World), Tokyo, 1981. Shoji Ito and Tamio Hattori's papers in the proceedings.

15. There are many small family companies on the lists of Toyota and Nissan subcontractors.

16. Shigeaki Yasuoka, *Zaibatsu no Keiei-shi* (History of Zaibatsu Management), Tokyo, 1978.

17. Nobuhiko Nakai, *Mitsui-ke no Keiei* (Management of the Mitsui's Business), *Shakai Keizaishigaku* (Socio-Economic History), Vol. 31, No. 6, 1966.

18. *Aruga Kizaemon Chosakushū* (Works of Aruga Kizaemon), Vol. 9, p. 186, Tokyo, 1970.

19. S. Yasuoka, *Zaibatsu no Keiei-shi* (History of Zaibatsu Management) Tokyo, 1978, S. Yasuoka, *Ownership and Management of Family Business: An International Comparison*, the United Nations University, Tokyo, 1982.

20. S. Yasuoka, ibid.

21. Zaidan Hōjin Mitsui Bunko, ed., *Mitsui Jigyō-shi* (Mitsui Enterprise History), No. 3 (1976) and Shigeaki Yasuoka, *Zaibatsu Keiseishi no Kenkyū* (A Study on the Formative History of the Zaibatsu), Minerva Shobō, Kyoto, 1970. The latter which contains all the articles of the Mitsui family code.

22. *Yasuda Hozensha to Sono Kankei Jigyō-shi* (Yasuda Family Company and the History of its Related Activities), Yasuda Real Estate Co. Ltd., 1974, pp. 114 ff.

23. The basis underlying the Kōnoike family code of 1889 was carried on to the revised one of 1899. The comparison of the two is found in Kensuke Hiroyama, "Meiji Taishō-ki ni okeru Kōnoike no Kigyō Katsudō, I" (Business Activities of the Kōnoike Family in the Meiji and Taisho Periods, I), *Osaka Daigaku Keizaigaku* (The University of Osaka, Department of Economics), Vol. 29, No. 1, 1979.

24. S. Yasuoka, "Shōka ni okeru Kaken no Seiritsu (Shiron)—Sumitomo Kahō no Kakureta Bubun tono Kanren ni oite" [The Establishment of Family Codes in Merchant Families—in relation to the hidden section of the Sumitomo family code], Doshisha University, Institute for the Study of Humanities and Social Sciences, *Shakai Kagaku* [Social Science], No. 24 (1978).

25. Shūko Shirayanagi, Sumitomo Monogatari (The Tale of Sumitomo), Chikura Shobō, Tokyo, 1931.

26. Compilation Committee on the biographies of Yataro and Yanosuke Iwasaki, *Iwasaki Yanosuke Den* (A Biography of Yanosuke Iwasaki), 1971, p. 297.

27. *Mitsubishi Shashi* (Mitsubishi Company History), Vol. 21, University of Tokyo Press, Tokyo, 1980, p. 961.

28. The following cases are primarily based on Shigeaki Yasuoka, *Zaibatsu no Keiei-shi* (op. cit.).

29. It is said that there are enough reference books regarding the history of the Rothschild family to fill a large library. However, the following are easily obtained: Jean Bouvier, *Rothschild*, trans. into Japanese by Ryūichirō Inoue (Kawade Shobō Shinsha, Tokyo, 1969), Frederic

Morton, *Rothschild Ōkoku* (The Rothschild Plutocracy), trans. into Japanese by Tomiyasu Takahara (Shinchōsha, Tokyo, 1975), Yasuo Nakagi, *Rothschild Ke* (The Rothschild Family), Seibun-do Shinkōsha, Tokyo, 1980.

30. W. H. A. Kerr, *Du Pont*, trans. into Japanese by Toshiko Morikawa (Kawade Shobō Shinsha, Tokyo, 1969).

31. J. K. Winkler, *Du Pont Dynasty*, 1935.

32. M. Duke, *The du Ponts*, 1976, p. 129.

33. This passage is based upon Minoru Morota, *Krupp* (Toyō Keizai Shinpō-sha, Tokyo, 1970).

34. Shigechika Urata, "Krupp-ke no Shūen" (The Final of the Krupp Family), *Sekai Shūhō*, Vol. 48, No. 36, September 1967.

35. Shoji Ito, "Indo ni okeru Zaibatsu no Shutsuji ni Tsuite" (Regarding the Emergence of a Financial Clique in India), *Keizai to Keizaigaku* (Economy and Economics), 1978. Isamu Hirota, "Indo ni okeru Kazokuteki Keiei no Seiritsu Jijō—Parsees Bourgeoisie o Sozai to shite" (Circumstances Pertaining to the Establishment of Family Management—with special reference to the Parsee bourgeoisie), *Shōgaku Ronshū* (Theories on Business), Doshisha University, Graduate School, No. 14, 1979. The passage here was mainly based on Hirota's thesis.

36. On the basis of Keiichiro Nakagawa's theory *Hikaku Keieishi Josetsu* (An Introduction to Comparative Management), University of Tokyo Press, 1981, p. 246. Hirota considers that a family business was first transformed into family management and then into a corporation.

# COMMENTS

Hidemasa Morikawa
*Hosei University*

## I.

We can begin our study of family enterprises with the Chandler model as a common framework. The Chandler model distinguished clearly four types of modern business enterprises along the historical transition: entrepreneurial, family, financially dominated and managerial. Chandler described, "The first type of modern business enterprise can then be labeled the entrepreneurial or family firm (it was, naturally, entrepreneurial in the first generation and family-dominated thereafter); the second type can be called the financially dominated firm. . . . Firms in which representatives of the founding families or financial interests no longer make top-level management decisions—where such decisions are made by salaried managers who own little of the companies' stock—can be labeled managerial enterprises."*

At the recent session of the Budapest congress, the Chandler model was often referred to by the attendents. I basically agree with this model, except for a few points.

1. Some scholars criticize the Chandler model because of its simple dichotomy: family enterprise and managerial enterprise. But they misunderstand. Chandler recognizes intermediate types of enterprise between family and managerial, such as financially dominated. And many scholars emphasize the ability of family enterprises to survive and question the transition from family to managerial enterprise as in the Chandler model. Surely, it is commonly overemphasized today that family enterprises seek, most of all, stability and permanency at the expense of their own growth

---

* Alfred D. Chandler, Jr. and Herman Daems, eds., *Managerial Hierarchies* (Cambridge, Massachusetts and London, 1980), pp. 13–14.

and innovation; and that once an industrial dynasty has been founded, the second and third generations, or even the founder himself, often lose interest in managing the firm and expend their energies and money on unrelated activities such as politics, social works, art, sports and the like.

However, there are also other advantages in family enterprises. They can make decisions rapidly and, free from the restrictions of stockholders, secure corporate royalties through kinship ties and train successors well in advance. Therefore, it is natural that many scholars point out the capability of family enterprises to survive. But it is meaningless to discuss whether the family enterprise is successful or not, because answers can be different according to the situation in which the enterprise operates. The Chandler model describes the long-term trend of transition from family to managerial enterprise.

2. Many scholars, including A. D. Chandler, fail to account for why the above mentioned transition occurred. They conclude that the enlargement of scale and the increasing number of units within the firm forced the family, as the owner, to offer stocks for public subscription and to consequently lose its controlling power within the firm, which is then taken over by salaried managers. Yet the public offering of stocks does not always indicate a transition to managerial enterprise. In prewar Japan, for instance, the Mitsui zaibatsu was a managerial enterprise, although it was owned entirely by the Mitsui family. We must be careful not to assume that shareholding corresponds directly to managerial authority within a firm. Furthermore, offering stocks to the public may bring about the participation in top management not of salaried managers but powerful capitalists from outside. Or, on the other hand, a family can still retain a large percentage of shares and dominate top management after selling shares in their company.

Rather, another reason Chandler proposes seems to be important. He points out that the development of large companies required a hierarchy of salaried managers that would take over top management and succeed the family members. But this is not sufficient to explain why salaried managers can rise into top management. Here, we must consider the need to motivate salaried managers and to utilize their managerial skills by drawing them up into top management.

3.  Ultimately, the long-term transition from a family to managerial enterprise occurs because the number of family members with managerial talents is limited, and by comparison, the number of salaried, talented managers is almost unlimited. If educational opportunity is so unequal that the upper class, to which the entrepreneurial family usually belongs, alone benefits, then this difference between family and salaried managers may not be so large. Still, the egalitarianization of education widens the gap.

## II.

1.  Professor Yasuoka regards the zaibatsu as representative of Japanese family enterprises. I would like to ask him, however, whether the zaibatsu developed because they were family enterprises, or in spite of this fact. By emphasizing the consistency and unchanging nature of specific features of Japanese family enterprises, such as closed ownership by a family or the delegation of authority from the family to the *bantō* type of salaried managers, Yasuoka succeeds in explaining the continuance of Japanese family enterprises for many years after the Tokugawa period until recent days. But he does not account for their development. After the Meiji Restoration, there occurred a fundamental transformation in the entrepreneurial situation. Family enterprises had to be able to respond to this and reorganize effectively in order to develop. They had to carry on new and modern businesses, and to succeed, they had to employ new salaried managers who were highly educated, as distinguished from the *bantō*, who were trained through experience alone within a narrow field.

2.  There is also the definitional problem of confusing professional managers with salaried managers. They are not the same. The former contrasts with an amateur manager, and refers to a full-time, specially trained, high-income-seeking individual. Full-time activity and specialized training can be found as well in the owner-manager. The type of manager that seeks high income by offering his specialized services and moves from company to company is rare in Japan, where lifetime employment is common. When we discuss the development of managerial enterprises, we must use

the term "salaried manager," as opposed to an owner or capitalist,
and not "professional manager."

3.  In modern Japan, three types of combinations of family enterprises and salaried managers developed. (a) In traditional family
enterprises, *bantō* salaried managers who were delegated top managerial authority from the family for a long period of time were
superseded by the highly educated and technocratic salaried managers. (b) In the family enterprises newly established after the Meiji
Restoration, the founder was in firm control, assisted by highly
educated, salaried middle-management personnel. After the founder
died, however, the top management of such companies was transferred to the cooperative efforts of family members and highly educated salaried managers. (c) In the joint-stock companies owned by
several capitalists, these salaried managers with specialized educa-
tions advanced into top management after the latter part of the
Meiji period (ca. 1905–1912), replacing capitalist managers who
took similar positions in other firms and consequently could not
concentrate on managing one company. Top salaried managers were
able to buy stock in their companies due to the high remuneration
paid to them and thus become large shareholders. They combined
the status of large shareholders with long experience in management
and influence over younger salaried managers, and as a result, transformed the firms in which they worked into a particular kind of
family enterprise that allowed them to bequeath the status of chief
executive, usually the presidency, to their sons.

4.  We can find a number of big family enterprises in present
day Japan. All of them are developing through the cooperation of
family and salaried managers. But they can be classified into four
groups according to the relationship between family member and
salaried managers in the top management.

   ①  Suntory:  family members always grasp powerful leader-
       ship of top management.

           Family declines to offer stocks for public subscription and
       holds 94% of total stocks. Family members secure each
       level of top management.

           President, Saji Keizo (second son of the founder, Torii
       Shinjiro)

Vice-president, Torii Nobuo (third son of the founder)

Semmu (Senior managing director), Torii Shih-ichiro (eldest son of Saji Keizo's elder brother)

Jōmu (Managing director), Torii Junji (nephew of the founder)

Director, Saji Nobutada (eldest son of Saji Keizo)

② Toyota Motor: the family's power is increasing.

Chairman, Toyoda Eiji (cousin of the founder, Toyoda Kiichiro)

President, Toyoda Shoichiro (eldest son of the founder)

Jōmu (Managing director), Toyoda Tatsuo (second son of the founder)

③ Ajinomoto: good balance between family and salaried managers continues.

Chairman, Suzuki Saburosuke the 4th (grandson of the founder, Suzuki Saburosuke, Jr.)

Vice-president, Suzuki Tadao (grandson of younger brother of the founder)

Senior Auditor, Suzuki Kyoji (grandson in law of the founder)

Auditor, Suzuki Michiyo (nephew of the founder)

④ Bridgestone: the power of the family is declining.

In 1973, family members were five, including the founder, Ishibashi Shoichiro. But in that year, president Ishibashi Kan-ichiro (eldest son of the founder) retired to become chairman; in 1976, Vice-president Narumo Shuichi (husband of the second daughter of the founder) died and then the founder died. In 1978, Semmu Hirakawa Ken-ichiro (nephew of the founder) resigned as director and in 1980, Semmu Ishii Koichiro (husband of the fourth daughter of the founder) was transferred to the presidency of a subsidiary company (Bridgestone Cycle) and became a director.

# The Position and Role of Family Business in the Development of the Japanese Company System

Matao Miyamoto
*Osaka University*

## I. Introduction

The aim of this paper is to investigate the changing position and role of family business in the development of the company system during the industrialization of Japan. More specifically, we will examine four topics as follows. First, we will look at the structure of firms, the ownership patterns and the management characteristics of big merchant houses in pre-modern Japan. Second, we will examine how the joint-stock company system was introduced into Japan after the Meiji Restoration (1868), what kinds of problems developed and how the position and role of family business changed in the process. Third, the distribution of family and non-family companies, and the relationship between ownership patterns and the legal forms of companies will be examined. Fourth, we will compare the financial performance of family and non-family companies, and of partnerships, limited partnerships and joint-stock companies, in order to reveal the management characteristics of family business.

Before discussing these topics, let us first examine the definition of "family business." The narrowest definition is "the family firm, in which the majority of capital is held by a single family or by a few families, and which is directly controlled and managed by these owner families." However, we should not restrict our discussion solely to typical and rather primitive forms of family business. Let us categorize the following types of firms as family businesses: 1) firms, in which the majority of capital is held by a single family or a few families, but which are managed by non-family members, 2) firms in which the share of capital held by a particular family is minor, but which are nonetheless controlled and managed by the family. More generally, let us define family businesses as follows: firms controlled, managed and/or majority-owned by a particular family.

## II. Ownership Patterns and Management Characteristics in the Merchant Houses of Tokugawa Japan

### 1. Ownership Patterns

Most Tokugawa merchant houses were individual proprietorships. Collective enterprises or joint investment ventures were not common. A few examples of collective enterprises can be found, although they were rather primitive. One was the joint investment or joint risk venture contracted among traders, ship captains and investors who were engaged in foreign trade before the age of national isolation (*sakoku*) which began in the 1630s. The practice went as follows: when the captain, authorized by the Government to engage in foreign trade, planned an overseas voyage, he would seek funds to meet the cost of the venture. These funds were usually offered by a trader who raised money from many other investors. In this case, the trader was not only a capitalist with unlimited liability but also the manager responsible for the venture, while the individual investors were merely financiers with limited liability who did not engage in business decisions. If the voyage succeeded, the profits were divided among the captain, the trader and the investors, with profit shares determined by the amount of their investment and the risks undertaken. When the voyage failed as a result of shipwreck or other accidents, the trader had no obligation to pay back the money to the investors, and could not ask the investors to bear the loss beyond their originally invested capital. The term of the investments was usually six months. Therefore, such investments may be understood to have been short-term risk ventures.[1]

Similar contracts are found for domestic long-distance trade and shipping in the latter half of the Tokugawa period. In this case, the captain and shipping agent with unlimited liability would raise funds from investors with limited liability. The profit and loss were divided among the three in the manner mentioned above.[2]

As an additional example, money exchangers (*ryogaeya*) in Osaka sometimes formed cooperative organizations for lending money to *Daimyo* (feudal lords), in which investors with unlimited and limited liability both participated. These cooperative ventures were called "*Kanyu Gashi*" (cooperative loans).[3] Ohmi merchants, a famous merchant group in the Tokugawa period, also formed collective enterprises in which several merchants jointly invested. These enterprises were generally short-lived, but in one case the enterprise lasted sixteen years.[4]

The above were all examples of joint investments in which capitalists with unlimited liability, who were responsible for management, and capitalists with limited liability, who had no responsibility for management, cooperated. Therefore, this type of joint investment might be called a limited partnership. However, most were temporary arrangements, and the number of members and the range of investors were limited. As a consequence, joint-stock companies and the like, in which all investors had limited liability, never emerged in the Tokugawa period.

The preceding examples of joint investments represents contracts between people who had no kinship relations. More popular than these, however, were family partnerships, of which the Mitsui house was typical. One of the most powerful Tokugawa merchant houses, the Mitsui engaged in drapery and money exchange on a nationwide scale. Originally under the founder, Takatoshi Mitsui (1622–94), the Echigoya (the name of Mitsui chain) was an individual proprietorship. After the death of Takatoshi, the Echigoya became a kind of partnership among his children. An organization called the *Ohmotokata* was set up to superintend the business interests of the Mitsui family in 1710. The fortune which Takatoshi left was not divided among his nine children, but was held by the *Ohmotokata* organization as the common assets of the Mitsui house. The heirs of the nine children's houses (afterwards expanded to eleven houses) continued for generations to be the co-owners of the *Ohmotokata*. However, no house could withdraw its shares or dispose of its assets individually. Every branch house had an equal right to speak regarding business decisions and management of the Mitsui business. And each branch had unlimited liability to the *Ohmotokata*. In this sense, the *Ohmotokata* of the Mitsui house can be called a kind of partnership.[5]

Another powerful merchant house in the Tokugawa period was the Konoike house in Osaka, which opened business as a *sake* brewer at the beginning of the seventeenth century, and afterwards became a powerful money exchanger. The Konoike adopted the practice of partible inheritance during the seventeenth century while business grew very rapidly. Moreover, the assets of the house were divided among the employees. As a result, many branch houses and branch stores were set up. But, unlike the Mitsui, Konoike branch houses carried on business independently. In other words, in the case of the Konoike house, family capital tended not to be consolidated but to be dispersed. This practice was finally abandoned after the middle of the eighteenth century when the Konoike, who had specialized in money lending to *Daimyo*, were suffering from declining profits. Thereafter, the house could no longer afford to divide its assets among its sons and employees. As a consequence, the creation of branch families was restricted, and further, the assets of small branch families tended to be amalgamated with those of the main house or the more powerful branch families. Most of the small branch families lost their independence from the main Konoike house, and instead participated in the money lending activities carried on by the main house or by the more powerful branch families. In this case, the former branch families became mere share-holders in the Konoike enterprise and did not take part in determining conditions for loans or in the selection of borrowers. The main house and the powerful branch houses were responsible for all business decisions. Therefore, the Konoike house enterprise may be viewed as a kind of limited partnership.[6]

As noted above, examples of kinship-based joint investment existed among the big merchant houses of Tokugawa Japan. However, we should pay attention to the fact that the aim of joint investments and the range of joint investors in the Tokugawa cases were somewhat different from those of modern joint-stock companies. In the latter case, capital is combined in order to enlarge the scale of business. In other words, the amalgamation of assets is directed to a growth-oriented strategy. Moreover, capital is raised from a more broadly defined social base. In contrast to this, as seen in the Mitsui and Konoike examples, the capital assets of the families were joined to defend against the dispersion of the capital accumulated among the families. Further, kinship was usually the base on which capital was raised. We may conclude from the above that as far as the structure of ownership is concerned, businesses in the Tokugawa period were under familial constraints.

We can point to many reasons why non-kinship-based and long-lived joint-stock companies did not emerge in the Tokugawa period. Among them the following three seem most important: 1) under the national isolation imposed by the Tokugawa Bakufu after the 1630s, international trade, which involved great risks and required large-scale capital investment, did not develop; 2) capital-intensive manufacturing industries did not emerge on a large scale; and 3) social overhead capital for such projects as canals and roads, which require large amounts of long-term capital investment, was usually provided not by the private sector but by feudal authorities. As a result, the demand for the kind of large-scale capital investment made possible by joint-stock companies was very limited and this form of enterprise did not develop in Tokugawa Japan.

## 2. Management Characteristics

Big merchant houses in the Tokugawa period were advanced with respect to the functional separation of household and firm. In the case of the Mitsui house, each family of the clan received two kinds of funds from the *Ohmotokata*, one for running their business and the other for living expenses. However, to use money from one for the purpose of the other was strictly forbidden.[7] The Mitsui, Konoike, Nakai (one of the famous Ohmi merchant houses) and other big merchant houses adopted highly developed methods of accounting, the principles of which were similar to double-entry bookkeeping. They employed clerks who were responsible for accounting and bookkeeping. The clerks administered house assets and the distribution of business profits. The House Code of the Konoike family prescribed that even the head of the house could not dispose of house assets without consultation with non-family managers and with other members of the family.

The head of the house was formally the manager of the business, but he was not allowed to make independent business decisions. In the 1713 Konoike House Code, the position of the house head was described as follows: "the heir of the main house (*Honke*) is to be responsible for maintaining and preserving house assets until he turns over his position to his successor. Therefore, he should follow the established traditions of the house on every matter."[8] Although the house headship was to be inherited by the eldest son in each successive generation, adopted sons sometimes assumed the office when real children were judged to be unqualified. In such cases, the person to be adopted was usually selected from among the most competent employees or from among the relatives of the house. Some examples have been reported from Kyoto merchant houses in which dissipated and unreliable house heads were purged by chief clerks employed to protect the long-range interests of the enterprise.[9] The house head occasionally made decisions on management. However, the most important decisions were usually made in a council of the house head and chief clerks.

As noted above, persons who were not related by blood to the merchant house could sometimes become the head or top managers of the family enterprise. Therefore, merchant houses in the Tokugawa period were not always family-controlled or family-managed enterprises, in spite of their structure as family-owned businesses. However, this does not mean that professional management prevailed in those days. The employees who were promoted to such top positions as chief clerk (*Banto* or *Shihainin*) as well as those adopted into the house were usually former apprentices who had entered the house during childhood or early adolescence and had been trained in the house. They were not promoted to important managerial positions until they had been recognized as quasi-members of the family who had demonstrated absolute loyalty to their host family. In this sense, the management of big merchant houses in the Tokugawa period might be characterized as a system based on management by fictive members of the house who could be counted on to protect the house assets from abuses by family members.

We may conclude this section by stating that in the merchant houses of Tokugawa Japan, familial constraints were stronger in the structure of ownership than in that of management and that these characteristics of the Tokugawa merchant houses provided the pre-conditions for the development of the company system after the Meiji Restoration of 1868.

## III. The Introduction and Development of the Company System and Family Business

### 1. Companies Prior to the Commercial Code of 1893

*Companies in the Early Meiji Period*

In 1867, the last year of the Tokugawa period, an organization for foreign trade named *Hyogo Shosha* (Hyogo Trading Company) was established with funds from the Konoike and other rich merchants in the Kansai area. The purpose of the organization was to prepare for opening the port of Hyogo. The Tokugawa Bakufu had promised the world powers, by the Commercial treaties of 1858, that they would open this port to trade. However, these merchants did not voluntarily join together to form this organization but were compelled to participate by the Tokugawa Bakufu which could not afford to cover the expenses for opening the port. The principles of the organization came from the Western company system. However, the organization cannot properly be called a company because the individual participants did not join together to carry on business, but were still independent in doing business. Therefore, this organization may be viewed as a kind of merchant association. Further, it lasted only six months, in large part because its sponser, the Tokugawa Bakufu collapsed.[10] In 1869, the new Meiji government urged the rich merchants in the major cities to form companies for trading and financing. As a result, companies, called *Tusho Gaisha* (Trading company) and *Kawase Gaisha* (Exchange company) were established in eight major cities. These companies were joint ventures among numbers of people and were independent legal entities with rights and duties separate from those of their investors. Moreover, they were the first companies that issued stock certificates, although the negotiability of the certificates was limited. In this sense, it is true that these were new types of collective enterprises in Japan. They were, however, not joint-stock companies in the strict sense for the following reasons: 1) limited liability was not established; 2) profits were divided not according to the performance of the companies but on a fixed rate basis; and 3) the board of directors was not organized in the fashion of joint-stock companies. In short, these companies may be viewed as prototypes of joint-stock companies. They failed within three or four years, partly because of the merchants' reluctance to participate in joint ventures. This may have been the result of their inexperience in collective enterprise and a lack of understanding of the Western company system.[11]

After the failure of these companies, the Meiji government continued to make various efforts to introduce the joint-stock company system as one of their measures to enrich and strengthen the country. In 1871, the Ministry of Finance published two explanatory books to help the promoters of companies: one was titled *"Rikkai Ryakusoku"* (Outline of Setting up Companies) written by Eiichi Shibusawa, an official of the Ministry at that time who later became one of the most powerful Japanese business leaders. Shibusawa wrote this book, having studied the Western company system during his stay in Europe. The other book was *"Kaisha Ben"* (On Companies), a translation of the chapter on banking in a Western book of economics. Aside from these two books, a number of enlightening pamphlets were written by the intellectuals in those days.[12] The contents of these books were rather primitive; nevertheless, many companies were established under their influence.

*The Case of the Horai-sha*

Some old merchants also formed joint-stock companies, for example, the Horai-sha, a company set up in 1873.[13] Three groups of promoters joined together in setting up this company. One group came from among Osaka and Tokyo merchants, namely the Konoike, Hirooka, Osada, Shimada and others, most of whom had been merchant-financiers and money lenders to *Daimyo* in the Tokugawa period. Another group was composed of ex-samurai, such as Shojiro Goto, Tsuna Takeuchi and others, who were high-ranking government officials or had special connections with important persons in the government. Two *Daimyo* families, the Hachisuka and the Ue-sugi, formed the third group. In the initial plan, promoters sought to raise capital in the amount of 4,450 thousand yen: 3,400 thousand yen from the merchant group and 1,050 thousand yen from the two *Daimyo*. The ex-samurai group was not expected to offer money. But why were these three groups joined together?

The merchant group had loaned a great deal of money to *Daimyo* by the end of the Tokugawa period. As creditors, they were anxious about how the *Daimyo* debts would be taken over by the new govern-ment. Moreover, they feared that they might lose their traditional rights to carry on business as authorized merchants, dealing in tax rice, money exchange, handling government money and other busi-nesses. They were appealing to the government to take proper mea-sures in their favor. The Osaka merchants, in particular, petitioned Shojiro Goto (a former governor of Osaka Prefecture and a councilor of the government at that time) for support. They urged him to use his position in the government to compel repayment of outstanding *Daimyo* loans. Goto agreed to this, but in return demanded that the merchants contribute funds to this joint venture. Goto acted, in effect, as the leader and organizer of the company. He obtained the participation of both the merchant families and the *Daimyo* as investors, though it is unclear how he persuaded the latter to join.

The range of business activities of the new company was expected to range from the traditional businesses, which had been carried on by the merchant group, to the new manufacturing industries, such as paper manufacturing, mining and sugar refining, in which the ex-samurai group was interested.

However, Goto's efforts did not achieve fruition. He succeeded in obtaining the rights to deal in tax rice and to handle government money, but failed to obtain full repayment of the merchants' loans to *Daimyo*. Although the Konoike, for example, had extended 1,200 thousand yen in loans, the amount of repayment was set at 300 thousand yen. When the merchants subsequently lost interest in the company, it became clear that their primary objective had not been to set up the company itself. Rather, they had seen this as an op-portunity to obtain repayment of outstanding loans. As a conse-quence, new arrangements had to be made in 1874 regarding

investments by the three groups: 1) the capital of the company was
reduced from 3,400 to 2,500 thousand yen; 2) the amount of capital
invested by Tokyo merchants and ex-samurai increased, while that
invested by Osaka merchants remained unsettled; and 3) two types
of stock certificates were to be issued: one was preferred stock which
guaranteed the stock holders dividends on a fixed rate basis and
guaranteed refundment of the principal, and the other was deferred
stock with limited liability, involving higher risk but also for higher
profitability. These arrangements reflected the conservative attitude
of the Osaka merchant group toward the company.

The *Horai-sha* opened business under these conditions. Shojiro
Goto was selected as the president and other ex-samurai assumed the
administrative posts. The merchants served on the board of directors
and sent their clerks to the company as managers. The two *Daimyo*
acted simply as investors; they did not engage actively in management. Not only had separation of ownership and management been
established, so, too, had a system of limited liability for all investors.

The *Horai-sha*, given its principles of organization, deserves to be
called a joint-stock company. However, it did not in reality work as
such. The Osaka merchants were not active in doing business carried
out under the name of the *Horai-sha*, but still clung to their own businesses. When the company happened to suffer a loss which was
clearly attributable to one of the Osaka merchants, other members of
the Osaka merchant group insisted that the expense be borne not by
the company but rather by the merchant directly responsible. It
would appear that the merchants did not understand the concept
of corporate responsibility.

Moreover, the Osaka merchants frequently tried to withdraw
their investments from the *Horai-sha*, since they were not interested
in such new businesses as paper manufacturing, sugar refining and
mining, which required large quantities of long term capital investment. As their interests were restricted to traditional businesses,
they did not have to promote the joint-venture type of business unless
they could obtain other benefits from doing so. As a consequence, the
*Horai-sha*, for all its advantages in corporate form, lasted only three
years.

The story noted above is, we believe, instructive in revealing how difficult it was for the old merchant houses to transform themselves into the joint-stock companies of the early Meiji period.

### National Banks

Learning from the American banking system, the Meiji government promulgated the National Banking Act in 1872, which declared that the national bank should be organized as a form of joint-stock company. This Act aimed at establishing modern banking institutions as well as giving work to ex-samurai who had by then been deprived of their right to feudal stipends. However, since the Act set rigid conditions on the establishment of national banks, only four were set up. The government revised the Act in 1876 to encourage people—especially ex-samurai—to promote the banks. The revised Act allowed them to pay up the capital of banks through government bonds which they had received as compensation for the feudal stipends they had previously been awarded. A total of 149 national banks were established in the period from 1876 to 1879. And the total amount of paid-up capital amounted to 4,211 million yen by the end of 1880. 44% of this was paid up by ex-*Daimyo*, 32% by ex-samurai and 24% by commoners.[14] Therefore, the national banks are sometimes called "samurai banks." We cannot deny that the promotion of the national banks was facilitated by the capitalization of samurai-held government bonds. However, in some cases merchants or landowners took the initiative in promoting the national banks. Moreover, the samurai's share (including that of *Daimyos'*) of the total capital gradually decreased, since it tended to be taken over by commoners as the banks themselves increased their holdings. By the end of 1896, the share invested by commoners had increased to 50% of the total amount of capital.[15]

In Osaka, thirteen national banks were set up between 1876 and 1880. Among them, the 13th, the 32nd, and the 148th national banks had been promoted by former money exchangers: the 13th by the Konoike, the 32nd by the Hirase and the 148th by the Yamaguchi. The 34th was set up by the wholesale merchants of drapery, and the 58th by rice brokers and others. It is indeed doubtful that these banks, set up as joint-stock companies, thoroughly escaped "familial" constraints. In the case of the 13th national bank, there were 34 stockholders in total. However, all of the stockholders came from the Konoike clan, including the Konoike main house and branch houses. Moreover, as the main house kept all of the stock certificates and forbade the stockholders to freely dispose of their certificates, the positions of all stockholders except those of the main house remained nominal.[16] The same was the case in the 148th national bank which was set up by the Yamaguchi house.[17]

As for the management in these banks, the employed clerks or the competent persons among the more powerful branch families continued to take charge of daily business decisions as had been the case in the Tokugawa period. The head of the main house remained a titular position. In short, it may be said that these old merchant houses adapted their family businesses to the legal form of the joint-stock company, but in fact maintained traditional patterns of ownership and management.

At any rate, the national banking mania from 1876 to 1879 represented the first phase in the diffusion of the joint-stock company system in Japan. Under the stimulus of the national banking mania, many companies were established during a few years of inflation around 1877. The word *Kaisha* (company) symbolized civilization to people in those days; it became fashionable to set up a company. However, not a small number of these companies were "bubble" companies. Most of them failed during the deflation period of 1881–1884 under the tight economic policy of the Minister of Finance, Masayoshi Matsukata.

*Railway, Cotton Spinning and the Zaibatsu Companies*
Again, after the Matsukata deflation, many new companies were established. The number of companies increased from 1,772 in 1883 to 4,067 in 1889. The nominal capital of the companies, which had been 30 million yen in 1883, reached 183 million yen in 1889.[18] Among the companies founded in those days, those in the fields of railway and cotton spinning quickly adopted the form of the joint-stock company. According to the statistics on these companies,[19] there were fifteen railway companies in 1889. Their paid-up capital amounted to 17,849 thousand yen and the number of investors was

7,381. Thus, the average paid-up capital and the average number of investors per company came to 1,189 thousand yen and 492 persons, respectively. As for cotton spinning, collectively the forty-one companies held 7,499 thousand yen in total paid-up capital and had 6,109 persons as investors. The average per company amounted to 182 thousand yen in paid-up capital and 149 investors. The average paid-up capital and the average number of investors per company for all companies amounted to 22 thousand yen and 55 investors, respectively. The railway and cotton spinning companies were the largest-sized companies at that time, both in terms of the amount of capital and the number of investors. We may assume that the capital of these companies was raised by a number of investors beyond the boundaries of kinship and local community, and that non-kinship based joint-stock companies prevailed in both the railway and cotton spinning fields. Much the same is true in such fields as electric lighting and insurance. The organizational structure as well as technology and know-how were transplanted from the West in these fields.

On the other hand, the situation was different in such fields as mining, foreign trade and shipbuilding. For example, the number of investors per mining company was only 2.9 persons, despite the relatively large amount of paid-up capital per company, amounting to 27 thousand yen. In the case of foreign trade, the number of investors per company was 9.6 while the paid-up capital per company was 88 thousand yen. Judging from the above, most of the companies in these fields were likely to take the form of partnership or kinship-based joint-stock companies. It may be interesting to recall that the companies of the *zaibatsu* cliques were prominent in these fields. The *zaibatsu* had enough family funds to finance their business activities while preserving the pattern of family ownership, even if they embarked on capital-intensive industries. In the fields of traditional craft industries, such as tobacco, bean paste and soy sauce manufacturing, small-size companies with a small number of investors prevailed. For example, the average capital of the companies in the fields of bean paste and soy sauce manufacturing was 5 thousand yen, and the average number of investors was 2.9 persons. As these industries did not require a large amount of capital and were less

risky, the family owners did not necessarily have to join their capital
with those of others even if their enterprises were formally joint-
stock companies.

## 2. The Development of the Company System after the Enforcement of the Commercial Code

*The Enforcement of the Commercial Code*[20]

During the first twenty years of the Meiji period, commercial
legislation consisted of ad hoc regulations and special enabling acts,
in spite of the rapid growth of the joint-stock company system. However, the government, which was enthusiastic to introduce the company system, made continuous efforts to prepare a comprehensive
Commercial Code from the beginning of the Meiji period. The
Commercial Code, commonly called the Old Commercial Code,
was finally promulgated in 1890. Nevertheless, as many businessmen
and lawyers pronounced that it was too early to enforce the Code,
the government could not help but postpone enforcement.

However, at the time of the panic in 1890, many companies became bankrupt and a number of legal disputes arose concerning the
interpretation of the limited liability system. In view of the circumstances, the government decided to enforce parts of the Commercial
Code, including the Company Law. The Company Law defined a
company as an independent entity with its own assets, rights and duties independent of those of the investors (although Company Law
did not expressly name companies legal entities). More importantly, companies were put into three categories under the Law: 1)
joint-stock companies (*Kabushiki Gaisha*), 2) limited partnerships
(*Goshi Gaisha*), and 3) partnerships (*Gomei Gaisha*). The Company
Law laid the legal foundation for the Japanese company system and
encouraged people to form and manage companies. But the Law
also had significant defects. It adopted licensing systems both with
regard to the promotion of joint-stock companies and the issuance of
company bonds, and the Law failed to provide regulations regarding
company mergers.

In 1899, the Old Commercial Code was abolished and replaced
by the New Commercial Code. This New Code itself was revised in

TABLE 1 Companies, Capital Assets and Capital per Company, 1896–1939.

| | Number of companies | | | | Paid-up capital | | | | | Paid-up capital per company | | |
| | Total | Percentage | | | Total million yen | Percentage | | | Average ¥1,000 | Average ¥1,000 | | |
| | | P. | L.P. | J.S. | | P. | L.P. | J.S. | | P. | L.P. | J.S. |
|---|---|---|---|---|---|---|---|---|---|---|---|---|---|
| 1896 | 4,596 | 7.5% | 36.3% | 56.2% | 397 | 3.1% | 6.9% | 89.9% | 87(100) | 43(100) | 19(100) | 139(100) |
| 1900 | 8,588 | 9.1 | 41.4 | 49.5 | 779 | 4.9 | 5.8 | 89.3 | 91(105) | 49(114) | 13( 68) | 164(118) |
| 1905 | 9,006 | 14.2 | 39.0 | 46.8 | 975 | 6.2 | 5.8 | 88.0 | 108(124) | 47(109) | 16( 84) | 203(146) |
| 1910 | 12,308 | 20.3 | 38.9 | 40.8 | 1,481 | 9.5 | 6.5 | 84.0 | 120(138) | 56(130) | 20(105) | 248(178) |
| 1915 | 17,149 | 17.8 | 40.2 | 41.8 | 2,167 | 8.4 | 5.9 | 85.7 | 126(145) | 60(140) | 20(105) | 258(186) |
| 1920 | 29,917 | 15.7 | 30.0 | 54.2 | 8,238 | 7.0 | 4.6 | 88.4 | 275(316) | 123(286) | 42(221) | 456(328) |
| 1925 | 34,345 | 15.1 | 33.6 | 51.1 | 11,160 | 8.0 | 6.6 | 85.3 | 324(372) | 171(398) | 63(331) | 543(391) |
| 1930 | 51,910 | 16.4 | 46.2 | 37.4 | 19,633 | 8.5 | 6.5 | 85.0 | 378(434) | 139(323) | 38(200) | 612(440) |
| 1935 | 84,146 | 19.5 | 52.8 | 27.7 | 22,352 | 7.8 | 6.9 | 85.3 | 266(305) | 79(184) | 26(137) | 610(439) |
| 1939 | 85,122 | 17.9 | 43.0 | 39.0 | 34,025 | 5.5 | 4.0 | 90.5 | 400(460) | 92(214) | 32(168) | 693(499) |

Notes:
1) Abbreviations: P.=Partnership, L.P.=Limited Partnership, J.S.=Joint-stock Company.
2) Figures in the parentheses are indices. 1896=100.

Sources: Before 1915, Noshomusho, *Noshomu Tokei Hyo* (The Department of Agriculture and Commerce: Statistical Report of the Department of Agriculture and Commerce).
After 1920, Shokosho, *Kaisha Tokei Hyo* (The Department of Industry and Commerce: Statistical Report of Company).

TABLE 2    Companies, Capital Assets and Capital per Company by Industry

| | Agriculture | | | Fishery | | | Mining | | |
|---|---|---|---|---|---|---|---|---|---|
| | P. | L.P. | J.S. | P. | L.P. | J.S. | P. | L.P. | J.S. |
| No. of companies | | | | | | | | | |
| 1896 | 6.0% | 49.6% | 44.4% | — | — | — | — | — | — |
| 1910 | 17.9 | 38.6 | 44.6 | — | — | — | — | — | — |
| 1920 | 19.3 | 39.6 | 41.1 | 10.8% | 14.9% | 74.3% | 6.1% | 16.4% | 77.5% |
| 1939 | 15.7 | 60.5 | 23.7 | 9.9 | 40.7 | 49.4 | 2.3 | 14.4 | 83.3 |
| Paid-up capital | | | | | | | | | |
| 1896 | 4.2% | 29.8% | 66.0% | — | — | — | — | — | — |
| 1910 | 20.3 | 12.6 | 67.1 | — | — | — | — | — | — |
| 1920 | 8.4 | 3.9 | 87.7 | 3.5% | 4.9% | 91.5% | 0.6% | 13.2% | 86.2% |
| 1939 | 3.8 | 6.4 | 89.2 | 0.5 | 1.8 | 97.7 | 1.4 | 0.5 | 98.1 |
| Paid-up capital per company (¥1,000) | | | | | | | | | |
| 1896 | 10 | 9 | 21 | — | — | — | — | — | — |
| 1910 | 50 | 15 | 66 | — | — | — | — | — | — |
| 1920 | 68 | 19 | 244 | 40 | 40 | 200 | 147 | 1,127 | 1,562 |
| 1939 | 25 | 11 | 385 | 31 | 29 | 1,664 | 1,111 | 57 | 2,054 |

Sources:   Same as for Table 1.

1911. The New Code demanded only that joint-stock companies act in accordance with the Company Law; it did away with licensing procedures and prescribed negotiability of the stock certificate. Further, the revised Commercial Code of 1911 defined the duties of promoters and directors, and strictly regulated company dissolution. The progress in company legislation noted above greatly contributed to the sound development of the company system in the subsequent period.

### Company Structure before 1920

Reliable statistics on companies are available for the period after 1896. Let us trace the development of the Japanese company system using these statistics.

Table 1 shows that as early as 1896, 56.2% of all companies were joint-stock companies and 89.9% of total paid-up capital was held by joint-stock companies. This illustrates how quickly the joint-stock company system spread in the Japanese economy after the enactment of the Commercial Code. Limited partnerships ranked second both

1896–1939.

| Manufacturing | | | Commerce | | | Transportation | | |
|---|---|---|---|---|---|---|---|---|
| P. | L.P. | J.S. | P. | L.P. | J.S. | P. | L.P. | J.S. |
| 8.4% | 41.0% | 51.6% | 7.2% | 32.2% | 60.6% | 6.0% | 45.8% | 47.6% |
| 20.3 | 44.4 | 35.3 | 21.6 | 35.2 | 43.2 | 10.3 | 47.3 | 42.4 |
| 14.3 | 29.3 | 56.4 | 18.3 | 31.6 | 50.1 | 18.3 | 31.6 | 50.1 |
| 16.4 | 41.6 | 41.9 | 21.4 | 45.9 | 32.7 | 21.4 | 45.9 | 32.7 |
| 4.6% | 13.0% | 72.4% | 4.2% | 7.4% | 88.4% | 0.1% | 0.7% | 99.2% |
| 13.3 | 8.0 | 78.7 | 8.5 | 6.4 | 85.1 | 0.7 | 1.9 | 97.4 |
| 2.5 | 3.0 | 94.5 | 18.3 | 4.9 | 81.7 | 0.9 | 2.1 | 97.4 |
| 2.0 | 2.8 | 95.3 | 21.4 | 7.7 | 78.1 | 0.8 | 1.7 | 97.5 |
| 36 | 21 | 107 | 41 | 16 | 101 | 2 | 6 | 706 |
| 104 | 28 | 352 | 93 | 17 | 183 | 16 | 9 | 527 |
| 45 | 27 | 433 | 181 | 39 | 404 | 51 | 29 | 572 |
| 49 | 26 | 901 | 119 | 30 | 430 | 37 | 17 | 549 |

in number of enterprises and in paid-up capital. The number of partnerships and the amount of capital held by them were relatively small. In terms of paid-up capital per company, joint-stock companies were three times bigger than partnerships and seven times bigger than limited partnerships.

Turning to the industry-by-industry figures shown in Table 2, we find that joint-stock companies were preponderant in the fields of commerce and transportation, in terms of number of companies and/or paid-up capital, in 1896. The number of investors per company in 1898 amounted to 113 in commerce, 154 in transportation, 60 in agriculture and 55 in manufacturing. We might say that the companies in the fields of commerce and transportation, on the average, raised their capital from a broader social base. The main reason why the joint-stock type of company was preponderant in the fields of commerce and transportation is that banks were included in commerce statistics, while railway and marine transportation companies came under transportation. Were we to remove banks, railway and marine transportation companies from the statistics, it is likely that partnerships and limited partnerships would represent the dominant companies in these two fields. In the field of manufacturing, a large number of limited partnerships and partnerships with small amounts of capital coexisted with large-scale joint-stock companies.

The preponderance of the joint-stock company, as seen in 1896, was not, however, maintained in subsequent years. As seen in Table 1, the percentage of joint-stock companies declined from 56.2 in 1896 to 40.8% in 1910, while that of partnerships increased from 7.5 to 20.3% in the same period. At the same time, the percentage of the paid-up capital of joint-stock companies decreased slightly, while that of partnerships increased from 3.1 to 9.5%. The average scale of joint-stock companies, in terms of capital per company, relative to that of partnerships and limited partnerships, increased: the ratios of the capital per joint-stock company to that of partnerships and to that of limited partnerships increased from 3.2 to 4.4 and from 7.3 to 12.4, respectively, between 1896 and 1910. These trends were found for every field of industry as seen in Table 2. How should these data be interpreted?

They do not mean that the joint-stock company system tended to retreat during the period, as the number and the capital of joint-stock companies continued to grow absolutely. We argue that the relative increase both in number and in paid-up capital of partnerships can be attributed to the increasing entry of corporate-style family businesses. In other words, family business, most of which had been individual proprietorships, gradually adopted the form of partnerships, under the influence to the Commercial Code. The tax reform of 1899[21] may also have provided incentives for family businesses to turn to corporate organization. In the reform, the corporation tax was introduced for the first time. At the same time, this reform strengthened the system of progressive taxation on personal income, making it advantageous for family businesses to become corporations. They would then come under corporate tax regulations rather than personal tax regulations. Comparatively speaking, these businesses paid less tax under the corporate tax system. One of the reasons that family business preferred partnerships or limited partnerships to joint-stock companies was that such companies were not required to disclose their assets and financial conditions. Aside from this, partnerships and limited partnerships were not limited in the number of investors they could seek.

The family businesses of the *zaibatsu* as well as those of less powerful families were reorganized into partnerships or limited partnerships during the period from 1896 to 1910. In 1893, the very year of the enforcement of the Commercial Code, the mining, banking, drapery and trading businesses of the Mitsui family were reorganized as separate partnerships. The liability of these partnerships was unlimited as a matter of course. According to Professor S. Yasuoka, the Mitsui were trying to find a way to avoid risks: "although the assets of these four partnerships were the joint property of eleven family members, Mitsui divided these eleven families into four groups consisting of five, two, two and two families, and each group took responsibility for one of the four partnerships."[22] By doing so, the Mitsui expected that the failure of any one of the four partnerships would not affect the Mitsui clan as a whole. Moreover, in 1909, the eleven Mitsui families established Mitsui *Gomei* (partnership) as an organization to hold the common assets of the families and to superintend the affiliated companies.

In the case of Mitsubishi, the Mitsubishi *Goshi* (limited partnership) was established by Hisaya Iwasaki and Yanosuke Iwasaki in 1893. The liability of these two partners was limited, as this type of limited partnership was allowed by the Commercial Code of 1893. The Mitsubishi *Goshi* did not divide its businesses but organized them into departments within Mitsubishi *Goshi*, initially, banking, mining, shipbuilding and coal marketing. The Ohkura and Fujita families also formed partnerships in 1893. As an example of a less powerful family business, the Konoike bank, which had been established as an individual proprietorship in 1897, was reorganized as a partnership in 1907.

Thus, through this period of Japan's Industrial Revolution, family businesses, although changing in appearance, survived vigorously. At the same time, joint-stock companies in the modern sector also grew steadily and continued to concentrate capital.

Let us return to Tables 1 and 2. During the period from 1910–20, when Japanese heavy industries really started to grow, the relative weight of joint-stock companies again increased, as seen in Table 1.

TABLE 3    Selected Joint-Stock Companies of the Largest Three Zaibatsu Reorganized around World War I.

| Name of Company | Year of establishment or reorganization | Former forms |
|---|---|---|
| Mitsui | | |
| Mitsui Bank | 1909 | Independent partnership |
| Mitsui Bussan (trading) | 1909 | Independent partnership |
| Toshin Warehouse | 1909 | Department of Mitsui Bank |
| Mitsui Mining | 1911 | Department of Mitsui Gomei |
| Mitsubishi | | |
| Mitsubishi Shipbuilding | 1917 | Department of Mitsubishi L.P. |
| Mitsubishi Iron and Steel | 1917 | Department of Mitsubishi L.P. |
| Mitsubishi Paper Manufacturing | 1917 | Independent limited partnership |
| Mitsubishi Mining | 1918 | Two departments of Mitsubishi L.P. |
| Mitsubishi Trading | 1918 | Department of Mitsubishi L.P. |
| Mitsubishi Warehouse | 1918 | Tokyo Warehouse Co., Ltd. |
| Mitsubishi Marine and Fire Insurance | 1919 | Department of Mitsubishi L.P. |
| Mitsubishi Bank | 1919 | Department of Mitsubishi L.P. |
| Mitsubishi Manufacturing of Internal Combustion Engine | 1920 | Department of Mitsubishi Shipbuilding Co., Ltd. |
| Mitsubishi Electrics | 1921 | Department of Mitsubishi Shipbuilding Co., Ltd. |
| Sumitomo | | |
| Sumitomo Bank | 1912 | Individual proprietorship |
| Sumitomo Cast Iron | 1915 | Direct management of Sumitomo Head Office |
| Osaka Hokko (land development) | 1919 | Newly established |
| Yoshinogawa Hydroelectric | 1919 | Newly established |
| Sumitomo Manufacturing of Electric Wire | 1920 | Direct management of Sumitomo Head Office |

Sources:    Shigeaki Yasuoka, ed., *Mitsui Zaibatsu*, 1982.
Yasuo Mishima, ed., *Mitsubishi Zaibatsu*, 1981.
Yotaro Sakudo, ed., *Sumitomo Zaibatsu*, 1982.
All three books were published by Nihon Keizai Shinbunsha.

This was especially true in the field of manufacturing, in which the percentage of joint-stock companies rose from 35.3 to 56.4, with a simultaneous increase in their share of paid-up capital from 78.7 to 94.5% (Table 2).

Needless to say, the first reason for this was the aggressive development of companies in the boom period during World War I—especially in the field of heavy manufacturing and the chemical and electrical industries—caused by the stoppage of imports of iron, steel and chemical products from the West. In these capital-intensive industries, the joint-stock company was preferred as a corporate form.

Moreover, larger family firms, including *zaibatsu* family enterprises, tried to expand their own businesses and/or tried to diversify their businesses by entering new fields. This inevitably led to an increasing demand for funds. Their substantial capital accumulation notwithstanding, the family enterprises could no longer afford to finance their extended or diversified businesses alone. As a consequence, many of them adopted the joint-stock company form in order to attract outside capital when undertaking such growth-oriented strategies as diversification, and vertical and lateral integrations.

The second factor contributing to the rapid growth of joint-stock companies was the tax reform of 1913. The corporate tax system had been based previously on proportional taxation, although progressive taxation was introduced to some degree for partnerships and limited partnerships in 1905 when the special tax was newly imposed on corporations. The tax reform, however, revised the progressive taxation system for all but joint-stock companies. The tax rate for partnerships and limited partnerships came to range from 4% to 13% of corporate income, depending upon the amount of income, while that for joint-stock companies with more than 21 stockholders was fixed at 6.25%.[23] Consequently, those enterprises which expected to earn more than 15 thousand yen in income could reduce their tax payments by adopting the joint-stock company form. It may be said that the tax reform of 1913 induced large family businesses to change their enterprises into joint-stock companies.

We can present many examples of this. Table 3 lists companies from the largest three *zaibatsu* which were established or reorganized into joint-stock companies around World War I. As for the other *zaibatsu*, Yasuda established two joint-stock companies, the Yasuda Bank and Yasuda Trading Company, as early as 1911. Furukawa reorganized two departments of the Furukawa Partnership into Furukawa Trading Co., Ltd. and Furukawa Mining Co., Ltd., in 1917 and in 1918, respectively. In the case of Asano, the Asano partnership which had been established in 1914, was transformed into a joint-stock company in 1918. Other *zaibatsu* families such as Ohkura, Fujita, Kuhara and Suzuki also established joint-stock companies or reorganized their existing businesses into joint-stock companies in the same period.[24]

Among less powerful families, the Konoike reorganized the Konoike Bank, which had been a partnership, into a joint-stock company in 1919,[25] and the Yamaguchi transformed the Yamaguchi Bank, formerly set up as an individual proprietorship, into a joint-stock organization in 1917.[26]

Interestingly, in most of these cases, such organizational changes were accompanied by changes both in the amount of capital raised and in the range of subscribers. For example, in 1917 Sumitomo Bank, in 1919 Mitsui Bank, and in 1920 Mitsubishi Mining offered some newly issued stocks for public subscription, although they represented only a small portion of total capital. On this occasion, the Sumitomo Bank increased its nominal capital from 15 million yen (150 thousand shares) to 30 million yen (300 thousand shares). Of the additional shares, 30 thousand were offered to the public and 120 thousand to the existing 25 stockholders. As a result, the number of stockholders increased from 25 at the end of 1916 to 896 by the end of 1917, while the percentage of shares held by the Sumitomo family declined from 97.5 to 76.4% during this same period.[27] In the case of the Mitsui Bank, the additional shares amounted to 80 thousand as its nominal capital was increased from 20 million to 100 million yen. Of the additional shares, 30 thousand were offered for public subscription and 50 thousand were issued to the existing stockholders.[28] Mitsubishi Mining increased its nominal capital from 50 to 100 million and paid-up capital from 30 to 62.5 million yen during 1920. Of the additional paid-up capital amounting to 32.5

million yen, more than 20 million yen was raised publicly. Consequently, the stockholdings of Mitsubishi *Goshi* (Limited Partnership)
declined to 60.8% of the total.[29]

The Konoike Bank increased its paid-up capital from 13 to 70
million yen and issued 140 thousand shares to 22 subscribers in 1919
when it was transformed from a partnership owned by seven investors into a joint-stock company.[30] In the case of the Yamaguchi
Bank, capital was increased in 1917 from one million to 20 million
yen, and the shares were offered to 975 subscribers when it was transformed from an individual partnership of the Yamaguchi house
into a joint-stock company.[31]

As seen above, many family businesses which had been characterized by closed ownership started to introduce outside capital by
offering a part of their stock to the public. However, we should pay
attention to the following two facts. One is that the companies opened
to the public at this stage were not the head offices of the family businesses, such as Mitsui *Gomei*, Mitsubishi *Goshi*, Sumitomo *Goshi* and
so on, but their affiliated companies. In other words, as will be discussed in the next section, larger families tried to maintain the "core"
of their ownership patterns by having their head offices reorganized
in the form of partnerships or limited partnerships with closed holdings and having the head offices hold a large majority of their affiliates' stocks.

The other noteworthy fact is that the non-family subscribers who
were offered stocks were not members of the general public, but
rather were individuals who had personal connections with the
companies, such as the managers and other employees of these firms.
This reveals how reluctant the families were to open their enterprises to the public.

*Company Structure, 1920–39*

Let us return to Table 1. During the period 1920–1935, the total
number of companies rose from 29,917 to 84,166, or increased 2.8-
fold. In the process, the number of partnerships and limited partnerships increased 3.5-fold and 4.9-fold, respectively, while the number
of joint-stock companies increased only 1.4-fold. As a result, the
percentage of limited partnerships rose from 30.0% in 1920 to 52.8%

TABLE 4   Number of Companies, Capital Assets, and Capital per Company for Holding Companies, 1925–1942.

| | Number of companies | | | | Paid-up capital percentage | | | (in million yen) | Paid-up capital per company (¥1,000) | | | |
|---|---|---|---|---|---|---|---|---|---|---|---|---|
| | P. | L.P. | J.S. | Total | P. | L.P. | J.S. | Total | P. | L.P. | J.S. | Average |
| 1925 | 44.7% | 30.2% | 24.8% | 427 | 60.6% | 25.2% | 14.1% | 834 | 2,649 | 1,634 | 1,104 | 1,953 |
| 26 | 43.2 | 32.6 | 24.0 | 475 | 63.5 | 22.9 | 13.5 | 999 | 3,097 | 1,479 | 1,185 | 2,103 |
| 27 | 42.8 | 31.4 | 25.4 | 500 | 63.0 | 21.5 | 15.4 | 1,041 | 3,066 | 1,431 | 1,263 | 2,082 |
| 28 | 42.1 | 29.1 | 28.4 | 563 | 62.2 | 20.4 | 17.3 | 1,087 | 2,852 | 1,358 | 1,179 | 1,930 |
| 29 | 40.4 | 30.1 | 28.8 | 631 | 58.6 | 19.6 | 21.7 | 1,154 | 2,652 | 1,193 | 1,376 | 1,828 |
| 30 | 41.6 | 30.3 | 27.6 | 620 | 56.9 | 18.3 | 25.0 | 1,194 | 2,633 | 1,170 | 1,751 | 1,934 |
| 31 | 39.8 | 31.7 | 28.0 | 621 | 52.7 | 19.9 | 27.2 | 1,161 | 2,481 | 1,176 | 1,818 | 1,869 |
| 32 | 37.0 | 33.1 | 29.7 | 683 | 53.2 | 20.2 | 26.5 | 1,164 | 2,450 | 1,034 | 1,526 | 1,704 |
| 33 | 38.8 | 32.0 | 29.3 | 707 | 51.3 | 20.9 | 27.7 | 1,151 | 2,154 | 1,069 | 1,542 | 1,628 |
| 34 | 36.0 | 32.7 | 31.2 | 776 | 48.1 | 20.8 | 30.9 | 1,233 | 2,128 | 1,011 | 1,578 | 1,589 |
| 35 | 35.6 | 32.5 | 31.6 | 744 | 47.9 | 19.9 | 45.9 | 1,218 | 2,200 | 1,054 | 1,610 | 1,637 |
| 36 | 35.6 | 32.2 | 31.8 | 733 | 52.5 | 22.7 | 24.6 | 1,112 | 2,241 | 1,068 | 1,176 | 1,517 |
| 37 | 36.5 | 31.6 | 31.7 | 838 | 42.6 | 12.0 | 45.2 | 1,406 | 1,957 | 641 | 2,394 | 1,677 |
| 38 | 36.2 | 29.9 | 33.6 | 853 | 43.5 | 11.1 | 45.2 | 1,426 | 2,011 | 625 | 2,245 | 1,672 |
| 39 | 32.8 | 26.6 | 40.4 | 918 | 43.9 | 11.0 | 44.9 | 1,386 | 2,026 | 626 | 1,677 | 1,510 |
| 40 | 29.5 | 26.8 | 43.6 | 912 | 26.8 | 12.8 | 60.1 | 1,109 | 1,110 | 584 | 1,734 | 1,216 |
| 41 | 27.3 | 25.6 | 47.0 | 958 | 26.6 | 11.0 | 62.1 | 1,174 | 1,194 | 530 | 1,688 | 1,225 |
| 42 | 27.0 | 24.4 | 48.3 | 945 | 25.2 | 10.9 | 63.9 | 1,134 | 1,122 | 539 | 1,689 | 1,203 |

Sources: Shokosho, *Kaisha Tokei Hyo*, op. cit.

in 1935 and, in contrast, that of joint-stock companies declined from 54.2 to 27.7%. However, when we look at the paid-up capital in different types of companies, we note that it did not undergo great change. The amount of paid-up capital held by joint-stock companies remained more than 85% during this period. This reflects the fact that the average scale of joint-stock companies, in terms of capital per company, tended to increase while those of partnerships and limited partnerships decreased. In short, small-scale partnerships and limited partnerships, while decreasing in scale, continued to increase in numbers. Joint-stock companies, on the other hand, tended to increase in scale through amalgamations and concentrations of capital while they decreased in number. The company structure came to be characterized by "dualism."

It is likely that the relative increases in partnerships and limited partnerships during this period were related to the tax reform of 1920. Before the tax reform, various tax rates had been imposed on corporations according to their legal form, making it advantageous for larger enterprises to form joint-stock companies. But the tax reform of 1920 made the tax rate uniform for every type of corporation; the rate varied only with the amount of corporate income. Thus, family businesses lost interest in forming joint-stock companies unless they could obtain benefits other than tax reduction.

Turning to the industry-by-industry figures shown in Table 2, we notice that the phenomenon noted above was especially true in the manufacturing, fishery, mining and transportation fields. In contrast, in the fields of commerce, the percentages of partnerships and limited partnerships increased both in numbers and in paid-up capital. This is partly because the number of holding companies which were classified as commercial companies in the company statistics increased. As seen in Table 4, holding companies grew very rapidly both in terms of number and total paid-up capital from 1925–1935. However, the paid-up capital per holding company decreased in the same period. It can be presumed that smaller business families as well as more wealthy business families increasingly set up holding companies. Secondly, we find that in the years from 1925 to 1934, more than 70% of holding companies, both in terms of number and total paid-up capital, were partnerships and limited partnerships. And during the period prior to 1930, the holding companies organized as partnerships were on the average the largest-scale holding companies in terms of paid-up capital per company, while the joint-stock type of holding companies ranked the lowest up to 1928 and second thereafter. It may be said that more wealthy families tended to prefer partnerships to joint-stock companies in the early stage of their growth as holding companies.

One incentive for family businesses to organize holding companies was provided by the tax reform of 1920 which introduced a system of composite taxation on income. As a consequence, taxes came to be imposed on dividends and bonuses paid to individuals, previously exempt from taxation. Moreover, the tax rate on large income earners was much higher than that on corporations. Therefore, the more wealthy families who held a number of their affiliates' stocks tried to find a way to save on tax payments. For this purpose, many of them had their head offices reorganized as holding companies, in the form of partnerships or limited partnerships. They placed most of their family assets under the control of the holding companies, including stocks in affiliates, and received the holding companies dividends and other income brought in by the family assets. For example, according to an estimate made by the Konoike family in 1921 when they set up a holding company, the tax amounts imposed on their total family incomes (as personal income) were estimated at about 110 thousand yen. In contrast, if they paid part of the taxes imposed on the same amount of income as corporate tax, the tax amounts were expected to decrease to about 43 thousand yen. In other words, they were able to save more than 60% of their tax payments by setting up their holding company.[32]

Of course, as many scholars have pointed out, the families' motives to save on tax payments did not alone account for the popularity of holding companies at this time. More powerful family businesses, such as the *zaibatsu*, which had diversified or were diversifying their businesses, aimed at controlling their subsidiaries more effectively by having holding companies as headquarters.

There are many examples of holding companies set up in this period. The Sumitomo family, for instance, reorganized the Sumitomo Head Office, which had not been incorporated, as Sumitomo

*Goshi* (Limited Partnership) in 1909. The Furukawa set up Furukawa *Gomei* (Partnership) as its holding company. The Asano established the Asano Family Corporation in 1918 which absorbed
the former Asano *Goshi* (Limited Partnership). In 1920, the Kuhara
and the Terada, in 1921 the Konoike, and in 1922 the Nomura, each
set up a holding company in the form of a partnership. In most of
these cases, the capital of the holding companies was raised exclusively from among the family members.[33]

However, the holding companies with closed family holdings
changed their ownership patterns after around 1935. As noted earlier, the number of joint-stock holding companies gradually increased
(see Table 4). At the same time, the average size of joint-stock holding companies became larger, while partnerships and limited partnerships tended to be smaller. It can be presumed that larger holding
companies gradually changed their corporate forms from partnerships or limited partnerships to joint-stock companies.

As examples, the cases of Sumitomo, Mitsui and Mitsubishi are
well known.[34] In 1937, Sumitomo dissolved their headquarters,
Sumitomo *Goshi* (Limited Partnership), to set up the Sumitomo
Head Office Co., Ltd., as a new holding company or headquarters.
At the end of the same year, Mitsubishi reorganized its holding
company (Mitsubishi *Goshi*) as a joint-stock company (Mitsubishi
Co., Ltd., and later Mitsubishi *Honsha* (Head Office) Co., Ltd.). In
the case of Mitsui, in August 1940, the head office of Mitsui, which
had been a partnership, was merged with the incorporated Mitsui
Bussan Company. As a result, Mitsui Bussan came to function not
only as a trading company under the Mitsui group but also as its
holding company. Nevertheless, the trading division of Mitsui
Bussan was again separated in 1944 as the new Mitsui Bussan Co.,
Ltd., and at the same time, the former Mitsui Bussan was reorganized
as the Mitsui *Honsha* (Head Office) Co., Ltd.

After these reorganizations, the big three *zaibatsu* offered stocks
in their incorporated holding companies for public subscription.
In 1940, Mitsubishi *Honsha* doubled its capital of 120 million yen
and on this occasion all of the newly issued stocks were offered to
subscribers outside the Iwasaki family. Consequently, the percentage
of total shares owned by the Iwasaki family in Mitsubishi *Honsha*

declined to 50%. In the case of Mitsui, 25% of the shares in Mitsui
Bussan, when it was holding company of the Mitsui *zaibatsu*, capitalized at 300 million yen, were offered to public subscription in
1942. As late as March 1945, when the Sumitomo Head Office doubled its capital of 150 million yen, one-sixth of newly issued shares
were offered to affiliated companies, namely, the Sumitomo Bank,
Sumitomo Trust and Sumitomo Life Insurance.

In addition, these three *zaibatsu* tried to raise funds through the
public issuance of company bonds during this period.

With regard to why these *zaibatsu* incorporated their head offices
and offered shares to the public, four main reasons are usually
cited:[35] 1) as the rate of income taxes and inheritance taxes on the
wealthy were raised substantially under the wartime government,
the capital resources of *zaibatsu* families tended to decrease; 2)
further, the demand for additional capital greatly increased since
the wartime economy required *zaibatsu* enterprises to enter into war-
related industries, especially heavy industries, even though the
*zaibatsu*'s financial organs, which had to subscribe to government
bonds, had difficulty meeting the capital requirements of the *zaibatsu* as a whole; 3) the partnership and limited partnership types of
holding companies could not easily raise outside capital, because
they were forbidden to issue company bonds and since the investment shares in these companies were not really liquid assets; and
4) as social criticism against the monopolization of national wealth
by the *zaibatsu* became more severe during the war, and the *zaibatsu*
were required to democratize their businesses by opening their companies to the public.

During this period, public stock offerings were limited to a small
circle. In the case of Sumitomo, all offered stocks were held by
related financial institutions. Mitsui and Mitsubishi offered stocks
preferentially to their subsidiaries and employees. Nevertheless, one
might say that there was a certain degree of progress in terms of
dissolving closed family ownership patterns. The traditional ownership pattern of big family businesses in Japan at last started to break
down in the wartime period. Needless to say, this provided the
preconditions for formal dissolution of the *zaibatsu* after the War.

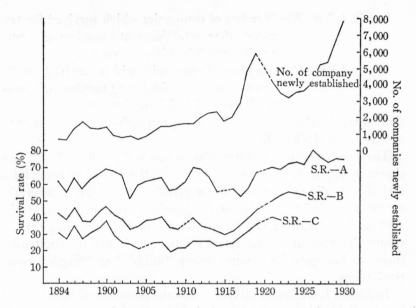

FIG. 1    Company Survival Rate and Number of Companies Newly Established, 1894–1930.

Notes:    S.R.—A    Survival Rate, 5 years after establishment.
S.R.—B    Survival Rate, 10 years after establishment.
S.R.—C    Survival Rate, 15 years after establishment.
Source:    Shokosho, *Kaisha Tokei Hyo*, op. cit.

## Survival Rate of Companies

The foregoing sections have examined the relationship between the development of the company system and the changing nature of family business. This section will look at how the company system became rooted in the Japanese economy from another point of view, namely, by examining how long the Japanese companies survived.

We can calculate statistics on the survival rates of firms by using company data. Three different rates have been calculated according to the length of survival as follows:

Survival Rate A= Number of companies which survived for five years after establishment / number of companies established in each year

Survival Rate B= Number of companies which survived for ten
years after establishment / number of com-
panies established in each year
Survival Rate C= Number of companies which survived for 15
years after establishment / number of companies established in each year
(hereafter, Survival Rate A, B and C, respectively, are referred to
as S.R.–A, S.R.–B, S.R.–C)

The survival rates of companies (S.R.–A, S.R.–B, S.R.–C) are
shown in Figure 1, with respect to the total number of companies
established. We assume that the survival rates reflect, to a certain
extent, the relative stability of the Japanese company structure in
each period. In other words, we assume that the survival rate of
companies goes up as the relative number of "sound" companies
increases but goes down when many "bubble" or "fragile" companies appear.

In Figure 1, we first of all notice that the period from 1894 to 1930
can be divided into two sub-periods in terms of the rate of survival:
namely the pre-1920 and the post-1920 periods. In the former,
S.R.–A remained below 70%. This means that more than 30%
of all companies did not survive five years after their establishment.
Moreover, more than 40% of all companies founded in the years
1895, 1897, 1903, 1908 and 1909 and in the several years after 1914
did not even last five years. In addition, S.R.–B and S.R.–C were
also lower during this period. On the average, more than 50% of
all companies established in this period disappeared within ten
years, while about three-fourths disappeared within fifteen years
after their establishment.

After around 1914, S.R.–A, S.R.–B and S.R.–C rose gradually.
In the post-1920 period, S.R.–A remained above 70%, and S.R.–B
over 50%. A smaller number of companies disappeared shortly
after establishment. More than 50% survived more than ten years.

Judging from the above, we can say that during the period after
1920 the number of "bubble" or "fragile" companies became smaller
and more "sound" companies appeared. In this sense, one might
argue that the company system actually took root in the Japanese
economy after World War I.

TABLE 5  Survival Rates of Partnerships, Limited Partnerships and Joint-Stock Companies, 1921–1933.

| Year of establish-ment | Survival rate A (%) | | | Survival rate B (%) | | |
|---|---|---|---|---|---|---|
| | P. | L.P. | J.S. | P. | L.P. | J.S. |
| 1921 | 50.5 | 40.4 | 80.3 | 36.1 | 26.6 | 59.8 |
| 22 | 71.4 | 51.8 | 90.5 | 52.7 | 35.6 | 67.3 |
| 23 | 71.6 | 56.0 | 89.3 | 52.4 | 40.1 | 72.9 |
| 24 | 72.9 | 61.1 | 92.9 | 55.8 | 44.9 | 73.0 |
| 25 | 85.3 | 60.3 | 93.2 | 75.6 | 45.8 | 81.1 |
| 26 | 78.1 | 58.7 | 100.8* | 60.1 | 39.2 | 80.1 |
| 27 | 86.2 | 69.1 | 106.9* | 62.5 | 47.1 | 91.9 |
| 28 | 80.7 | 67.3 | 96.1 | 51.3 | 40.6 | 76.1 |
| 29 | 82.9 | 64.5 | 89.9 | — | — | — |
| 30 | 85.9 | 68.5 | 90.4 | — | — | — |
| 31 | 80.8 | 70.7 | 88.0 | — | — | — |
| 32 | 64.8 | 53.7 | 75.1 | — | — | — |
| 33 | 62.3 | 53.7 | 83.2 | — | — | — |

Notes: 1) Survival Rate A = $\dfrac{\text{No. of companies which survived five years after est.}}{\text{Total no. of companies established in each year}}$

Survival Rate B = $\dfrac{\text{No. of companies which survived ten years after est.}}{\text{Total no. of companies established in each year}}$

2) * The reason that these figures exceed 100 is, we suspect, that the enterprises established as a single company sometimes were divided into several companies afterwards.

Source: Shokosho, *Kaisha Tokei Hyo*, op. cit.

Second, we would like to examine the comparative survival rate of partnerships, limited partnerships and joint-stock companies, shown in Table 5. The survival rates of joint-stock companies were clearly the highest, as less than 10% failed within five years. On the other hand, the average life of limited partnerships was the shortest. It is also obvious that the difference in survival rates among partnerships, limited partnerships and joint-stock companies was related to differences in their scale. In addition, it should be taken into consideration that partnerships and limited partnerships mainly consisted of family companies, as will be seen later. It may be said that smaller-size and/or family companies, many of which were organized as partnerships or limited partnerships, were on the average much shorter-lived.

TABLE 6   Distribution of Companies and Assets, 1931–1941.

| Year | Number of companies | | | Paid-up capital (million yen) | | |
|---|---|---|---|---|---|---|
| | Family company | Non-family company | Total | Family company | Non-family company | Total |
| 1931 | 48,813 | 23,152 | 71,965 | 5,087 | 8,879 | 13,966 |
| 1932 | 56,431 | 21,298 | 77,729 | 5,193 | 8,876 | 14,075 |
| 1933 | 61,635 | 21,493 | 83,128 | 5,415 | 8,979 | 14,389 |
| 1934 | 67,016 | 21,507 | 88,523 | 5,863 | 9,712 | 15,576 |
| 1935 | 72,387 | 21,755 | 94,592 | 6,315 | 10,077 | 16,392 |
| 1936 | 74,750 | 21,510 | 96,250 | 6,737 | 10,650 | 17,387 |
| 1937 | 71,050 | 21,205 | 92,255 | 7,603 | 11,770 | 19,374 |
| 1938 | 68,722 | 19,122 | 87,844 | 8,418 | 13,241 | 21,659 |
| 1939 | 68,357 | 19,968 | 88,835 | 8,585 | 15,405 | 23,989 |
| 1940 | 68,060 | 22,968 | 91,028 | 8,668 | 18,261 | 26,930 |
| 1941 | 69,690 | 27,507 | 97,023 | 9,677 | 20,775 | 30,452 |
| 1931 | 67.8% | 32.2% | 100% | 36.4% | 63.6% | 100% |
| 1932 | 72.6 | 27.4 | 100 | 36.9 | 63.1 | 100 |
| 1933 | 74.1 | 25.9 | 100 | 37.6 | 62.4 | 100 |
| 1934 | 75.7 | 24.3 | 100 | 37.6 | 62.4 | 100 |
| 1935 | 77.0 | 23.0 | 100 | 38.5 | 61.5 | 100 |
| 1936 | 77.7 | 22.3 | 100 | 38.8 | 61.2 | 100 |
| 1937 | 77.0 | 23.0 | 100 | 39.2 | 60.8 | 100 |
| 1938 | 78.2 | 21.8 | 100 | 38.9 | 61.1 | 100 |
| 1939 | 77.0 | 23.0 | 100 | 35.8 | 64.2 | 100 |
| 1940 | 74.8 | 25.2 | 100 | 32.2 | 67.8 | 100 |
| 1941 | 71.7 | 28.3 | 100 | 31.8 | 68.2 | 100 |

Source:   Ohkurasho Shuzeikyoku, *Shuzeikyoku Tokei Nenpo-sho*, Vol. 58–68, 1932–1942
          (Tax Bureau, Ministry of Finance, *Annual Statistics of Tax Bureau*, Vol. 58–68).

## IV.   Family Companies and Non-Family Companies

Reliable statistics on family companies compared to non-family companies are available for the period after 1931. This section will first examine the distribution of family and non-family companies and, second, the relationship between ownership patterns and the legal forms of companies. Third, the performance of family companies will be compared with that of non-family companies, although the scope of research is limited. Fourth, this same approach will be applied to a comparative study of partnerships, limited partnerships

TABLE 7.  Number of Investors per Company, Capital per Company and Capital per Investor, 1931–1941.

|  | No. of investors per company (persons) | | Paid-up capital per company (¥1,000) | | Paid-up capital per investor (¥1,000) | |
|---|---|---|---|---|---|---|
|  | F.C. | N.F.C. | F.C. | N.F.C. | F.C. | N.F.C. |
| 1931 | 7.8 | 183.9 | 104 | 383 | 13.3 | 2.1 |
| 32 | 7.9 | 187.0 | 92 | 417 | 11.6 | 2.2 |
| 33 | 7.5 | 191.5 | 85 | 417 | 11.6 | 2.2 |
| 34 | 7.6 | 185.1 | 88 | 452 | 11.5 | 2.4 |
| 35 | 7.7 | 200.7 | 87 | 463 | 10.5 | 2.3 |
| 36 | 7.3 | 242.8 | 90 | 495 | 12.4 | 2.0 |
| 37 | 8.1 | 243.1 | 107 | 555 | 13.2 | 2.3 |
| 38 | 8.6 | 297.8 | 123 | 693 | 13.9 | 2.3 |
| 39 | 8.3 | 319.8 | 126 | 771 | 15.2 | 2.4 |
| 40 | 8.2 | 313.8 | 127 | 795 | 15.5 | 2.5 |
| 41 | 9.8 | 284.2 | 139 | 755 | 14.1 | 2.7 |

Note:  Abbreviations: F.C.=Family Company, N.F.C.=Non-family Company.
Source:  Ohkurasho Shuzeikyoku, *Shuzeikyoku Tokei Nenpo-sho*, op. cit.

and joint-stock companies. Last, the same kind of comparative study of holding companies will be made. The purpose of these comparative analyses is to suggest some of the characteristics of management in Japanese family businesses.

## 1.  Distribution of Family and Non-Family Companies

To begin with, the term "family company" (*dozoku gaisha*) is used here as defined by the tax law, which states, "if more than half of the capital stock or invested capital of the corporation is held by a single stockholder or a single partner and those who have particular connections with him, such as his relatives or employees, the corporation is regarded as a family company."[36]

Table 6 shows the distribution of family and non-family companies from 1931 to 1941. It indicates that the number of family companies was about 70%, representing around 36% of all paid-up capital during this period, although after 1938 the percentages slightly declined. It may be said that family companies were still growing during this period, except after 1938, and keeping pace with non-family companies in terms of aggregate figures.

Table 7 shows the number of investors per company, the paid-up

TABLE 8   Family Companies and Non-Family Companies by Industry, 1931.

| | Number of companies | | | | | | | | Composition of paid-up capital | | Notes (Dominant companies) |
|---|---|---|---|---|---|---|---|---|---|---|---|
| | F.C. | | | | N.F.C. | | | | | | |
| | P. | L.P. | J.S. | Sub-total | P. | L.P. | J.S. | Sub-total | F.C. | N.F.C. | |
| Agriculture | 15.2% | 47.0% | 4.7% | 67.0% | 4.1% | 11.3% | 17.6% | 33.0% | 39.8% | 60.2% | F.C.–L.P. |
| Fishery | 15.5 | 24.8 | 6.9 | 39.9 | 3.9 | 9.9 | 46.3 | 60.1 | 14.5 | 85.5 | N.F.C.–J.S., F.C.–L.P. |
| Mining | 3.2 | 15.5 | 26.3 | 45.0 | 1.1 | 8.6 | 45.3 | 55.0 | 45.2 | 54.8 | N.F.C.–J.S., F.C.–J.S. |
| Manufacturing | 12.6 | 39.8 | 10.4 | 62.7 | 1.8 | 8.1 | 27.4 | 37.3 | 23.1 | 76.9 | F.C.–L.P., N.F.C.–J.S. |
| Commerce | 15.6 | 54.7 | 6.8 | 77.0 | 1.7 | 7.9 | 13.3 | 23.0 | 57.9 | 42.1 | F.C.–L.P. |
| Financing & Insurance | 9.9 | 21.8 | 9.6 | 41.2 | 1.6 | 7.3 | 49.8 | 58.8 | 17.5 | 82.5 | N.F.C.–J.S. |
| Transportation | 5.2 | 21.9 | 9.3 | 36.5 | 2.8 | 12.1 | 48.7 | 63.5 | 13.8 | 86.2 | N.F.C.–J.S. |
| Others | 23.5 | 27.1 | 13.6 | 54.3 | 2.1 | 5.0 | 28.6 | 45.7 | 87.2 | 12.8 | F.C.–P, F.C.–L.P., F.C.–J.S. |
| (Holding Co.) | (17.3) | (17.0) | (9.5) | (43.9) | (—) | (—) | (—) | (—) | (—) | (—) | |

Note: Abbreviations: P.=Partnership, L.P.=Limited Partnership, J.S.=Joint-stock Company.

Source: Ohkurasho Shuzei Kyoku, *Shuzeikyoku Tokei Nenpo-sho*, op. cit.

TABLE 9   Number of Investors per Company, Capital per Company and Capital per Investor by Industry, 1931.

| | No. of investors per company (persons) | | | Paid-up capital per company (¥1,000) | | | Paid-up capital per investor (¥1,000) | | |
|---|---|---|---|---|---|---|---|---|---|
| | F.C. | N.F.C. | Average | F.C. | N.F.C. | Average | F.C. | N.F.C. | Average |
| Agriculture | 5.8 | 49.3 | 20.1 | 41 | 124 | 68 | 7.1 | 2.5 | 3.4 |
| Fishery | 6.2 | 114.3 | 71.1 | 81 | 350 | 54 | 13.1 | 2.8 | 3.1 |
| Mining | 57.6 | 293.1 | 183.0 | 2,252 | 2,237 | 2,244 | 39.1 | 7.6 | 12.0 |
| Manufacturing | 12.1 | 155.5 | 65.6 | 112 | 626 | 304 | 9.3 | 4.1 | 4.6 |
| Commerce | 5.5 | 46.0 | 14.8 | 48 | 118 | 64 | 8.8 | 1.1 | 4.3 |
| Financing & Insurance | 21.1 | 1,042.8 | 621.8 | 276 | 910 | 649 | 13.1 | 0.9 | 1.0 |
| Transportation | 10.4 | 123.1 | 82.0 | 99 | 357 | 263 | 9.5 | 2.9 | 3.2 |
| Others | 8.7 | 71.2 | 29.9 | 156 | 225 | 627 | 3.2 | 20.9 | 42.1 |
| (Holding Company) | 6.2 | — | — | 1,171 | — | — | 187.6 | — | — |

Note:   Abbreviations:   F.C.=Family Company,   N.F.C.=Non-family Company.
Source:   Ohkurasho, *Shuzeikyoku Tokei Nenpo-sho,* op. cit.

capital per company and the paid-up capital per investor for family
and non-family companies, respectively. It shows a striking differ-
ential between family and non-family companies. The average
family and non-family companies can be summarized as follows:

|  | No. of investors per company (persons) | Paid-up capital per company (¥1,000) | Paid-up capital per investor (¥1,000) |
|---|---|---|---|
| Family Co. | 8 | 111 | 13 |
| Non-family Co. | 246 | 578 | 2 |

The average non-family company had 30 times the number of
investors and 5 times the capital of the average family company,
while the average holdings of the former were much smaller than
those of the latter. Generally speaking, non-family companies in this
period raised their capital from members of the general public who
had smaller quantities of funds to contribute.

Industry-by-industry figures are shown in Tables 8 and 9. As
evident from Table 8 in terms of number, family companies were
preponderant in fields such as agriculture, manufacturing and commerce, while in terms of capital amount, family companies occupied
substantial shares in agriculture, mining, commerce and others
fields. From the above, it may be said that agriculture, commerce
and others (including holding companies) were the typical industries
in which family companies were dominant. As evident from Table 9,
fisheries, manufacturing, financing, insurance as well as transportation were characterized by the coexistence of numerous small-scale
family companies owned by a small number of investors and many
large-scale non-family companies owned by more than 350 investors.
A "dual structure" thus prevailed in these fields. Interestingly, however, the situation was different in mining. In this field family companies stood shoulder to shoulder with non-family companies both in
number and in the average amount of capital, although the number
of investors per company were different between the two. Recall that
in this field the affiliated *zaibatsu* companies were prominent and
it can be argued that this affected the structure of mining companies.

TABLE 10   Legal Variants of Family and Non-Family Companies, 1931–1941.

| Year | Family companies | | | | Non-family companies | | | |
|---|---|---|---|---|---|---|---|---|
| | P. | L.P. | J.S. | L.R. | P. | L.P. | J.S. | L.R. |
| 1931 | 20.6% | 67.3% | 12.2% | — | 5.9% | 25.7% | 68.4% | — |
| 1932 | 19.9 | 68.1 | 12.1 | — | 5.9 | 24.6 | 69.4 | — |
| 1933 | 20.6 | 67.5 | 11.9 | — | 6.1 | 25.3 | 68.5 | — |
| 1934 | 21.5 | 66.2 | 12.3 | — | 6.0 | 24.7 | 69.2 | — |
| 1935 | 22.8 | 64.2 | 12.9 | — | 6.0 | 24.1 | 69.8 | — |
| 1936 | 23.3 | 62.6 | 14.2 | — | 6.6 | 22.5 | 70.8 | — |
| 1937 | 22.8 | 60.5 | 16.7 | — | 6.6 | 21.2 | 72.1 | — |
| 1938 | 22.7 | 57.6 | 19.8 | — | 4.8 | 16.7 | 78.5 | — |
| 1939 | 22.2 | 54.6 | 23.2 | — | 4.6 | 15.2 | 82.6 | — |
| 1940 | 21.7 | 50.8 | 26.5 | 1.0 | 4.0 | 13.1 | 78.0 | 4.9 |
| 1941 | 20.3 | 46.5 | 29.2 | 4.1 | 3.2 | 11.0 | 69.0 | 16.8 |

Notes:  1)  Abbreviation:  P.=Partnership,  L.P.=Limited  Partnership,  J.S.= Joint-stock Company, L.R.=Limited Responsibility Company.
　　　　 2)  Numbers of family and non-family companies are obtained in Table 6.
Source:  Same as for Table 6.

## 2.  Relationships between the Ownership Patterns and Legal Forms of Companies

Table 10 shows the distribution of partnerships, limited partnerships and joint-stock companies among family companies as well as in non-family firms. Table 11 shows the distributions of family and non-family companies according to their legal forms.

In Table 10, as expected, the percentage of joint-stock companies that were also family companies was the smallest until 1938, while most family companies were partnerships and limited partnerships. In contrast, among non-family companies, joint-stock companies accounted for more than 68%, and the percentage of partnerships was extremely small among non-family companies. It is evident that the limited partnership was the dominant form of family company and that joint-stock companies outnumbered other forms among non-family companies in this period. However, after 1938 the percentage of joint-stock companies among family as well as non-family firms continued to increase. This reflects, perhaps, that family companies tended to shift in legal forms from partnerships, and especially

TABLE 11 Family and Non-Family Distribution of Partnerships, Limited Partnerships and Joint-stock Companies, 1931–1941.

| | Partnership | | | Limited partnership | | | Joint-stock | | | Total | | |
|---|---|---|---|---|---|---|---|---|---|---|---|---|
| | Total | F.C. | N.F.C. | Total | F.C. | N.F.C. | Total | F.C. | N.F.C. | Total | F.C. | N.F.C. |
| 1931 | 11,390 | 88.1% | 11.9% | 38,753 | 84.7% | 15.3% | 21,771 | 27.3% | 72.7% | 71,965 | 67.8% | 32.2% |
| 1932 | 12,472 | 89.9 | 11.1 | 43,650 | 88.0 | 12.0 | 21,399 | 31.5 | 68.5 | 77,729 | 72.6 | 27.4 |
| 1933 | 13,984 | 90.7 | 9.3 | 47,040 | 88.5 | 11.5 | 22,058 | 33.7 | 66.3 | 83,128 | 74.1 | 25.9 |
| 1934 | 15,712 | 91.8 | 8.2 | 49,691 | 89.3 | 10.7 | 23,116 | 35.6 | 64.4 | 88,523 | 75.7 | 24.3 |
| 1935 | 17,935 | 92.7 | 7.3 | 52,047 | 89.9 | 10.1 | 24,604 | 38.3 | 61.7 | 94,592 | 77.0 | 23.0 |
| 1936 | 18,807 | 92.5 | 7.5 | 51,613 | 90.6 | 9.4 | 25,826 | 41.0 | 59.0 | 96,250 | 77.0 | 23.0 |
| 1937 | 17,595 | 92.0 | 8.0 | 47,499 | 90.5 | 9.5 | 27,157 | 43.7 | 56.3 | 92,255 | 77.7 | 22.3 |
| 1938 | 16,497 | 94.5 | 5.5 | 42,754 | 92.5 | 7.5 | 28,589 | 47.5 | 52.5 | 87,844 | 78.2 | 21.8 |
| 1939 | 16,069 | 94.3 | 5.7 | 40,372 | 92.5 | 7.5 | 32,390 | 49.0 | 51.0 | 88,835 | 77.0 | 23.0 |
| 1940 | 15,663 | 94.2 | 5.8 | 37,592 | 92.0 | 8.0 | 35,964 | 50.2 | 49.8 | 91,028 | 74.8 | 25.2 |
| 1941 | 15,035 | 94.1 | 5.9 | 35,405 | 91.5 | 8.5 | 39,309 | 51.7 | 48.3 | 97,203 | 71.7 | 28.3 |

Note: Abbreviation: F.C.=Family Company, N.F.C.=Non-family Company.
Source: Same as for Table 6.

limited partnerships, to joint-stock companies or limited liability companies introduced as one of the legal forms after 1940.

Next, looking at Table 11, we notice that family companies overwhelmed non-family companies in number of partnerships and limited partnerships through this period, especially in the later years. However, the percentage of family firms among all joint-stock companies was not small, and it increased in later years.

Another noteworthy fact is that the rates of increase in the number of companies varied by type as follows:

| Type of Company | Rate of increase in no. of companies during the period 1932 to 1941 |
|---|---|
| Partnership—family company | 26 (%) |
| Partnership—non-family company | −34 |
| Limited partnership—family company | −16 |
| Limited partnership—non-family company | −43 |
| Joint-stock company—family company | 202 |
| Joint-stock company—non-family company | 30 |

The rate of increase in the number of joint-stock family companies was remarkable. In other words, the absolute increase in the number of joint-stock family companies during the period from 1932 to 1941 amounted to 13,582: around 70% of additional companies were joint-stock family companies. This demonstrates the extent to which family businesses shifted their corporate form from partnerships or limited partnerships to joint-stock companies.

The characteristics of company structures by industry, some of which have been discussed above, are indicated in Table 8, especially in the column "Notes."

### 3. Comparative Performance of Family and Non-Family Company

The central question in this section is whether the ownership patterns of firms affected their behavior in any particular direction. On this point, Professor Leslie Hannah[37] noted, "for the United States, the dichotomous classification [dichotomy between "owner-controlled" and "managerially controlled" firms] has produced statistically significant results: between 1952 and 1963, for example, owner-controlled firms among the largest 500 showed higher profits than managerially controlled ones.[38] For Europe, however, the evidence is mixed, with some studies suggesting family firms have a good profit or growth performance and others being inconclusive or showing the opposite."[39]

Regarding the Japanese case, did family companies pursue security and stability at the expense of profitability? To which items did Japanese managers attach importance when dealing with disposal of profits, dividends, reserves or bonuses? Was there any significant difference between the behavior of family companies and non-family companies in these matters?

Table 12 compares the aggregate performance of family and non-family companies during the period from 1931 to 1941. From this table we can make the following observations:

1)   a significant difference is not seen between the profit rate of family companies and non-family companies (see Column A);

2)   the dividend rate (dividend/capital), the reserve rate (reserve/capital) and the payout ratio (dividend/profit) of family companies are lower than in non-family companies (see Columns B, C and D);

3)   bonus/profit ("bonus" refers to the portion of profit paid to managers) in family companies is much higher than in non-family companies (see Column E);

4)   with regard to coefficients of variation for each time series figure, which is computed as a standard deviation/mean, those for family companies are higher than for non-family companies, except the coefficient for reserve rates; this means that the profit rate, the dividend rate, the payout ratio and the bonus ratio for family companies were subject to wider fluctuations compared to those of non-family companies.

It seems important that the profit rates were not so different between family and non-family companies, indicating that despite their relative smallness in scale, family companies were comparable to non-family companies in terms of profitability. It is likely that the lower dividend rates, lower payout ratios and higher bonus ratios of family companies were reflections of their managerial behavior. In other words, it can be presumed that the managers of family companies were inclined to hold down outflow of profits, hence maintain-

TABLE 12  Comparative Performance of Family and Non-Family Companies, 1931–1941.

| Year | Profit/Capital | | Dividend/Capital | | Reserve/Capital | | Dividend/Profit | | Bonus/Profit | |
|---|---|---|---|---|---|---|---|---|---|---|
| | Family Co. | Non-family Co. | Family Co. | Non-family Co. | Family Co. | Non-family Co. | Family Co. | Non-family Co. | Family Co. | Non-family Co. |
| 1931 | 3.6% | 5.9% | 2.5% | 4.6% | 21.4% | 25.5% | 70.2% | 79.4% | n.a | n.a |
| 1932 | 4.7 | 6.6 | 2.8 | 4.9 | 21.6 | 26.0 | 60.1 | 74.9 | n.a | n.a |
| 1933 | 6.9 | 7.9 | 3.7 | 5.2 | 21.5 | 27.7 | 54.6 | 66.7 | n.a | n.a |
| 1934 | 8.0 | 9.4 | 4.2 | 5.8 | 21.5 | 27.7 | 52.8 | 62.1 | n.a | n.a |
| 1935 | 7.9 | 10.2 | 4.3 | 6.5 | 21.8 | 29.5 | 54.2 | 64.0 | n.a | n.a |
| 1936 | 9.2 | 11.0 | 4.9 | 6.9 | 25.1 | 30.2 | 53.4 | 62.6 | 11.0% | 4.9% |
| 1937 | 12.2 | 12.0 | 5.6 | 7.2 | 23.0 | 31.0 | 46.1 | 60.3 | 8.9 | 4.9 |
| 1938 | 11.7 | 12.4 | 5.9 | 7.2 | 23.8 | 32.4 | 50.1 | 58.0 | 12.6 | 5.0 |
| 1939 | 13.4 | 12.5 | 6.0 | 7.1 | 25.8 | 33.7 | 45.0 | 57.2 | 13.8 | 5.0 |
| 1940 | 12.7 | 13.1 | 5.3 | 6.9 | 23.1 | 35.0 | 41.6 | 52.6 | 14.2 | 4.6 |
| 1941 | 13.3 | 11.5 | 4.9 | 6.3 | 22.6 | 31.8 | 37.1 | 55.0 | 15.2 | 5.6 |
| Mean | 9.4 | 10.2 | 4.6 | 6.2 | 22.8 | 30.0 | 51.4 | 63.0 | 12.6 | 5.0 |
| S.D. | 3.3 | 2.4 | 1.1 | 0.9 | 1.5 | 3.0 | 8.7 | 7.8 | 2.1 | 0.3 |
| C.V. | 35.1 | 23.5 | 23.9 | 14.5 | 6.6 | 10.0 | 16.9 | 12.4 | 16.7 | 6.0 |

Note:    Abbreviations:  S.D. = Standard Deviation,  C.V. = Coefficient of Variation.
Source:  Same as for Table 6.

TABLE 13  Comparative Performance of Family and Non-Family Companies by Industry, 1931 and 1934.

| | Profit/Capital | | Dividend/Capital | | Reserve/Capital | | Dividend/Profit | |
|---|---|---|---|---|---|---|---|---|
| | F.C. | N.F.C. | F.C. | N.F.C. | F.C. | N.F.C. | F.C. | N.F.C. |
| **1931** | | | | | | | | |
| Agriculture | 3.0% | 1.2% | 2.7% | 0.9% | 22.0% | 8.4% | 88.6% | 77.8% |
| Fishery | 1.6 | 3.7 | 1.1 | 3.2 | 8.5 | 17.0 | 68.1 | 86.3 |
| Mining | 1.6 | 2.0 | 1.9 | 1.5 | 19.7 | 13.2 | 120.8 | 75.8 |
| Manufacturing | 4.0 | 6.0 | 2.5 | 5.3 | 18.3 | 19.6 | 63.1 | 89.6 |
| Commerce | 3.9 | 4.6 | 2.6 | 2.8 | 15.6 | 12.0 | 66.9 | 61.0 |
| Financing & Insurance | 7.8 | 9.9 | 6.1 | 6.8 | 65.7 | 67.2 | 77.5 | 68.5 |
| Transportation | 1.4 | 4.0 | 0.9 | 3.4 | 8.4 | 13.9 | 67.6 | 83.9 |
| Others | 2.3 | 2.3 | 1.2 | 1.0 | 12.1 | 4.5 | 54.0 | 56.6 |
| (Holding Companies) | 2.7 | — | 2.0 | — | 22.6 | — | 72.1 | — |
| **1934** | | | | | | | | |
| Agriculture | 3.0 | 4.3 | 1.9 | 2.4 | 9.9 | 12.0 | 61.8 | 55.7 |
| Fishery | 4.7 | 11.6 | 3.1 | 6.2 | 12.8 | 10.8 | 66.9 | 54.2 |
| Mining | 10.5 | 9.0 | 5.9 | 6.7 | 22.0 | 14.1 | 56.2 | 74.9 |
| Manufacturing | 9.8 | 13.6 | 5.1 | 6.9 | 19.1 | 21.7 | 51.2 | 63.8 |
| Commerce | 7.6 | 5.9 | 4.0 | 3.1 | 17.8 | 12.9 | 52.7 | 52.7 |
| Financing & Insurance | 13.8 | 13.1 | 5.3 | 7.9 | 63.6 | 73.4 | 38.6 | 60.5 |
| Transportation | 3.1 | 4.9 | 1.6 | 3.2 | 8.8 | 14.1 | 53.6 | 66.2 |
| Others | 5.0 | 13.0 | 3.3 | 6.0 | 20.3 | 18.2 | 65.3 | 50.0 |
| (Holding Companies) | 5.1 | — | 3.3 | — | 20.9 | — | 65.4 | — |

Source:  Same as for Table 6.

ing a lower dividend. Yet, if so, why did they not raise the reserve rate to a higher level comparable to that of non-family companies? They did not because additional taxes were imposed on excessive reserves of family companies.[40] The stability of family companies' reserve rates, shown in Table 12, probably relates to this. Consequently, family companies adopted a financial policy characterized by larger bonuses, lower dividends and reserves.

The fourth observation noted above suggests that family firms were relatively more influenced by business fluctuations and could share risk with their investors, while non-family firms were required to meet the interests of their existing and potential investors, most of whom desired to get constant returns on investment, hence stabilizing the corporate performance.

Next, let us compare the corporate performance of family and non-family companies by industry. The results of calculations for 1931 and 1934 are presented in Table 13. This comparative analysis by industry reveals somewhat different characteristics from the analysis of companies in the aggregate. The main observations from Table 13 can be summarized as follows.

1) In the fields of manufacturing and transportation, there exists a distinction between the performance of family and non-family companies; in these two fields, family companies showed lower profit rates, lower dividend rates, lower payout ratios and lower reserve rates than non-family firms; comparative performance in fishery has the same characteristics except for the payout ratio.

2) In the field of mining, the reserve rate of family companies was much higher than that of non-family firms.

3) The analysis by industry does not suggest any other notable differences between family and non-family companies.

We can suppose that the first observation noted above relates to the dual structure in the company system seen in the fields of manufacturing and transportation, which has been mentioned earlier. To put this another way, in these two fields, large-scale non-family and small-scale family firms coexisted, with the former showing a better performance and distributing more profits to their investors.

The higher reserve rate seen in family companies engaged in min-

TABLE 14  Comparative Performance of Partnerships, Limited Partnerships and Joint-Stock Companies, 1925–1942.

|  | Profit/Capital | | | Dividend/Capital | | | Reserve/Capital | | | Dividend/Profit | | |
|---|---|---|---|---|---|---|---|---|---|---|---|---|
|  | P. | L.P. | J.S. | P. | L.P. | J.S. | P. | L.P. | J.S. | P. | L.P. | J.S. |
| 1925 | 6.3% | 5.6% | 10.5% | 2.0% | 2.1% | 6.9% | 19.5% | 8.8% | 23.7% | 32.3% | 39.2% | 65.5% |
| 1926 | 4.9 | 5.0 | 9.7 | 3.4 | 2.1 | 6.6 | 15.8 | 9.4 | 23.4 | 70.4 | 41.3 | 68.3 |
| 1927 | 5.0 | 4.7 | 9.3 | 3.5 | 2.0 | 6.1 | 15.9 | 10.2 | 23.3 | 70.2 | 43.3 | 65.1 |
| 1928 | 4.7 | 4.6 | 9.4 | 3.4 | 2.3 | 6.3 | 16.2 | 10.7 | 22.0 | 71.6 | 49.7 | 66.9 |
| 1929 | 4.5 | 4.6 | 8.8 | 3.4 | 2.3 | 6.2 | 15.7 | 10.9 | 21.8 | 76.3 | 50.0 | 70.1 |
| 1930 | 3.6 | 4.0 | 7.0 | 3.0 | 2.2 | 5.0 | 15.7 | 11.5 | 21.6 | 82.7 | 54.9 | 71.5 |
| 1931 | 2.6 | 2.4 | 5.7 | 1.9 | 1.4 | 4.3 | 15.4 | 11.4 | 21.6 | 72.5 | 58.2 | 76.1 |
| 1932 | 2.7 | 2.4 | 6.4 | 2.1 | 1.3 | 4.3 | 14.5 | 11.0 | 21.9 | 79.5 | 56.4 | 67.1 |
| 1933 | 3.9 | 3.2 | 8.0 | 2.8 | 1.7 | 4.8 | 14.6 | 11.9 | 21.7 | 70.5 | 52.8 | 59.6 |
| 1934 | 7.3 | 4.3 | 8.9 | 3.2 | 2.5 | 5.3 | 12.4 | 10.8 | 22.1 | 44.0 | 58.4 | 59.1 |
| 1935 | 4.3 | 4.8 | 9.6 | 2.7 | 2.8 | 5.9 | 12.1 | 11.0 | 22.8 | 64.0 | 58.0 | 61.0 |
| 1936 | 5.0 | 6.5 | 9.8 | 3.4 | 2.8 | 6.1 | 11.9 | 11.6 | 23.6 | 68.3 | 42.4 | 62.0 |
| 1937 | 6.8 | 6.6 | 10.3 | 4.9 | 3.1 | 6.3 | 12.0 | 7.0 | 22.5 | 72.1 | 46.9 | 60.9 |
| 1938 | 7.8 | 7.3 | 11.0 | 5.0 | 3.4 | 6.4 | 12.3 | 7.6 | 22.6 | 63.6 | 46.6 | 58.7 |
| 1939 | 8.8 | 9.2 | 11.4 | 5.1 | 3.5 | 6.2 | 12.7 | 8.7 | 22.5 | 58.0 | 37.6 | 54.7 |
| 1940 | 8.9 | 9.4 | 12.1 | 3.7 | 3.3 | 6.1 | 9.9 | 9.9 | 23.7 | 41.8 | 35.4 | 50.7 |
| 1941 | 8.8 | 6.1 | 12.8 | 3.4 | 2.0 | 5.8 | 11.4 | 7.2 | 25.3 | 38.1 | 32.8 | 45.7 |
| 1942 | 9.2 | 9.1 | 11.6 | 3.2 | 2.9 | 5.4 | 12.6 | 11.3 | 23.6 | 34.7 | 31.5 | 46.1 |
| Mean | 5.8 | 5.5 | 9.6 | 3.3 | 2.4 | 5.8 | 13.9 | 10.1 | 22.8 | 61.7 | 46.4 | 61.6 |
| S.D. | 2.1 | 2.1 | 1.9 | 0.9 | 0.6 | 0.7 | 2.3 | 1.5 | 1.0 | 15.7 | 8.7 | 8.1 |
| C.V. | 36.2 | 38.2 | 19.8 | 27.3 | 25.0 | 12.1 | 16.5 | 14.9 | 4.3 | 25.4 | 18.8 | 13.1 |

Note: Abbreviations:  P.=Partnership, L.P.=Limited Partnership, J.S.=Joint-stock Company, S.D.=Standard Deviation, C.V.=Coefficient of Variation.
Source:  Same as for Table 1.

Table 15 Comparative Performance of Holding Companies by Partnerships, Limited Partnerships and Joint-Stock Companies, 1925–1942.

| | Profit/Capital (%) | | | Dividend/Capital (%) | | | Reserve/Capital (%) | | | Dividend/Profit (%) | | |
|---|---|---|---|---|---|---|---|---|---|---|---|---|
| | P. | L.P. | J.S. | P. | L.P. | J.S. | P. | L.P. | J.S. | P. | L.P. | J.S. |
| 1925 | 6.4 | 6.1 | 3.5 | 1.9 | 1.6 | 2.1 | 26.4 | 11.4 | 5.9 | 29.4 | 27.0 | 62.4 |
| 26 | 5.2 | 5.8 | 4.5 | 4.3 | 1.9 | 3.7 | 19.9 | 13.2 | 7.1 | 81.5 | 32.7 | 83.0 |
| 27 | 5.6 | 5.2 | 3.6 | 4.6 | 1.6 | 2.4 | 19.9 | 16.6 | 5.3 | 81.1 | 30.2 | 66.5 |
| 28 | 4.9 | 5.1 | 4.3 | 4.0 | 2.2 | 3.2 | 19.9 | 20.1 | 7.5 | 83.3 | 43.4 | 74.8 |
| 29 | 4.7 | 6.7 | 3.4 | 3.9 | 2.6 | 2.7 | 20.4 | 21.8 | 5.4 | 82.1 | 40.3 | 78.2 |
| 30 | 4.3 | 7.5 | 1.3 | 3.8 | 3.8 | 1.1 | 21.3 | 26.0 | 10.9 | 89.4 | 47.3 | 86.9 |
| 31 | 3.0 | 3.9 | 1.2 | 2.3 | 2.1 | 0.9 | 22.8 | 28.2 | 9.6 | 76.2 | 53.0 | 80.5 |
| 32 | 2.5 | 2.3 | 1.6 | 2.6 | 1.6 | 1.4 | 21.5 | 28.5 | 11.0 | 101.8 | 70.6 | 84.3 |
| 33 | 3.7 | 2.4 | 3.8 | 3.3 | 1.5 | 2.9 | 22.0 | 26.6 | 9.9 | 88.8 | 59.0 | 74.8 |
| 34 | 10.7 | 3.9 | 8.1 | 4.1 | 3.1 | 4.1 | 18.6 | 25.2 | 12.8 | 38.7 | 78.0 | 50.7 |
| 35 | 3.9 | 3.0 | 6.1 | 3.1 | 3.2 | 4.3 | 19.1 | 26.3 | 14.1 | 77.5 | 108.0 | 70.2 |
| 36 | 4.4 | 7.0 | 3.7 | 4.1 | 3.9 | 2.4 | 19.4 | 28.2 | 6.9 | 91.3 | 56.3 | 64.7 |
| 37 | 7.0 | 8.2 | 4.6 | 6.2 | 3.5 | 3.2 | 19.2 | 14.1 | 11.4 | 89.0 | 43.0 | 70.2 |
| 38 | 6.9 | 5.3 | 5.2 | 5.8 | 3.0 | 3.5 | 19.2 | 15.2 | 12.4 | 84.0 | 56.2 | 67.9 |
| 39 | 6.7 | 8.4 | 6.4 | 5.9 | 3.1 | 3.8 | 19.7 | 15.9 | 15.1 | 88.0 | 36.6 | 59.3 |
| 40 | 4.8 | 5.8 | 5.7 | 3.0 | 3.3 | 2.8 | 12.3 | 21.2 | 15.5 | 62.5 | 56.4 | 48.7 |
| 41 | 4.9 | 4.7 | 13.6 | 2.9 | 2.7 | 3.3 | 12.2 | 22.6 | 18.4 | 60.1 | 58.4 | 23.9 |
| 42 | 5.3 | 5.9 | 6.5 | 3.2 | 3.0 | 3.8 | 14.4 | 25.0 | 8.4 | 60.0 | 51.1 | 58.4 |
| Mean | 5.3 | 5.4 | 4.8 | 3.8 | 2.6 | 2.9 | 19.3 | 21.5 | 10.4 | 75.8 | 52.6 | 67.0 |
| S.D. | 1.8 | 1.8 | 2.8 | 1.2 | 1.0 | 1.0 | 3.5 | 5.6 | 3.7 | 17.8 | 18.7 | 14.9 |
| C.V. | 33.9 | 33.3 | 58.3 | 31.6 | 38.5 | 34.5 | 18.1 | 26.0 | 35.6 | 23.5 | 35.6 | 22.2 |

Sources: Shokosho, *Kaisha Tokei Hyo*, op. cit.

ing might be explained by the fact that *zaibatsu* subsidiaries were prominent in this field. The reason for this is that most *zaibatsu* companies were eager to accumulate equity capital for future growth.

## 4. Comparative Performance of Partnerships, Limited Partnerships and Joint-stock Companies

Table 14 compares the performance of partnerships, limited partnerships and joint-stock companies. The main observations can be summarized as follows.

1) With regard to the rates of profit, dividends and reserves, those in joint-stock companies were higher than in partnerships and limited partnerships.

2) Limited partnerships were lowest in every type of performance variable.

3) The payout ratio of partnerships was as high as that of joint-stock companies, although their other three rates (profits, dividends and reserves) were as low as those of limited partnerships.

4) As for the coefficients of variation, partnerships and limited partnerships showed a higher value than joint-stock companies for every variable.

The findings above are on the whole consistent with those in the previous section. The characteristic features found in this section for partnerships and limited partnerships correspond with those for family companies. This is quite natural, because more than 90% of partnerships and limited partnerships were family companies, as seen in Table 11.

However, we should pay particular attention to the high payout ratio of partnerships noted above. This implies that partnerships, which included many larger-scale family companies, tended to adopt a dividend policy which favored their investors, as did joint-stock companies.

## 5. Performance of the Holding Companies

Needless to say, holding companies in pre-war Japan were usually family-owned and family-controlled. This section will examine the performance of holding companies. Table 15 suggests the following.

1) For profit and dividend rates, holding companies, except

joint-stock types, were comparable to other companies as a whole; profit and dividend rates in joint-stock holding companies were much lower than those of joint-stock companies as a whole.

2) With regard to the reserve rate, holding companies, except joint-stock companies, showed a higher rate than companies as a whole, while that of joint-stock holding companies was much lower than that of joint-stock companies as a whole.

3) The payout ratio of holding companies was much higher than those of companies as a whole; that of partnership holding companies was especially high.

From the above, we might say that holding companies, except the joint-stock types, were comparable to companies as a whole in terms of profitability, but they tended to reserve much more funds and to allocate a much greater proportion of profits to investors, compared to companies as a whole. It is significant that partnership and limited partnership holding companies—as typical family companies—displayed such behavioral patterns.

## 6. Comparative Performance of the Largest 200 Companies

It is difficult to draw a simple conclusion from the above with regard to the characteristics of financial performance in family companies compared to non-family companies. When we compared the corporate performance of family and non-family companies *in the aggregate*, we found a notable difference between the two. Specifically, dividend rates, payout ratios and reserve rates in family companies were lower, while their bonus ratios were higher. And the difference between family and non-family companies coincided on the whole with that between partnerships and limited partnerships, and joint-stock companies. However, the comparative analysis *by industry* reveals different things than the analysis of companies in the aggregate. For example, in mining, where many large-scale family companies existed, family companies showed a higher reserve rate than non-family companies. Moreover, partnership and limited partnership holding companies, which were on the average large-scale family companies with closed holdings, displayed a higher reserve rate and higher payout ratio than any other type of company, including joint-stock holding companies. Judging from this, it is

TABLE 16   Financial Performance of the Largest 200 Companies (1936).

| Fields | Ownership patterns | No. of companies | Profit capital | Dividend capital | Reserve capital | Dividend profit |
|---|---|---|---|---|---|---|
| Manufacturing | Type A | 12 | 23.1% | 10.3% | 27.9% | 46.5% |
| | Type B | 42 | 19.5 | 9.6 | 36.7 | 54.3 |
| | (Types A+B) | (54) | (20.3) | (9.8) | (34.7) | (52.6) |
| | Type C | 38 | 20.3 | 10.3 | 28.3 | 50.8 |
| Railway | Type A | — | — | — | — | — |
| | Type B | 8 | 7.8 | 6.4 | 8.8 | 84.1 |
| | Type C | 23 | 6.5 | 5.2 | 9.6 | 70.7 |
| Electric power and Gas | Type A | 3 | 7.1 | 6.0 | 4.2 | 85.7 |
| | Type B | 12 | 11.3 | 8.3 | 10.8 | 75.3 |
| | (Types A+B) | (15) | (10.5) | (7.8) | (9.5) | (77.4) |
| | Type C | 27 | 9.9 | 7.5 | 9.4 | 75.2 |
| Mining | Type A | — | — | — | — | — |
| | Type B | 6 | 17.2 | 10.3 | 14.1 | 63.2 |
| | Type C | 3 | 16.5 | 5.6 | 11.4 | 36.2 |
| Others | Type A | 2 | 6.1 | 4.0 | 37.0 | 33.0 |
| | Type B | 8 | 14.0 | 7.0 | 25.3 | 52.6 |
| | (Types A+B) | (10) | (12.4) | (6.4) | (27.6) | (48.7) |
| | Type C | 4 | 1.7 | 3.8 | 19.5 | 26.3 |
| All | Type A | 17 | 18.3 | 8.8 | 24.8 | 51.8 |
| | Type B | 76 | 16.2 | 8.8 | 26.7 | 61.3 |
| | (Types A+B) | 93 | (16.6) | (8.8) | (26.4) | (59.6) |
| | Type C | 95 | 13.0 | 7.8 | 16.8 | 61.0 |

Note: Type A=Majority-owned (more than 50% of capital) by particular families (one or more), or jointly by families and companies.

Type B=Minority-owned (less than 50% of capital) by particular families (one or more), or jointly by families and companies.

Type C=Owned (minority or majority) by managers, companies or government.

Sources: 1) Osakaya Shoten, *Kabushiki Nenkan* (A Yearbook of Joint Stock Companies), 1936, 1941.

2) For the selection of the largest 200 companies and the classification of ownership patterns, we owe Professors K. Mito and H. Masaki. See, K. Mito and H. Masaki, "Wagakuni Daikigyo ni okeru Shoyu to Shihai" ("Ownership and Control in Japanese Big Business), *Soshiki Kagaku*, Vol. 3, No. 3, 1969.

probable that the difference in corporate performance seen between family and non-family companies in the aggregate did not result from the difference in ownership patterns but rather differences in scale between these firms. In order to substantiate this hypothesis, we did a more detailed study by using the data of individual firms, as follows.

We analyzed the financial performance of the largest 200 companies in 1936, as seen in Table 16. In this analysis, 188 of the largest 200 companies for which financial data are available were classified by industry and by ownership pattern. Regarding ownership pattern, we categorized companies from respective fields into three types: "Type A" is a company which is majority-owned (more than 50% of capital) by particular families (one or more), or jointly by families and companies; "Type B" is minority-owned (less than 50% of capital) by particular families (one or more), or jointly by families and companies; and "Type C" is owned (minority or majority) by managers, companies or government. Roughly speaking, Types A and B may be regarded as family companies and Type C as non-family companies. The profit rates, dividend rates, reserve rates and payout ratios were calculated for each type by industry, as seen in Table 16.

To be brief, this classification did not reveal significant results with respect to differences in corporate performance, except in the category of researve rates: with regard to the rates of profit and dividend, and payout ratios, notable differences were not necessarily seen among the three types for almost every field of industry; the results were inconclusive as far as this analysis is concerned. However, we might say that the reserve rates of Types A and B—namely family companies—were on the average higher than those of type C, non-family companies (railway, electric power and gas companies excepted). From the above, it might, then, be arguable that in large-scale firms the ownership patterns do not affect financial policy in any particular direction except reserve policy. But this remains to be thoroughly substantiated. At this stage, our study suggests at most that small-scale family firms might have a peculiar financial structure and that as family firms became large in scale, their financial structure might come to resemble that of other large firms.

## NOTES

\* The author of this article would like to thank Professors Shigeaki Yasuoka, Masaru Udagawa and Kenjiro Ishikawa for their valuable comments
and suggestions. He is also grateful for comments and English corrections
on the manuscript from Professor William B. Hauser; for English corrections made by Mr. Michael A. Cusmano and Mr. Jeffrey E. Hanes; and
for research assistance and typewriting from Mr. Vichian Chakepaichayon.

1. Tsuneharu Egashira, "Kyodo Kigyo Genryu Ko" ("On the Origins
   of Collective Enterprises"), *Sangyo Keizai Ronsho* No. 1–2, 1966.
2. Hiroshi Shimbo, "Tokugawa-koki, Ishin-ki ni okeru Kyodo Kigyo"
   ("Collective Enterprises in the Latter Half of the Tokugawa Period
   and in the Early Meiji Era"), *Kokumin Keizai Zasshi*, Vol. 119, No. 4,
   1969.
   Manabu Yunoki, "Kinsei Kaiungyo no Hatten to sono Keiei"
   ("Development of Marine Transportation and Its Management"),
   *Keiei Gaku Ronkyu*, Vol. 14, No. 4, 1961.
3. H. Shimbo, ibid.
4. T. Egashira, op. cit.
5. Shigeaki Yasuoka, *Zaibatsu Keisei-shi no Kenkyu* (The Study on the
   Formation of Zaibatsu), pp. 196–229, Minerba, 1970.
6. S. Yasuoka, ibid., pp. 140–154, Matao Miyamoto, "Konoike Zenemon" in Yotaro Sakudo, eds. *Edo-ki Shonin no Kakushinteki Kigyosha
   Katsudo* (Innovative Entrepreneurship by Tokugawa Merchant), pp.
   93–94, Yuhikaku, 1978.
7. S. Yasuoka, op. cit. p. 214.
8. Mataji Miyamoto, "Konoike-ke no Kakun to Tensoku" ("The
   House Codes and Business Rules of the Konoike House")
   Mataji Miyamoto, ed., *Osaka no Kenkyu* (The Studies on Osaka),
   Vol. 3, p. 73, Seibundo, 1969.
9. Masao Adachi, "Kyoto ni okeru Sinise no Keiei Rinen" ("Business
   Ideology of Old Kyoto Merchants"), *Nihon Shisoshi*, Vol. 14, 1980.
10. Wataro Kanno, *Nihon Kaisha Kigyo Hassei-shi no Kenkyu* (The Study
    of the Formation of the Company System in Japan), pp. 69–109,
    Keizai Hyoron-sha, 1931.
    Hiroshi Shimbo, *Nihon Kindai Shinyo Seido Seiritsu Shiron* (The
    History of The Modern Financial Institutions in Japan), pp. 35–53,
    Yuhikaku, 1968.

90                                      *M. Miyamoto*

11. W. Kanno, ibid., pp. 110–257. H. Shimbo, ibid. pp. 54–198.
12. W. Kanno, ibid., pp. 33–68.
13. Matao Miyamoto, "Meiji Shoki no Kigyo to Kigyo-ka—Horai-sha no Baai—" ("On the Corporation and Entrepreneurship in the Early Meiji Era—In the case of the Horai Company"), *Keiei-shi Gaku*, Vol. 4, No. 3, 1970.
14. Shin'ichi Goto, ed., *Nihon no Kinyu Tokei* (Financial Statistics of Japan), p. 43, 1970.
15. S. Goto, ibid.
16. S. Yasuoka, op. cit., pp. 172–177.
17. Sanwa Bank, *Sanwa Ginko no Rekishi* (The History of the Sanwa Bank), pp. 34–36, 1974.
18. Naikaku Tokeikyoku, *Nihon Teikoku Tokei Nenkan* (Annual Statistics of the Japanese Empire), Vol. 10.
19. Ibid. As a study which uses these company statistics, Professor T. Imuta's work is very valuable: Toshimitsu Imuta, "Meiji Chu-ki ni okeru Kaisha Kigyo no Kosei" ("Company Structure in the Mid-Meiji Period"), Osaka City University, *Kenkyu to Shiryo*, Vol. 25, 1967; and Toshimitsu Imuta, "Meiji-ki ni okeru Kabushiki Kaisha no Hatten to Kabunushi-so no Keisei" ("The Development of Joint-stock Companies and the Formation of a Stockowner Class"), Osaka City University, ed., *Meiji-ki no Keizai Hatten to Keizai Shutai*, 1968.
20. As for the Commercial Code, see Shin'ichi Takayanagi and Isamu Fujita, eds., *Shihonshugi Ho no Keisei to Tenkai* (The Formation and Development of Capitalistic Law), University of Tokyo Press, 1973. Also see Ichiro Kobashi, "Wagakuni ni okeru Kaisha Hosei no Kei-sei" ("The Formation of Company Legislation in Japan"), United Nations University Discussion Paper, HSDRJE-67J/unup-387, 1981.
21. Ohkura-sho Shuzeikyoku, "Zeiho Enkaku Yoko" ("Outline History of the Tax Law") in *Shuzeikyoku Tokei Nenpo-sho*, 1938.
22. Shigeaki Yasuoka, "The Tradition of Family Business in the Strategic Decision Process and Management Structure of Zaibatsu Business: Mitsui, Sumitomo and Mitsubishi" in Keiichiro Nakagawa, ed., *Strategy and Structure of Big Business* (Proceedings of the First Fuji Conference on Business History, Vol. 1), University of Tokyo Press, 1976, p. 84.
23. Ohkura-sho Shuzeikyoku, op. cit.
24. Hidemasa Morikawa, *Nihon Zaibatsu Shi* (History of the Japanese Zaibatsu), Kyoikusha, 1978, pp. 164–175.

25. Matao Miyamoto and Kensuke Hiroyama, "Meiji Koki Showa Shoki Konoike ni okeru Takakuka Zasetsu to Sengyo Shiko" ("Diversification and Specialization in the Konoike House during the Period 1867–1933"), *Keiei-shigaku*, Vol. 15, No. 1, 1980, p. 64.

26. Sanwa Bank, op. cit., pp. 69.

27. Sumitomo Bank, *Sumitomo Ginko Hachijunen Shi* (80 Year History of the Sumitomo Bank), 1979, pp. 195–196.

28. Shigeaki Yasuoka, ed., *Mitsui Zaibatsu*, Nihon Keizai Shinbunsha, 1982, pp. 235–236.

29. Yasuo Mishima, ed., *Mitsubishi Zaibatsu*, Nihon Keizai Shinbunsha, 1981, pp. 275–277.

30. Kensuke Hiroyama, "Meiji Koki Taisho-ki ni okeru Konoike no Kigyosha Katsudo" ("Entrepreneurship by the House of Konoike during the Second Half of the Meiji Era and the Taisho Era (3)"), *Osaka Daigaku Keizaigaku*, Vol. 30, No. 1, 1980, p. 27.

31. Sanwa Bank, op. cit., p. 69.

32. M. Miyamoto and K. Hiroyama, op. cit., p. 80.

33. Shigeaki Yasuoka, "Zaibatsu no Kyodaika", ("Enlargement of Zaibatsu"), in Masaaki Kobayashi and others eds., *Nihon Keieishi o Manabu*, Yuhikaku, 1976. Morikawa, op. cit.

34. As for these cases, see Mishima, op. cit., S. Yasuoka, *Mitsui Zaibatsu*, op. cit., and Y. Sakudo, op. cit.

35. For example, S. Yasuoka, ibid., Morikawa, op. cit., and Yoshio Togai, "Senji Keizai to Zaibatsu" ("Wartime Economy and Zaibatsu"), M. Kobayashi and others, op. cit.

36. Ohkurasho Shuzeikyoku, op. cit.

37. He was the organizer of the session on "From family firm to professional management: structure and performance of business enterprise" at the Eighth International Economic History Congress held at Budapest in 1982.
   See, Leslie Hannah, "Introduction" in *From Family Firm to professional Management: Structure and Performance of Business Enterprise*, edited by L. Hannah, Akademiai Kiado, Budapest, 1982, pp. 4–5.

38. Hannah quoted this from R. J. Monsen, John S. Chiu and D. E. Cooley, "The Effect of the Separation of Ownership and Control on the Performance of the Larger Firm", *Quarterly Journal of Economics*, Vol. 82, 1968.

39. According to Hannah, the references for this are works by Jacquemin and de Ghellinick, Nyman and Silberston, and Dean Savage.

40. Ohkurasho Shuzeikyoku, op. cit.

# COMMENTS

Masaru Udagawa
*Hosei University*

In his very interesting paper, Professor Miyamoto has traced the process of development of the Japanese company system from the Edo era to World War II, focusing mainly on the changing position and role of family business in this process. Furthermore, after comparing the financial performance of family and non-family companies during 1931–1941, he discusses several important characteristics of the management of family businesses.

I have no major disagreements with the views expressed by Professor Miyamoto, but would like to bring up some additional problems.

Firstly, both the big merchant houses before the Meiji Restoration and those founded afterwards were family businesses, although between the two groups, there was no basic difference in ownership patterns or management characteristics. While the family held the ownership, they not only delegated authority for operational activities but also responsibility for most long-term policy making to the salaried managers. Therefore, the fate of big family enterprises depended on the managerial abilities of the salaried managers. This was particularly true after the Meiji Restoration. In fact, after 1868 many big merchant houses which had originated in the Edo period went bankrupt after they failed to find able salaried managers. And where bankruptcy was avoided, growth did not occur and they remained as smaller zaibatsu, such as the Konoike. On the other hand, the Mitsui and Sumitomo families succeeded in recruiting talented salaried managers who had a strong interest in the progress of industrialization. As a result, both became large zaibatsu. To some extent this was also true for newly formed family enterprises established after the Meiji Restoration.

Consequently, I would like to ask Professor Miyamoto a few questions. What was the function of salaried managers in big family enterprises? How did that function change in the periods before and after the Meiji Restoration? Comparing the Mitsui and the Konoike after 1868, did their recruitment policies toward salaried managers differ?

Secondly, after the Meiji Restoration, when the joint-stock company system was introduced, certainly, the big merchant houses or zaibatsu did not adopt immediately to this system. But it is well known that many of them participated in the foundation of large stock companies in new business fields such as banking, railways and cotton-spinning, and became large stockholders in those companies. In this sense, they also played an important part in the introduction and establishment of the stock company system. In general, did they become stockholders in those companies by their own will or due to the advice of the government, or figures such as Shibusawa and Fukuzawa who hoped to introduce this system into Japan? And how did these investments influence their main businesses?

Afterwards, these big family enterprises, including the zaibatsu, reorganized into corporate form, particularly into stock companies. As the main motives of their reorganization, Professor Miyamoto pointed out savings in tax payments, mobilization of outside capital, rationalization of management and avoidance of social criticism against monopolization. To add to these motives, I think that they expected to add posts for salaried managers through that reorganization because, as said above, the success of their firms depended on the devotion of these individuals to management. Therefore, big family enterprises were very eager to get able salaried managers and to keep them in their firms. In order to do this, it was necessary to increase the opportunities for promotion and posts for employees, in particular managers, through the diversification and reorganization of their business.

Thirdly, Professor Miyamoto reveals that the joint-stock company developed along with limited partnerships or partnerships that were mostly family business. And he also points out that non-family business and family business coexisted in some fields. In such cases, how did this influence the course of industrialization and the characteristics of management in Japan?

Finally, Professor Miyamoto compares the financial performance
of family and non-family companies, and partnerships, limited
partnerships and joint-stock companies. Furthermore, the data and
analysis presented appears for the first time in Japan and will be of
considerable use in the future. Some further compilations of data
and analyses should also prove useful, for example, classifying companies by firm scale. I hope Professor Miyamoto undertakes such
projects as well.

# Financing of the Japanese Zaibatsu
## —Sumitomo as a Case Study—

Shoichi Asajima
*Senshu University*

## I. Introduction

The aim of this conference is to clarify the difference between family business and non-family business by means of comparison. My paper will be in alignment with this through its underlying theme of fund raising in family business. Sumitomo, which I am presently researching, can be considered an example of fund raising in a family business due to the fact that it is typical of zaibatsu family businesses in Japan, and because Sumitomo is representative of Japan's zaibatsu as one of the four largest general zaibatsu. I therefore submit this paper as material for discussing fund raising in the Sumitomo zaibatsu. I will adhere to Professor Yasuoka's opinion in defining the concept of zaibatsu.[1]

One would desire first to inquire into any special characteristics which distinguish the fund raising in a zaibatsu, because it is a family business, from ordinary firms. However, clarification of zaibatsu fund raising has not progressed much as a field of study within zaibatsu research. Mitsui and Sumitomo are the most thoroughly understood to date; however, as research on others still lags behind, we are not at the point of constructing a general theory of fund raising in zaibatsu.

Having made this point, let us take a closer look at the issue at hand through my research studies of the Sumitomo zaibatsu from 1920.[2]

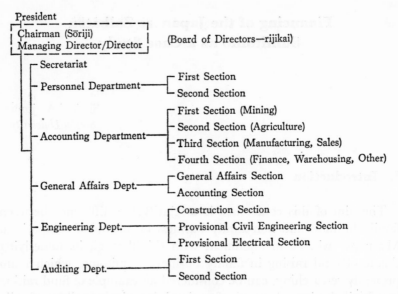

FIG. 1   The Head Office Structure of the Sumitomo Limited Partnership
(The Sumitomo Goshigaisha).

## II.  Funding Control by the Zaibatsu Head Office (Honsha)

### 1.  General Controlling Function of the Head Office

Fund raising in the Sumitomo zaibatsu was overseen by the head
office or "Honsha," the headquarters of the Sumitomo zaibatsu, a
part of the Sumitomo limited partnership (the Sumitomo Goshigaisha). Let us look at this general control.[3]

The Sumitomo Goshigaisha was established in 1921 after reorganizing what was a private enterprise. The new arrangement was
composed of the head office and directly managed enterprises. Also
included in the Sumitomo zaibatsu were several independent companies which were not a part of the Goshigaisha.

The head office of the Goshigaisha exercised a general controlling
function over the entire Sumitomo zaibatsu. In other words, while
this was obvious with respect to the directly managed enterprises,
the head office also required that the independent subsidiaries sub-

mit plans for equipment investment and operations to the head office annually before the fiscal year began. The head office reviewed these plans in detail, adjusted them from the standpoint of the entire zaibatsu and submitted them for approval to the board of directors (rijikai). The head of the Sumitomo family, Kichizaemon, lead a symbolic existence. He had nothing to do with actual operations and he simply gave formal approval on matters that came before him. The significant decision making was done by the board of directors, where especially the chairman (soriji), who held the highest responsibility, wielded the most influential authority. The necessary funds for each department within the zaibatsu were submitted along with the plans for equipment investment and operations. The necessary amounts and fund raising methods were decided within the context of the approval and revision of these plans, which contained instructions from the head office to the directly managed enterprises and subsidiaries.

General control of the head office was strict. Two reports had to be handed in biannually. One was the "Accounting Forecast and Fund Raising Plan." The other was the follow-up "Biannual Report" which explained changes in the enterprise, the progress of equipment investments and so on. In addition, there were monthly and ten-day reports. Through these, the head office established a system whereby it was possible to grasp in detail the actual conditions of all the enterprises under its jurisdiction. The head office had a particularly strong interest in equipment investment and the funding plans for these investments. The head office conducted a rigorous check on the content of the plans submitted from each department under its control and would not readily allow changes once a plan was in operation.

At Sumitomo, detailed operating regulations were incorporated into the Sumitomo Kahō (the Sumitomo family constitution and company manual) and later into the Shasoku (a revised version of the Sumitomo Kahō). A look at these regulations reveals an extremely limited delegation of authority, the necessity of reporting in detail to the upper ranks when anything out of the ordinary occurred and a dependence on instructions. In other words, Sumitomo, even compared to other zaibatsu, operated under a particu-

larly strong centralized power structure. The general controlling
function with respect to funds was performed by the accounting
department (keiribu) and the accounts section of the general affairs
department (sōmubu kaikeika) of the head office. The organization
was comparatively simple, with the elite personnel located throughout the zaibatsu.

## 2.  Funds Adjusting Function of the Head Office

There were not many independent corporations in the form of a
company within the Sumitomo zaibatsu during the Taishō period.
There were only three companies: Sumitomo Bank, Sumitomo Electric Wire & Cable Works and Sumitomo Steel Works. The other
enterprises under the zaibatsu were all directly managed by the
Sumitomo Goshigaisha. Those under direct management covered
a wide variety of enterprises, such as the Besshi Mine Office, Waka-
matsu Coal Mining Office, Sumitomo Copper Works and Sumitomo
Fertilizer Works. In comparison to other zaibatsu head companies,
this overseeing of such a wide variety of enterprises managed directly
by the Sumitomo Goshigaisha, in addition to its head company
functions for the zaibatsu, is a significant characteristic. The directly
managed enterprises became corporations and separated from the
Sumitomo Goshigaisha one after another up until the early Showa
period (1928). Sumitomo Steel Tube & Copper Works, Ltd., Sumitomo Fertilizer Works, Ltd., Sumitomo Besshi Mine Co., Ltd.,
Sumitomo Kyushu Colliery Co., Ltd. and Sumitomo Warehouse
Co., Ltd. were added as subsidiaries. Additionally, Sumitomo Building Co., Ltd. and Sumitomo Trust Co., Ltd. were newly established; Ban Colliery Co., Ltd. and Hinode Life Insurance Co., Ltd.
were purchased, while Tosa Yoshinogawa Hydro Electric Power
Co., Ltd. and Osaka North Harbour Co., Ltd. became recognized
as affiliated companies. In this way, the Sumitomo zaibatsu was
composed of numerous subsidiary companies, with the Sumitomo
Goshigaisha as the nucleus, and a reduced number of enterprises
directly managed by the Goshigaisha. The enterprises that had been
directly managed became independent units within the Goshigaisha
and a distinction was made as to funds and financial profits and
losses. However, even though numerous subsidiaries took the form of

TABLE 1  Loans and Deposits in the Sumitomo Ltd. Partnership.

Transition of Loans (Balance)                                            (unit: ¥1000)

| | 1922 | 1923 | 1924 | 1925 | 1926 | 1927 | 1928 | 1929 | 1930 | 1931 |
|---|---|---|---|---|---|---|---|---|---|---|
| Sumitomo Warehouse | 2181 | | 1180 | 1180 | 780 | 1080 | 1080 | 2180 | 2180 | 2180 |
| Sumitomo Building | 1530 | | | | 1290 | 1160 | 1310 | 1310 | 1240 | 1180 |
| Sumitomo Copper Works | | | | 2675 | | | | | | |
| Sumitomo Ban Colliery | 270 | | | | | 888 | | | | |
| Sumitomo Hospital | 1568 | | | | | | | | | 3526 |
| Sumitomo family | | | | | | | 204 | 194 | 188 | 182 |
| Housing loans | | | | | | | 305 | 321 | 400 | 264 |
| Other | | 1974 | 1878 | 1861 | 627 | 794 | 409 | 458 | 917 | 502 |
| Total | 5549 | 1974 | 3058 | 5716 | 2697 | 3922 | 3308 | 4463 | 4925 | 7834 |

Transition of Deposits (Balance)                                         (unit: ¥1000)

| | 1922 | 1923 | 1924 | 1925 | 1926 | 1927 | 1928 | 1929 | 1930 | 1931 |
|---|---|---|---|---|---|---|---|---|---|---|
| Sumitomo Electric Wire & Cable Works | ⟵ | 2600 | 2800 | 3300 | 3300 | 3300 | 5800 | 5200 | 4000 | 4600 |
| Sumitomo Steel Works | | 2800 | 3200 | 4250 | 4300 | 4700 | 5400 | 4700 | 4500 | 1370 |
| Osaka North Harbour | | | | | 850 | 750 | 350 | 410 | 580 | 1460 |
| Simitomo Besshi Mine | ? | | | | | 250 | | | | |
| Sumitomo Hospital | | | | | | | 45 | 65 | | |
| Sumitomo Steel Tube & Copper Works | | | | | | | | | 750 | |
| Sumitomo family | ⟵ | | | 1050 | 2200 | 2200 | 4391 | 2300 | 1400 | 3050 |
| Savings | | | | | | 900 | 900 | 970 | 1102 | 1195 |
| Other | ⟶ | 2541 | 2483 | 1653 | 1238 | 515 | 650 | 787 | 944 | 1047 |
| Total | 5616 | 7941 | 8483 | 10253 | 11888 | 12615 | 17536 | 14432 | 13276 | 12722 |

joint-stock companies, they were treated on the same level as directly managed enterprises with respect to the head office's general control within the zaibatsu.

The head office completely supplied the necessary funds to the directly managed enterprises, but collected any surplus that arose. The subsidiaries were also made to deposit any surplus funds with the head office rather than with a bank. When a deficit arose, the money was returned to them or they borrowed from the head office. In short, the head office performed an adjustment function for the supply and demand of funds for the firms under its jurisdiction. Interest was calculated for this borrowing and lending of money, but it was probably necessary to internal control. In other words, interest was calculated only to evaluate the performance of each management unit, not to actually charge interest. This kind of funds adjustment by the head office did not extend to all the firms within the entire zaibatsu; there were a few exceptions (see Table 1).

The head office performed the adjustment function of taking in interest funds from company A and disbursing them to company B that was short of funds. However, it often utilized these funds, as it found necessary, within the head office when it suffered from a lack of funds due to investments in subsidiaries and the holding of negotiable securities. When the head office itself slipped into a fund deficit due to its numerous investments, it borrowed from financial institutions within the zaibatsu, especially from the Sumitomo Bank.

It was important for the head office to anticipate the maximum level of funds necessary for the entire zaibatsu for the year and how to adjust for that level. To that end, the head office required enterprises and companies under its jurisdiction to file a report on the maximum amount of funds necessary for the year. I would like to emphasize that the adjustment function of the head office is conducted based on these funding estimates.

## III.  Fund Raising Methods in Zaibatsu Firms

Fund raising in the Goshigaisha's directly managed enterprises was simple: lending and borrowing funds from the head office—an increase or decrease in deposit funds. There was no other method allowed.

TABLE 2.    Summary of Financial Income and Expenditures during the Sumitomo Goshgaisha Period.

(unit: ¥1000)

| | Business income and expenditures/* (deficit) | Payments | Other deposit withdrawals/* (savings increase) | Methods of increase borrowing/* (refunding) | Handling issue notes payable/* (account settled) | Issue bonds/* (bond redemption) |
|---|---|---|---|---|---|---|
| 1922 | * 1884 | 1250 | 645 | | | |
| 1923 | 294 | 2275 | * 2565 | | | |
| 1924 | * 610 | 975 | * 1532 | 597 | | 572 |
| 1925 | 937 | 3250 | * 3594 | * 591 | | |
| 1926 | * 938 | | * 238 | 700 | | |
| 1927 | * 2118 | 2750 | * 1567 | 699 | 235 | |
| 1928 | * 7330 | 3000 | * 509 | * 272 | 5106 | |
| 1929 | * 8698 | 4000 | * 552 | 4691 | 570 | |
| 1930 | * 8933 | 5000 | * 1057 | 1910 | 3070 | |
| 1931 | * 1086 | | 1989 | 1877 | *2782 | |
| 1932 | 2554 | | * 1389 | * 690 | * 467 | |
| 1933 | 3636 | 4200 | * 1421 | * 833 | *5013 | *572 |
| 1934 | *16963 | 23000 | 493 | *3555 | 2975 | |
| (1935) | (*10238) | (6500) | (* 143) | (2680) | (1200) | |
| 1936 | * 7733 | 6250 | * 1707 | 1434 | 1757 | |
| Total | *59110 | 62450 | *12671 | 8622 | 701 | 0 |

(Parentheses for 1934 indicate estimated values)

A problem lies in financing subsidiaries which have taken on the joint-stock company form. Fund raising methods included (1) increasing paid-up capital, (2) borrowing and depositing with the head office, (3) borrowing from financial institutions, (4) issuing notes payable, (5) issuing bonds. The fund raising method varied with the rapid development of the Sumitomo zaibatsu and the fluctuations in the economy. Tables 2 and 5 indicate the fund raising totals for group subsidiaries by period: the Sumitomo Goshigaisha period (1921–1936) and the Sumitomo Honsha period (1937 on).

**1.  The Sumitomo Goshigaisha Period**
The financing of subsidiaries in this period relied mainly on paid-up capital. Companies which showed a deficit repaid their loans, redeemed their notes payable and recovered deposits by biding their time and increasing their capital, whether by reliance on (1) increasing paid-up capital, (2) withdrawing funds deposited with the head office or borrowing from it, (3) issuing notes payable, or other fund raising methods. This can be referred to as self-capital centrism. Even though incurring business liabilities was inevitable, it was believed that equipment and negotiable securities investments should be handled by equity capital. Thus, a firm's outstanding loans and notes payable were able to be liquidated by collections of paid-up capital.

However, this kind of fund raising must not be evaluated in the same manner as ordinary firms because it involved a closed investment. In other words, among the subsidiaries in the Sumitomo zaibatsu, there have been extremely few examples of any opening of stocks to the public. These exceptions were Sumitomo Bank (went public in 1917), Sumitomo Trust Co. (1925), Sumitomo Chemical Co. (1934), Sumitomo Metal Industries, Ltd. (1935), and Sumitomo Electric Wire & Cable Works, Ltd. (1937). Sumitomo Bank did not increase its capital during this period. Sumitomo Trust Co. went public at the time of its establishment and remained as such without any capitalization increases after that. Therefore, only three of the five companies listed above opened their stocks to the public after they were incorporated and thereby took in external funds.

Non-Sumitomo stockholders acquired shares in Sumitomo Ban

Colliery Co., Osaka North Harbour Co., and Sumitomo Life Insurance Co., but Osaka North Harbour Co. and Sumitomo Life Insurance Co. did not increase their capitalization at all and Sumitomo itself subscribed to the entire amount of the capitalization increase for Sumitomo Ban Colliery Co. Therefore, no external capital was introduced into any of these three companies through capital increases.

All of the other companies (Sumitomo Warehouse Co., Sumitomo Building Co., Tosa Yoshinogawa Hydro Electric Power Co., Sumitomo Steel Tube & Copper Works, Sumitomo Steel Works, Sumitomo Besshi Mine Co., Sumitomo Kyushu Colliery Co., Sumitomo Aluminium Reduction Co., Sumitomo Machinery Co. and Manchurian Sumitomo Metal Industries) had no stockholders outside of Sumitomo. They maintained a purely closed system under family and kinship group control.

Therefore, the only three companies which received capital payments from outside the zaibatsu were Sumitomo Chemical Co., Sumitomo Metal Industries and Sumitomo Electric Wire & Cable Works. Although accurate calculations have not been possible as to the amount of subscriptions from stockholders outside the zaibatsu since opening stocks to the public, most fund raising came from within the zaibatsu when the three companies are totalled together. Companies other than these that had capital increases during this period were Sumitomo Building Co., Sumitomo Steel Tube & Copper Works, Tosa Yoshinogawa Hydro Electric Power Co., Sumitomo Aluminium Reduction Co., Manchurian Sumitomo Steel Tube Co., Sumitomo Machinery Co., Sumitomo Colliery Co., and Sumitomo Metal Industries and Sumitomo Chemical Co. before they opened their stocks to the public. In any case, all fund raising was done inside the zaibatsu because the companies were not public. Judging from these circumstances, it can be assumed that almost all of the ¥62,450,000 in paid-up capital listed in Table 2 is fund raising within the zaibatsu.

(a) The next question is: who are the investors within the zaibatsu? To give us something to work from, let us look at the composition of stockholders in the Sumitomo Steel Works at the end of 1924. There were a mere 15 people holding a total of 240,000 shares, of

TABLE 3   Estimate of Dividends Received by Kichizaemon Sumitomo.

(unit: ¥1000)

| | Dividends from the Goshigaisha | Dividends from the affiliates | Total |
|---|---|---|---|
| 1925 | 592 | | |
| 1926 | | | |
| 1927 | 1,727 | 394 | 2,121 |
| 1928 | 1,826 | ↑ | |
| 1929 | 1,234 | | |
| 1930 | 2,122 | average | |
| 1931 | 247 | taken as | |
| 1932 | 1,974 | 400 | |
| 1933 | 2,023 | | |
| 1934 | ? | | |
| 1935 | 5,626 | ↓ | |
| 1936 | 2,467 | 417 | 2,884 |
| subtotal | 19,838 | 4,800 | 24,638 |
| 1937 | | 523 | |
| 1938 | 675 | 711 | |
| 1939 | 675 | 804 | |
| 1940 | 675 | 1,028 | |
| 1941 | 675 | 1,070 | |
| subtotal | 2,700 | 4,136 | 6,836 |

which the Sumitomo Goshigaisha held 89%, Kichizaemon Sumitomo 10.4%, and thirteen Sumitomo executives 0.6%. Although the thirteen executives each held 100 stocks on paper, it is supposed that these stocks were, in effect, owned by the Goshigaisha.

Many examples of closed investment can be found among firms in the Sumitomo zaibatsu, with the exception of those whose stocks were open to the public. The above stockholder composition, with the Sumitomo Goshigaisha or Kichizaemon and Sumitomo executives holding the stocks, formed the basis of shareholding even in firms that had links to outside capital, where the external capital was added as large stockholders. There are also incidences where Kichizaemon's name does not appear at all, simply "Goshigaisha." Therefore, we can conclude that the paid-up capital within the zaibatsu was actually investments of the Goshigaisha, with Kichizaemon Sumitomo occasionally joining in.

The next question concerns where the Goshigaisha and Kichi-zaemon Sumitomo acquired the paid-up capital funds.

First of all, Kichizaemon owned 98.7% of the capital of the Goshigaisha as well as stock in six companies (of which three did not pay dividends) as of 1927: The dividends that Kichizaemon received for that year are calculated at ¥2,120,000, a large part being dividends from the Goshigaisha. Looking at the year 1936 in the same manner, in addition to the Goshigaisha, he owned stock in eight companies (of which two did not pay dividends), and the dividends Kichizaemon received that year are calculated at ¥2,880,000. In effect, Kichizaemon's dividend income came largely from the Goshigaisha—which changed greatly from year to year as can be seen in Table 3—with approximately ¥400,000 from affiliated firms each year. Moreover, perhaps some of the dividends which Kichizaemon received from the Goshigaisha totalled ¥19,830,000 for 1925–1936, for the years for which figures are available. If we estimate dividends over the same period from subsidiaries at ¥4,800,000 (¥400,000 × 12 years), then the total can be considered approximately ¥25,000,000. The amount of paid-up capital judged to have been paid to subsidiaries by Kichizaemon during the same period is calculated at a mere ¥1,170,000. Therefore, Kichizaemon's paid-up capital funds could be raised adequately from the dividends he received, and the balance was probably used either for the Sumitomo family budget or put into savings.

On the other hand, the amount paid-up by the affiliated companies totals ¥106,270,000 over the years 1922–36, for which the figures are known. When the figure for spot goods investment is subtracted, the amount totals ¥62,400,000 (see Table 4). The Goshigaisha received ¥73,550,000 in dividends from subsidiaries during this period and over ¥14,390,000 in dividend interest from its holdings in negotiable securities. In short, the Goshigaisha made payments to the subsidiary companies with the dividends received from them, which would result in a small amount of excess being generated.

Among the dividends received from subsidiaries, the largest amounts were received from Sumitomo Bank, 44% of the total, followed by Sumitomo Electric Wire & Cable Works at 16%, with the remaining 40% contributed by a large number of affiliates.

TABLE 4    Breakdown of Paid-up Capital during the Sumitomo Goshigaisha
Period.

| | Payment amounts | | | Breakdown of the Goshigaisha payments | |
|---|---|---|---|---|---|
| | Total | Goshigaisha | Other | Investment in goods | Cash investments |
| 1922 | 1,250 | 778 | 472 | | 778 |
| 1923 | 17,275 | 16,087 | 1,188 | 14,950 | 1,137 |
| 1924 | 975 | 487 | 488 | | 487 |
| 1925 | 10,050 | 4,823 | 5,227 | | 4,823 |
| 1926 | 9,000 | 9,000 | | 9,000 | |
| 1927 | 19,000 | 18,481 | 519 | 14,950 | 3,531 |
| 1928 | 8,000 | 7,975 | 25 | 4,975 | 3,000 |
| 1929 | 4,000 | 4,000 | | | 4,000 |
| 1930 | 5,000 | 4,959 | 41 | | 4,959 |
| 1931 | 2,500 | 1,875 | 625 | | 1,875 |
| 1932 | | | | | |
| 1933 | 6,700 | 5,624 | 1,076 | | 5,624 |
| 1934 | 28,000 | 20,287 | 7,713 | | 20,287 |
| 1935 | 16,500 | 10,509 | 5,991 | | 10,509 |
| 1936 | 6,750 | 1,392 | 5,358 | | 1,392 |
| total | 135,000 | 106,277 | 28,723 | 43,875 | 62,402 |
| Component ratio | (100) | (78.7) | (21.3) | | |

Sumitomo Bank never increased its capital and Sumitomo Electric
Wire & Cable Works received a capital stock payment only once in
1922. In other words, the Goshigaisha absorbed the profits of Sumitomo Bank, Sumitomo Electric Wire & Cable Works and others
through dividends and then provided funds to other subsidiaries that
needed funds through capital stock payments. The adjustment
function was performed through this structure.

(b)   The next subject I would like to look at is savings with-
drawals. However, there are surprisingly few in Table 2. Instead,
the table shows many years in which savings increased (years marked
with *). When the companies are analyzed according to their commercial base, there is a parallel between companies which withdrew
from their savings and those which increased their savings. Table 2
shows the results in which both types cancel out each other. The
companies with large deposits in the head office included Sumitomo

(unit: ¥1000)

| | Dividends received by affiliated companies | | | | Interest on other dividends |
|---|---|---|---|---|---|
| | Total | Bank | Sumitomo Wire & Cable Works | Other | |
| 1922 | (3,237) | 2,565 | 278 | 394 | 697 |
| 1923 | (3,477) | 2,565 | 525 | 387 | 488 |
| 1924 | 3,521 | 2,586 | 547 | 388 | 484 |
| 1925 | 3,513 | 2,579 | 547 | 387 | 492 |
| 1926 | 3,285 | 2,564 | 547 | 174 | 549 |
| 1927 | 4,446 | 2,386 | 1,372 | 688 | 622 |
| 1928 | 3,718 | 2,226 | 657 | 835 | 742 |
| 1929 | 5,719 | 2,226 | 657 | 2,836 | 831 |
| 1930 | 4,987 | 2,100 | 657 | 2,230 | 1,285 |
| 1931 | 4,304 | 1,897 | 2,005 | 402 | 1,042 |
| 1932 | 3,255 | 1,769 | 325 | 1,161 | 1,152 |
| 1933 | 5,577 | 1,765 | 1,829 | 1,983 | 1,343 |
| 1934 | (8,918) | (1,765) | 577 | 6,576 | ? |
| 1935 | 9,078 | (1,765) | 547 | 6,766 | 2,266 |
| 1936 | 6,516 | 1,765 | 584 | 4,167 | 2,398 |
| total | 73,551 | 32,523 | 11,654 | 29,374 | 14,391 |
| Component ratio | | | | | |
| | (100) | (44.2) | (15.8) | (40.0) | |

Steel Works, Sumitomo Electric Wire & Cable Works and North Harbour Co. These companies were representative of those relying on deposits, as their fund raising was conducted only through taking from or adding to their deposits in the head office. Also, since capital increases and capital stock payment were done in round figures, deposits would often increase due to the temporary surpluses that arose.

(c)  The reliance of subsidiaries on borrowing began from 1924, according to Table 2. The companies reliant on borrowing were quite limited. There were only two companies that relied on the head office for their borrowings, Sumitomo Warehouse Co. and Sumitomo Building Co.; and there were only three companies that relied on Sumitomo Bank and Sumitomo Trust Co. for borrowing—Sumitomo Fertilizer Works, Tosa Yoshinogawa Hydro Electric Power Co. and Sumitomo Building Co. Only one company, Osaka

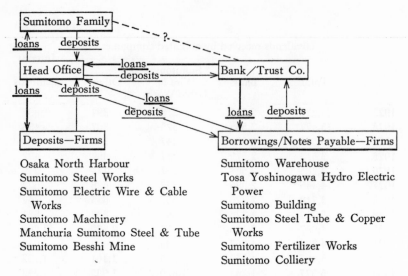

Osaka North Harbour
Sumitomo Steel Works
Sumitomo Electric Wire & Cable
  Works
Sumitomo Machinery
Manchuria Sumitomo Steel & Tube
Sumitomo Besshi Mine

Sumitomo Warehouse
Tosa Yoshinogawa Hydro Electric
  Power
Sumitomo Building
Sumitomo Steel Tube & Copper
  Works
Sumitomo Fertilizer Works
Sumitomo Colliery

FIG. 2   Funding Structure during the Sumitomo Goshigaisha Period.

North Harbour Co., relied on sources from outside the zaibatsu and
this can be considered a special case. Therefore, it can be said that,
in effect, the borrowing during this period was handled exclusively
within the zaibatsu.

(d)   The only firms that issued notes payable were Sumitomo
Fertilizer Works and those belonging to the mining divison. Even
so, these notes payable were not issued in order to settle accounts
with customers. They were drawn on Sumitomo Bank for the
purpose of fund raising; and it is thought they were, in fact, considered as borrowings. Moreover, the notes payable that were issued
were almost all redeemed during this period and are presumed to
have been simply short term borrowings. Also, Sumitomo Warehouse
Co. issued bonds in small denominations, but bond issues were not
yet an important means of fund raising for the Sumitomo zaibatsu
as a whole during this period. In fact, a distinction should probably
be made between the above companies that relied mainly on external
liabilities for fund raising, i.e. borrowing and notes payable, and
companies that operated through savings deposits.

The funding structure of the Sumitomo zaibatsu during this
period is outlined in Figure 2.

TABLE 5   Summary of Financial Income and Expenditures of the Sumitomo Honsha Period.

(unit: ¥1000)

| | Business income and expenditures (*deficit) | Fund raising methods | | | | |
|---|---|---|---|---|---|---|
| | | Paid-up capital | Honsha | Loans Bank/ Trust Co. | Other | Bonds |
| 1937 | * 53,180 | 45,630 | 3,850 | 3,690 | | |
| 1938 | * 34,050 | 32,240 | *10,250 | 12,060 | | |
| 1939 | *100,070 | 57,100 | * 9,430 | 52,400 | | |
| 1940 | *150,230 | 55,000 | 19,460 | 31,910 | 13,860 | 30,000 |
| 1941 | *187,310 | 29,000 | 750 | 73,160 | 9,600 | 74,800 |
| 1942 | *301,400 | 71,500 | 500 | 127,950 | 22,450 | 79,000 |
| 1943 | *391,830 | 65,000 | 600 | 88,290 | 147,250 | 90,700 |
| Sub-total | *1,218,070 | 355,470 | 5,480 | 389,460 | 193,160 | 274,500 |
| Component ratio | (100) | (19.2) | (0.4) | (32.0) | (15.9) | (22.5) |

## 2.  The Sumitomo Honsha Period

The Sumitomo zaibatsu developed dramatically in this period due to the boom in military production. The scale of fund raising expanded accordingly, giving rise to changes in fund raising methods. A look at the years from 1937 to 1943 shows that 48% of total fund raising was done through borrowings. Bond issues also became more prevalent and accounted for 23%, whereas the use of capitalization increases and capital stock payments was limited to 29% (see Table 5). This meant that since expansions in equity could not meet the increasing demand for funds, reliance on external liabilities was unavoidable.

Let us look in closer detail at the fund raising methods during this period in the same manner as we examined those for the Sumitomo Goshigaisha period.

(a)   First, Table 5 shows capitalization increases and capital stock payments, according to Sumitomo data. The Sumitomo Honsha made payments of ¥59,890,000 to its subsidiaries over the years 1937–41. The Honsha only received ¥35,350,000 in dividends from subsidiaries during the same period. Therefore, the simple reinvestment of these dividends resulted in large deficits. There were larger

TABLE 6   Breakdown of Paid-up Capital of the Sumitomo Honsha Period.
(unit: ¥1000)

| | | Paid-up amounts | | | Honsha dividends | |
|---|---|---|---|---|---|---|
| | Total | Honsha | Main family and relatives | Affil-iates | Banks and other external sources | From affil-iates | From other |
| 1937 | 45,630 | 11,490 | 3,470 | (4,120) | 30,670 | 6,019 | 1,714 |
| 1938 | 32,240 | 9,460 | 4,160 | (4,760) | 18,620 | 5,421 | 2,416 |
| 1939 | 57,100 | 18,420 | 6,490 | (5,400) | 32,190 | 6,507 | 1,939 |
| 1940 | 55,000 | 13,480 | 5,770 | 12,440 | 23,310 | 8,260 | 1,853 |
| 1941 | 29,000 | 7,040 | 9,020 | 10,290 | 2,650 | 9,143 | 2,016 |
| Total | 218,970 | 59,890 | 28,910 | 22,730 | 107,440 | 35,350 | 9,938 |

deficits even when the dividends from sources other than affiliated firms were invested; and so the Honsha relied on borrowing. This was because the rapid expansion of subsidiaries far exceeded the paid-up capital capacity of the head office.

While it is not possible to single out Kichizaemon Sumitomo, the column "main family and relatives" in Table 6 probably consisted almost entirely of Kichizaemon. The total for a five-year period was ¥28,910,000 and the paid-up capital amount had grown so large as to be incomparable with that of the Goshigaisha period. The dividends received by Kichizaemon during the same period are calculated at ¥6,830,000, which amounted to only one-fourth of the paid-up capital figure. The dividends received from the Sumitomo Honsha were only ¥2,700,000 and the dividends from the developing subsidiaries were calculated at ¥4,130,000, and were increasing annually. It is not clear what Kichizaemon did about this gap between the amount received in dividends and the paid-up capital. Also, if all the income from dividends was channelled into paid-up capital, the question arises as to what the Sumitomo family depended on for income. This is also unclear at present.

The important point is that the main category of paid-up capital during this period shifted from the Sumitomo Honsha and Kichi-zaemon to the category "banks and other external sources." Included in this category are paid-up capital from affiliated financial institutions, in particular, Sumitomo Bank, and paid-up capital received from stockholders outside the zaibatsu. This category became the largest single source of paid-up capital. The mutual stock ownership among affiliated companies gradually increased, but never became a source of fund raising for the overall zaibatsu.

(b) Next, we will look at borrowings. The fund adjustment function of the Sumitomo Honsha declined and Sumitomo Bank and Sumitomo Trust Co. gradually increased their importance with the zaibatsu. The decisive factor in this was that funds from outside the zaibatsu were substantially introduced into the zaibatsu from 1940 on, due to external borrowings and bond issuings. Even though there were external borrowings, the borrowings were from special financial institutions like Industrial Bank of Japan, Yokohama Specie Bank, Industrial Bank of Manchuria, Wartime Credit Bank and special national policy companies like Nippon Gold Mining and Teikoku Fuel. It was not the case that funds were sought from city banks of other affiliations. In this way, even though funds had to be sought outside the zaibatsu, funds were introduced in a manner which did not influence the zaibatsu control structure.

During this period, the affiliated companies that depended on external sources for borrowings and on bonds were those related to military demand, such as Sumitomo Metal Industries, Sumitomo Electric Industries, Sumitomo Chemical Co., Shikoku Central Electric Power Co., Sumitomo Mining Co., Manchurian Sumitomo Metal Industries, Sumitomo Machinery Co. and Nippon Electric Co. On the other hand, there were also debt-free companies with no direct relationship to military demand, such as Sumitomo Warehouse Co. and Osaka North Harbour Co.

## IV. Characteristics of Zaibatsu Fund Raising

The fund raising in the Sumitomo zaibatsu has been described above. However, from the results obtained through the Sumitomo case, I would like to generalize about other zaibatsu like Mitsui and Mitsubishi to the extent possible.

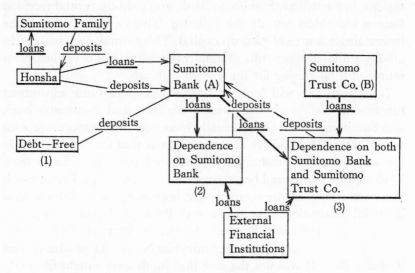

FIG. 3   The Funding Structure of the Sumitomo Period.
   (1)   Osaka North Harbour
         Sumitomo Warehouse
   (2)   Sumitomo Aluminium Reduction
         Sumitomo Electric Wire & Cable Works
         Sumitomo Metal Industries
         Manchurian Sumitomo Metal Industries
   (3)   Sumitomo Mining
         Sumitomo Chemical
         Shikoku Central Electric Power
         Nippon Electric

## 1. Fund Raising and Joint-Stock Companies within the Juris-diction of the Zaibatsu

The Sumitomo zaibatsu was late in reorganizing the Honsha into a company structure and in making the firms under its jurisdiction into joint-stock companies. Mitsui's four directly managed companies, Mitsui Bank, Mitsui Bussan Kaisha, Mitsui Warehouse Co. and Mitsui Mining Co., became joint-stock companies after 1910. Mitsubishi Shipbuilding & Engineering Co., Mitsubishi Iron Manufacturing Co., Mitsubishi Mining Co., Mitsubishi Trading Co., Mitsubishi Warehouse Co., Mitsubishi Bank and others became joint-stock companies one after another during the period between

1917 and 1920. The changeover to the joint-stock company structure in Sumitomo got fully underway in the 1920s, with the exception of Sumitomo Bank and Sumitomo Steel Works which were relatively early. While there is a slight discrepancy in the periods, there were points in common with respect to the conscious reorganization of the important firms into joint-stock companies, all within a concentrated period of time.

Looking at this changeover to the joint-stock structure of the firms under zaibatsu jurisdiction from the point of view of fund raising, all three zaibatsu had in common the elimination of what is inherently a function of the joint-stock company system, i.e. a concentration of public money. It was a general practice in Mitsui and Sumitomo for the zaibatsu head office and family actually to own all the stocks, and there seems to have been a similar phenomenon in Mitsubishi, too. As long as they persisted in this type of closed investment, the introduction of public money was impossible. However, as the zaibatsu of that time relied mainly on their own savings to develop business, the changeover to joint-stock company structure was not the result of financial necessity. As Professor Yasuoka pointed out, the joint-stock structure functions to "rationalize the holdings and management of the various enterprises" and to "organize a system that can expand to giant size."[4] Of course, the periods of incorporation and the reasons for using stocks are slightly different for each zaibatsu.

However, after the changeover to the joint-stock structure, as long as they maintained the system of closed investment, the expansion of enterprises under zaibatsu jurisdiction depended on capital stock payments from the Honsha or family, and took the form of expanding capitalization. Siphoning off profit was mainly done in the form of dividends, and was accumulated by the Honsha or the zaibatsu family and then reinvested in firms, as needed, in the form of capital stock payments. The matter of whether to handle capital accumulation at the enterprises under zaibatsu jurisdiction or to handle it on the family side was dependent upon the dividend rate. This can be called a mechanism wherein the zaibatsu expanded and reinvested within the limits of its own accumulations. It was a matter of course for the Honsha to control funds strictly to try to improve the effective use of the funds as a whole, since giving too much managerial freedom to the firms would destroy the fund raising mechanism for the zaibatsu as a whole. Of course, in the Sumitomo case, we can see this strictness, but would it not seem to also be the case with the fund raising regulations between the Honsha and the affiliates in the Mitsubishi case,[5] and then again the same with Mitsui?

## 2. The Fund Adjustment Function of the Head Office

Fund control is one aspect of the zaibatsu controlling structure. On a daily management basis, the effects of the fund adjustment function of the head office were directly apparent. The head office took precedence at Sumitomo in place of Sumitomo Bank and depended on the bank and other financial institutions within the zaibatsu for the excessive deficits that arose as a result of fund adjustments. Mitsubishi appears to have been somewhat similar, but the Mitsui case is not clear. It seems rather that the Mitsui Bank operated in the forefront and performed the adjustment function. The differences in the structure of each zaibatsu are reflected here also. Sumitomo carried many directly managed divisions over a long period, and the head office conducted the fund raising for them so that even after they became joint-stock companies, the former customs were probably maintained. It also depended on the speed of development in the enterprises under zaibatsu control and would seem to be connected to the fact that at Mitsui and at Mitsubishi, affiliated enterprises' jurisdiction expanded earlier and were separated from the control of the head office. It was also a problem of the control structure whether to centralize or decentralize authority. For the head company of a zaibatsu to handle fund adjustment, as in the manner of the Sumitomo Honsha, seems to have been a passing phase in the development process of the zaibatsu. This function gradually weakened and all enterprises were eventually converted into joint-stock companies.

There is also a problem in the relationship between the zaibatsu and the zaibatsu family when using the phrase "family business." At Sumitomo, when the Sumitomo Goshigaisha was established, there was a separation between the firms and the household, but it is not clear how much of the assets were designated for the household. Afterwards, the zaibatsu family received large amounts of dividends from the zaibatsu firms, as we have already seen. A part of this was reinvested in subsidiaries. However, Table 1 confirms the fact that the Honsha lent the Sumitomo family funds whenever needed and the family deposited funds with the Honsha in times of plenty. Here, too, it is noted that it was the Honsha, rather than Sumitomo Bank, that had direct access to the Sumitomo family. I would be interested to know how Mitsui and Mitsubishi handled this point.

## 3. The Position of the Bank in the Zaibatsu

It is commonly assumed that fund raising in zaibatsu is taken on singlehandedly by the zaibatsu bank (or, in a wider sense, the zaibatsu-affiliated financial institutions). However, as was seen in the case of the Sumitomo zaibatsu, fund raising in zaibatsu was basically provided by internal accumulations. The head office handled the adjustment function, and the bank was involved in the final arrangements. Therefore, as long as this structure existed, the zaibatsu bank was not the main actor but rather performed a supporting role unobtrusively in the background. It definitely did not handle fund raising singlehandedly. While a family business does not necessarily have a bank under its control, it is an interesting question as to whether or not a zaibatsu, which is one type of family business, has a bank. Those zaibatsu which have a bank are certainly of considerable interest with respect to their character and function.

The banks in Japan are different from the banks in England or Germany with respect to the above point. The opinion is well-known that states that Japanese banks have the character of a so-called "kikanginko" (organ bank) and that zaibatsu banks are not an exception to this.[6] However, Professor Kazuo Sugiyama asserts that expanding the idea of "kikanginko" to apply to zaibatsu banks "involves determining to what extent the bank is included in the zaibatsu organization and whether the decision making is controlled by the head office mechanism," and advocates an approach from the firm structure or management organization point of view.[7]

The decision making on fund raising in Sumitomo is done by the head office with its eye on the overall zaibatsu; Sumitomo Bank and the others abide by the Honsha's instructions. The positions of Sumitomo Bank and Sumitomo Trust Co. are shown in Figs. 2 and 3. Even if the zaibatsu bank is not providing many funds to the zaibatsu firms, it has the capability to act if necessary, by virtue of the fact that it is reflecting the demand for funds within the zaibatsu at that time, and it adheres to the control of the head office. That is precisely the reason that when demand for funds suddenly increased during the war, loans to zaibatsu firms increased dramatically. In this respect, the bank had the character of an "organ bank."

On the other hand, the bank set rules on loan limits, collateral, etc., with respect to the head office and the zaibatsu firms and made efforts to protect the soundness of the bank management. This was because the family was aware of criticism from society, thus they opened their stock to the public and probably did so with the approval of the top management in the zaibatsu. In this respect, the bank was different from the minor banks which became unsound and declined through their lack of any check on their operations due to their "kikanginko" character. Sumitomo Bank displays the "soundness" that is representative of Japanese banks. As long as this was the case, can it really be said that there was a check on the bank's behavior as an "organ bank?" Mitsui and Mitsubishi are thought to have operated similarly in this respect.

## NOTES

1. Shigeaki Yasuoka, "Nihon no Zaibatsu" ("Zaibatsu of Japan"), Vol. 3 of *Nihon Keieishi Kōza* (Lectures on the Business History of Japan), 1976, p. 14.

   "A zaibatsu contains a nucleus parent company (holding company) that is invested in by a family or kinship group and forms an enterprise group that has the firms it controls (subsidiaries) doing business in a wide variety of industries. The large scale subsidiaries have a monopolistic position in their respective industrial sectors."

2. The following are offered as reference bibliographies for fund raising in the Sumitomo zaibatsu.

   Shoichi Asajima, "1920 nen iko no Sumitomo zaibatsu ni kansuru ikkosatsu" ("An Observation of the Sumitomo Zaibatsu from 1920"),

*Senshu Keieigaku Ronshu* (Business Review of Senshu University) 24th ed., Mar. 1978.

Shoichi Asajima, "Senji taiseiki no Sumitomo zaibatsu" ("Sumitomo Zaibatsu of the Wartime System"), *Senshu Keieigaku Ronshu* (Business Review of Senshu University) 30th ed., Aug. 1980.

Shoichi Asajima, "Ryotaisenkan niokeru Sumitomo zaibatsu no shushi kōzo" ("The Structure of Income and Expenditure in the Sumitomo Zaibatsu during the Two World Wars"), *Shakaikagaku Nenpo* (The Annual Bulletin of Social Science), Senshu Daigaku Shakaikagaku Kenkyujo (The Institute for Social Sciences, Senshu University), 15th ed., 1981.

Shoichi Asajima, "Sumitomo zaibatsu niokeru shikinchotatsu no seikaku" ("The Character of Fund Raising in the Sumitomo Zaibatsu"), *Keieishigaku* (Business History Review), vol. 26, 2nd ed., July 1981.

3.  For detailed reference on the controlling function of the Sumitomo zaibatsu, see:

Shoichi Asajima, "Zaibatsu niokeru keieitosei no ikkosatsu" ("An Observation of Management Control in Zaibatsu"), *Senshu Keiei Kenkyu Nenpo* (The Annual Bulletin of the Senshu University), 6th ed., 1981.

4.  Shigeaki Yasuoka, "4. Zaibatsu no kyodaika" ("The Expansion of the Zaibatsu"), *Nihon Keieishi o Manabu 2* (Studying Japanese Business History 2), 1976, pp. 61–2.

5.  This problem has been made clear to the extent where the following is available.

Keizaikikakucho (Economic Planning Agency) ed., "Mitsubishi zaibatsu niokeru shikinchotatsu to shihai" ("Fund Raising and Control in the Mitsubishi Zaibatsu"), 1958.

6.  see Toshihiko Katoh, *Honpo ginko shiron* (Japanese Bank History), University of Tokyo Press, 1957.

7.  Kazuo Sugiyama, "Gomeigaisha Mitsui ginko no kikanginkoteki seikaku" ("The Organ Bank Character of Mitsui Bank Partnership"), *Gendai Kinyu* (Modern Financing), vol. 3 of Gendai Shihonshugi to Zaisei / Kinyu (Modern Capitalism and Financial Affairs / Financing), p. 254.

# COMMENTS

Yasuo Mishima
*Konan University*

Professor Asajima's paper explains various processes and types of fund raising by the Sumitomo zaibatsu, one of the largest zaibatsu in Japan. I shall try to explain the Mitsubishi zaibatsu, another major zaibatsu, then compare the two of them.

## I. The Mitsubishi Zaibatsu

### 1. 1893–1907
When the profits of the Mitsubishi Limited Partnership (M. L. P.), the holding company of the Mitsubishi zaibatsu, were limited, funds were raised mainly through borrowing from the Iwasaki family. When the profits increased, they were accumulated as an inner reserve fund (¥11,480,000 in this period). These profits were generated from the mining and colliery sections at first, and the shipbuilding and banking sections later.

### 2. 1908–1919
In this period, Mitsubishi set up its modern decentralized, product-defined division system. Fund raising depended mainly upon inner reservation of profits of the M. L. P. and each of the sections. In the first half of this period, the main stream of funds was: mining section —M. L. P.—mining, colliery, marketing sections. And, in the later half of this period (World War I): shipbuilding, colliery sections—M. L. P.—iron-manufacturing, shipbuilding sections, plus borrowing from the banking section. As dependence upon the banking section increased, borrowing and notes payable increased.

From 1917 to 1921, each division of the M. L. P. changed its form to an independent corporation.

## 3.  1920–1931

The long depression influenced the Mitsubishi zaibatsu strongly in this period. The paid-up capital of M. L. P. increased from ¥30 million to ¥120 million, but the resources were funds of the Iwasaki family and inner reserve funds of the M. L. P. Because of the depression, most of the affiliated companies were unable to score any profits, with the exception of the Banking, Shipbuilding and Mining companies, so dividends were vary few. New profits came mainly from the premiums of public stock offerings of the Mitsubishi Banking Co. The amount of security holdings of M. L. P. did not change in this period, but capital amounts of all the affiliated companies increased from ¥156 million in 1921 to ¥235 million in 1931. As a result of the public stock offerings of the affiliated companies, the controlling power of M. L. P. decreased. Its rate of stock holding decreased from 85.5% in 1921 to 69.0% in 1928. That is, the practice of fund centering in M. L. P. and of concentrating investment in special divisions decreased. The affiliated companies with much interest (Banking, Mining and Shipbuilding) could enlarge their business by using their inner reserve funds.

## 4.  1932–1945

The resources of fund raising to increase military production in this period were many-fold:

1)  acquiring of premiums by public stock offerings

2)  borrowing from the Mitsubishi Bank and the Mitsubishi Trust Company

3)  issuing of bonds by Mitsubishi-sha (Mitsubishi Limited Partnership changed its name to Mitsubishi-sha Corporation in 1937) and many of the affiliated companies

4)  increasing dividends of the affiliated companies. Mitsubishi-sha received ¥24 million in 1940 and ¥41 million in 1945 as dividends from Banking, Mining, Heavy Industry, Electric Appliances, and the Trading Co. which were recording high profits. The total amount of all profits registered by the affiliated companies was ¥24 million in 1932, ¥100 million in 1940, and ¥231 million in 1944.

## II.  Comparing Mitsubishi with Sumitomo

(A)   President Koyata Iwasaki of M. L. P., who was a son from
a branch house of the Iwasaki family, invested only 17–25% of the
capital of M. L. P. He did not wish to own the Mitsubishi group
under closed investment. When the decentralized, product-defined
divisions of M. L. P. changed to corporations, Mr. Koyata thought
it good to gather public funds. Stock in the Mining Co. was the first
to be offered to the public in 1920. Therefore, it appears that Mitsubishi was more eager to gather public funds from the beginning
than Sumitomo.

(B)   After 1920 the rate of capital accumulation in the affiliated
companies increased at Mitsubishi. It seems to me that the controlling power of M. L. P. was smaller than Sumitomo Honsha. Of
course, "the treaty between M. L. P. and the affiliated companies
for fund raising" established very strict relations between the affiliated companies and M. L. P. in 1918. But, this was revised in 1929,
and the controlling power of M. L. P. for fund raising of the affiliated
companies was weakened. The reasons for this were:

(1)   imbalance of development and differences in profits of the
affiliated companies;

(2)   by public stock offering, and importation of foreign capital
for the affiliated companies, the controlling power of M. L. P. decreased for fund raising of each of the affiliated companies. It is
definite that the decentralization of the division system of the
M. L. P. before 1917 had a strong effect.

After 1895, the item "Iwasaki Family Account" was important in
the M. L. P.'s balance sheet. The dividends which the Iwasaki family
received from M. L. P. were redeposited in M. L. P. and reinvested
in the Mining and Shipbuilding sections. But the "Iwasaki Family
Account" disappeared after 1918.

In the Mitsubishi zaibatsu, like Sumitomo, it was the M. L. P.
rather than the Bank that had direct access to the Iwasaki family.

(C)   Regarding the characteristics of the zaibatsu bank, I think
the Mitsubishi Bank was very similar to the Sumitomo Bank, as
Professor Asajima has pointed out.

# The Relationship between Zaibatsu and Family Structure: The Korean Case

Tamio Hattori
*Institute of Developing Economies*

## Introduction

Recently, the remarkable development of the Korean economy is regarded as a model of LDC economic development. Many economists and politicians have been amazed at the wonderful progress the Korean economy has made in the last two decades. In these twenty years, the Korean per capita GNP has grown from less than US $100 to over US $1,500, and exports have increased from US $40 million to US $15 billion.

The existence of zaibatsu, or chaebol, is one of the important reasons why the Korean economy has developed with such rapid speed. In the same 20-year period, growth for the five biggest zaibatsu was 30.1% annually. Furthermore, the growth rate for the ten largest was 28.0% as against 9.9% for the national average.[1] The zaibatsu have played the important role of locomotive in Korean's economic growth.

Before analyzing the characteristics of Korean zaibatsu, it is necessary to know the status of the Korean economy.

After the end of colonial rule by Japan, Korea started economic development on its own supported by American aid. But the Korean War erupted in 1950 and the entire Korean industrial setting was almost destroyed. In 1953, when the war ended, the Korean government decided on an import-substitution economic development policy. Many zaibatsu, for instance *Sumsung*, *Hyundai* and *Lucky*, started developing at that time. In 1960, student power ousted president Lee Sung-man from public office, and the following year

*121*

the Militalist Revolution took place. The new militarist government opted for an export-oriented economic growth policy; they also prepared a five-year economic plan, which was initiated in 1962. As a result of this five-year plan, Korean economic growth began to accelerate from the early 70's, coinciding with the accelerated economic growth experienced by the zaibatsu.

From the 1960's to the 70's, the Korean industrial structure, following the government's five-year plan, changed drastically. In line with that drastic change, the order of major zaibatsu have fluctuated depending on which company was the main industry of that zaibatsu. In the mid 50's, following the social disorder of the Korean War (1950–53), the basic industries in Korea shifted from cotton spinning, electric machinery, electronics and construction to chemical and heavy machine industries. Almost all private companies have tried to advance into new industrial fields under the government's active support.

Under such government leadership, private companies were encouraged toward multiple operation. A private company which failed to develop in multiple fields was destined to retain a relatively low status and was even risking bankruptcy.

For instance, the S zaibatsu, which has maintained the top spot among the zaibatsu, is made up of many kinds of companies: general trading, sugar manufacturing, cotton spinning, synthetic fibers, paper manufacturing, general construction, electric machinery and electronics, precision machinery, petrochemicals, heavy industry, insurance, newspapers, hotels and department stores. And, by knowing the date of establishment, we can easily see that the S zaibatsu has developed in accordance with the government's industrial policy. Regarding scale, there is no other case such as S zaibatsu, but others have also achieved a similar kind of broad, multiple development.

Now, let us decide on a working definition of zaibatsu. It is generally held that the term zaibatsu is defined differently by each researcher, but when comparing the many definitions, there are roughly two required conditions that emerge. One condition is "under closed control by a family or kinship group" and the other is "involved in multiple development."

TABLE 1.

| Nos. of "zaibatsu" | 5 | Average | 10 | Average | 20 | Average | 46 | Average % |
|---|---|---|---|---|---|---|---|---|
| Industries: | | | | | | | | |
| Agriculture, forestry and fishing | 0.05% | 0.01% | 0.05% | —% | 0.08% | 0.003% | 0.08% | —% |
| Mining | 4.56 | 0.92 | 4.56 | | 5.54 | 0.01 | 5.54 | |
| Manufacturing | 18.39 | 3.68 | 23.42 | 1.01 | 33.24 | 0.98 | 42.98 | 0.37 |
| Construction | 15.51 | 3.10 | 29.35 | 2.77 | 31.73 | 0.24 | 37.01 | 0.20 |
| Electricity, water service | 0.64 | 0.13 | 0.64 | | 0.64 | | 0.64 | |
| Transportation, communication | 12.57 | 2.51 | 15.75 | 0.64 | 17.39 | 0.16 | 17.92 | 0.02 |
| Wholesale, retail | 2.22 | 0.44 | 2.37 | 0.03 | 4.29 | 0.19 | 4.63 | 0.01 |
| Finance, insurance | 22.96 | 4.59 | 24.30 | 0.27 | 26.87 | 0.26 | 32.17 | 0.20 |
| Others | 2.06 | 0.41 | 2.29 | 0.05 | 2.76 | 0.05 | 2.87 | |

Source: Sagong, Il "Economic Growth and Chaebol", *Chuson*, Sep., 1980 [in Korean].

With respect to multiple development, as mentioned above, the Korean Chaebol also can be called a "zaibatsu." But it is very difficult to recognize whether major affiliated enterprises have a monopolistic or oligopolistic share in their field or not, because of insufficient research into materials.

The second aspect is "closed control by a family or kinship group." The former condition applies to Korean zaibatsu but the latter is a problem, because the structure of the Korean family and kinship system is different from the Japanese structure. One of the biggest differences is the inheritance system. Division of succession is common in Korean society. In this sense, there is no traditional concept of "Kasan," or family property, in Korea.[2]

The first objective of this paper is to analyze the relation between the formation of Korean zaibatsu and the traditional structure of the Korean family. The second is to analyze how the zaibatsu prevented any division in scale, despite the existence of traditional custom law.

I wish to advance an hypothesis concerning the relationship between the formation and maintenance of the zaibatsu and the family or kinship structure in Korea.

## I. The Zaibatsu in the Korean Economy

Before analyzing the characteristics of the Korean zaibatsu, it is necessary to know what status or role the zaibatsu have in the Korean economy.

First of all, let us try to understand the role of zaibatsu in the Korean industrial field by examining published data (Table 1). According to Table 1, zaibatsu have a large share in the manufacturing, construction and finance and insurance fields. Particularly, in manufacturing, the 46 zaibatsu have 42.98% of the total. But the difference between the five largest zaibatsu and the big ten zaibatsu is very clear, because the former have a 3.68% average share of manufacturing industries, and the latter have only a 1.01% average. This is similar to that for the top twenty zaibatsu (0.98%). In construction, the total share of the 46 zaibatsu is 37.01%, the average share of the five largest is 3.10% while the big ten's is 2.77%.

TABLE 2.

| Scale | No. of companies | | Ratio $\left(\dfrac{A}{B}\right)$ |
|---|---|---|---|
| | Total (A) | Zaibatsu-affiliated (B) | |
| Small (less than 2 billion won) | 89 | 17 | 19.1% |
| Medium (2 billion to 5 billion won) | 116 | 64 | 55.2 |
| Large (more than 5 billion won) | 92 | 62 | 67.4 |
| Total | 297 | 143 | 48.1 |

Source: "The Report on Listed Companies" 1981 Autumn [in Korean].

TABLE 3.

| Scale | Ratio of stockholders* | | | | | | |
|---|---|---|---|---|---|---|---|
| | F | A | I | C | B | S | O |
| Small | 58.0% | 10.9% | 11.3% | 5.5% | 4.6% | 5.9% | 3.8% |
| Medium | 48.8 | 19.8 | 12.5 | 5.9 | 2.6 | 6.3 | 4.0 |
| Large | 37.8 | 32.3 | 4.3 | 7.5 | 4.3 | 5.1 | 8.7 |

Source:  Same as Table 2.
* F: Family, A: Affiliated Company, I: Individual, C: Company, B: Bank, S: Securities Company, O: Others.

In the construction field, the difference between the big ten and the top twenty is large. The finance and insurance field shows that the five largest zaibatsu have a huge share—4.59% average—and the others have only from 0.20–0.27%.

From the above analysis, we can divide the zaibatsu by scale and classify affiliated companies into 3 kinds. Large-scale zaibatsu are composed of large-scale and diverse affiliated companies, with manufacturing, construction and finance & insurance as the central figures. Middle-scale zaibatsu are organized similarly to the large scale zaibatsu. Thus, middle-scale zaibatsu are clearly marked off from small-scale zaibatsu, which however are still larger in size and range than small family businesses.

Next, it is very important to know the pattern of stockholding. In Korea, the number of listed companies is 297, excluding finance

& insurance and other services (as of the end of June 1981). Among
the 297, 143 companies (48.1%) are zaibatsu-affiliated companies.
Table 2 shows the scale of listed companies. In the case of small
companies, only 19.1% (17 among 89) are zaibatsu affiliated companies, but in contrast to this, 67.4% of the large-scale companies
are zaibatsu-affiliated companies.[3]

Next, let's try to check the characteristics of the principal stockholders. Table 3 shows the composition of the first, second and
third principal stockholders. According to the scale of company
growth, the ratio of a family's or individual's stockholdings decreases
and, conversely, the ratio of affiliated companies and foundations
increases. In the case of "more than 5 billion" shares, the highest
ratio (37.8%) is also family, but affiliated companies and foundations have an almost equal ratio to the controlling family (32.3%).
The ratio of a family's stockholdings is in inverse proportion to the
scale of the company (37.8%, 48.8%, 58.0%).

## II. The Characteristics of Stockholding

From the preceding analysis, it is easy to see that the zaibatsu
have a huge influence in the Korean economy and take on a strong
familistic coloration.

In this section, I wish to analyze the pattern of stockholding in
the zaibatsu. First, it is necessary to explain two points. One concerns research material. In Korea, the financial statements of listed
companies are not publicly available and for this reason I used
listed stock reports (*Sanjang-Jusig*), such as Quarterly Reports
on Listed Companies (*Kaisha Shiki Ho*). The second point concerns
the number of listed companies. Zaibatsu-affiliated companies are
partially listed; on average 1/5 to 1/2 of all companies are listed.
Because of these reasons, an analysis of zaibatsu through stockholding
has its limits, but to get an idea the changing pattern of stockholding,
we can approach the available facts.

First, there are three kinds of patterns in Korean zaibatsu's
stockholding.[4]

A.   Pattern I  :   Monopolized by a proprietor (or family)

B.   Pattern II  :   Controlled by a stockholding company

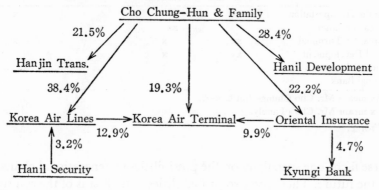

Fig. 1.

C. Pattern III: Reciprocal stockholding by an affiliated company

The classifications above are relative concepts, not absolute. Most cases of stockholding are based on zaibatsu family consequently.

Let us try to explain these stockholding patterns in detail.

*A. Pattern I: Monopolized by a Proprietor*

The main characteristic of this pattern is the fact that the proprietor and/or his family have huge shares of stock directly in their name. Almost all the small zaibatsu adhere to this pattern. In this paper, I will take up *Hanjin* as a model of pattern I.

Figure 1 shows the stockholding structure in *Hanjin* zaibatsu as of March 1981. Although *Hanjin* has at least 14 affiliated companies, only six are listed. According to Fig. 1, Mr. Cho, the owner of this zaibatsu, directly owns a large share of stock, with the exception of the Kyungi Bank; Oriental Insurance holds the stock. This basic stockholding structure in *Hanjin* has not changed since 1976. In the case of Oriental Insurance, the top stockholder is, of course, Mr. Cho (15.4%), and the second largest stockholders are his four sons (1.7% each). The first son has an advantage as the second largest stockholder of Hanjin Transportation (4.3%). Looking at

|  | Chairman | President | Executive Dr. | Director |
|---|---|---|---|---|
| Hanjin Transportation | xx |  |  | x |
| Korea Air Lines |  | xx | x |  |
| Korea Air Turminal | xx | x |  | x |
| Hanil Development | xx | x |  |  |
| Oriental Insurance |  |  |  | xx, x |
| Kyungi Bank |  |  |  |  |

xx means Mr. Cho Chung-Hun himself.
x means Mr. Cho's Family.

Fig. 2.

these facts, one speculates on the possibilities of generational changes in the future. There are two probabilities—the first is of the son succeeding to his father's status, and the other is a division of the zaibatsu. These two are equal possibilities, because in Korean society, there are equally strong principles about a son's succession to his father's status and the succession of property. I will discuss this problem in the next section.

From the aspect of management, Mr. Cho has the status of Chairman, President or Executive Director in five out of the six listed affiliated companies. Moreover, his brothers and sons all have status as Vice-Chairmen, Presidents and Executive Directors in the same five companies (Fig. 2). In this case, *Hanjin* zaibatsu is completely controlled through stockholding and management by Mr. Cho and his family.

### B.   Pattern II: Controlled by a Stockholding Company

The characteristic of Pattern II is the fact that there is a stockholding company serving as the headquarters of a zaibatsu, and the proprietor has stock mainly in that stockholding company. Generally in Korea, stockholding companies are not engage purely in stockholding but also carry on their own business as well. A typical example of Pattern II is the *Dae Woo* zaibatsu. *Dae Woo* is a very young company which was founded only 15 years ago. This case is a special and more indirect example of Pattern II because Mr. Kim Woo-Jung, the founder of this zaibatsu, established a Foundation and he donated all of his stock to it. Now, he retains the status of Chairman of the Board of Directors.

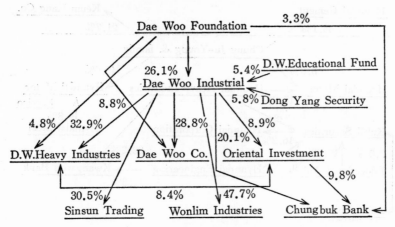

FIG. 3.

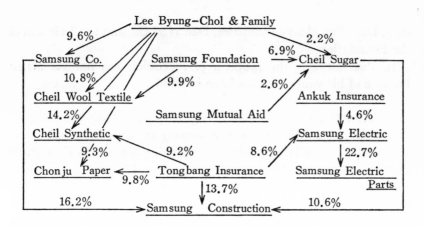

FIG. 4.

The structure of *Dae Woo* is illustrated in Fig. 3. Dae Woo Industrial is the biggest stockholder in five out of the seven listed affiliated companies. Dae Woo Foundation has a 26.1% share of Dae Woo Industrial.

From the aspect of management, Mr. Kim and his elder brother participate in their business only. In the management of affiliated companies, Mr. Kim has status as a top manager of Dae Woo Indus-

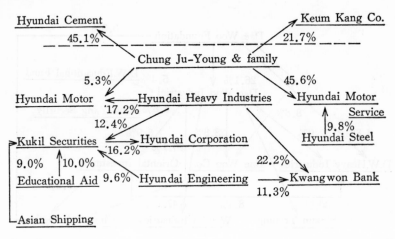

Fig. 5.

trial, Dae Woo Heavy Industries, Dae Woo Co. and as Chairman of the Foundation.

In this instance, the problem of succession has not yet arisen because of his youth (he was born in 1936).

### C.  Pattern III: Reciprocal Stockholding by Affiliated Companies

It would be suitable to use the *Samsung* zaibatsu as a typical example of Pattern III. But, before analyzing *Samsung* in detail, it is necessary to explain the meaning of "reciprocal." In recent Japanese big business groups (for example Mitsubishi), a perfect "reciprocal" relationship is seen in stockholding. These "reciprocal" relationships make a kind of closed circle. On the contrary, in Korea, stockholding is consequently controlled by the zaibatsu family. Because of this fact, the meaning of "reciprocal" is limited.

Figure 4 shows the structure of stockholding of *Samsung*. According to Fig. 4, Mr. Lee and his family have a relatively small share of stock (by Korean standards). The Foundation and Mutual Aid's holdings make up for the family's small holdings. Tongbang Insurance has a semi-central role in stockholding, but because it is unlisted, it is impossible to know the structure of that company.

Although the size of the Foundation's and Mutual Aid's stockholdings has decreased recently, their role in stockholding has been very

important. In my analysis, this fact is related to the succession of
the Chairmanship from Mr. Lee Byong-Chol to his third son,
Gon-Hi. In the following section, I will discuss this matter more
thoroughly.

Looking at management, Mr. Lee has the status of Chairman of
Samsung and Cheil Wool Textile. His son is Vice-Chairman of these
same companies, as well as of Samsung Electronics and Samsung
Construction, and Director of Chonju Paper and Cheil Sugar.

As pointed out above, it is suitable to classify Korean zaibatsu's
stockholding in 3 patterns. According to the size of the zaibatsu,
Pattern III is generally larger than Pattern I or II. But it is difficult
to conclude that with growth, the pattern of a zaibatsu changes from
I to II, or II to III. It is likely that a zaibatsu will be divided by the
sons in line with their age.

From this point of view, the example of the *Hyundai* zaibatsu is
very interesting. The structure of stockholding is shown in Fig. 5.
In this case, Hyundai Heavy Industries has a very important role,
but it is not listed. It is my guess that Mr. Chung and his family have
a large share in this company. A characteristic in this case is that the
structure of stockholding is a mixture of Pattern I and III. Above
the broken line in Fig. 5, the structure resembles a Pattern I zaibatsu, and below (except for the Motor Service) a Pattern III
zaibatsu is reflected. With regard to Hyundai Cement, the figure
shows that Mr. Chung and family possess some stock, but in actuality, one of Mr. Chung's brothers, Sun-Young, holds all of the
family's stock and also holds the status of President of that company.
Another of Mr. Chung's brothers, Sang-Young, has 21.7% of the
stock in Keum Kang Co., and he is the acting President. If, in the
future, the *Hyundai* separates these two companies, this zaibatsu
will change to a purely Pattern III zaibatsu.

The problem is the unmanageable relationship between uncle
and nephew in the traditional Korean family structure. In the
following section, we shall discuss the relationship of family structure and the formation of a zaibatsu.

## III.  Korean Family Structure and Zaibatsu

Up to this point, I have at times referred to the structure of the

Korean family, which has a strong effect on the structure of the
Korean zaibatsu. It would be wise here to name certain characteristics of the Korean family structure. For easier understanding, I
will compare it with the Japanese family.

First, it will be stressed that the Korean family is purely patrilineal.
Although the Japanese family is usually termed patrilineal, there is
sometimes a factor of bilaterality mixed into its structure. The use
of "pure" in this context means a true blood relation. A person who
does not have an actual blood relationship cannot be considered
a true member of the family. Under this condition, a successor must
be an actual blood relation to the father. This strict principle leads
us to at least two points below.

One is the regulation of an adopted son. An adopted son must be
a blood relative of the adoptive father. In addition to that, an
adopted son is required to *not* disturb the order of age in the offspring
of the father and to be of the proper generation. Under these
strict rules, almost all adopted sons are the sons of an adoptive
father's brother. In contrast to this Korean family structure, Japanese adopted sons are not always required to have a biological blood
tie. As a consequence of this rule, a person who marries into the
family of his bride is not unusual in Japan, especially in a merchant
family. Even in cases where there is a living son, under certain circumstances an adopted son is taken by a Japanese family as heir.
From this point of view, a Japanese family or "ie" is not exclusively
made up of a biological family, but can also be a sort of social institution. The meaning of this "institution" is that the role of family
members are divided into head of the family, wife of the head,
successor of head and so on, and these roles of family members are
changeable irrespective of blood relation.[5] I believe this aspect of the
Japanese family is a unique and basic characteristic of Japanese
familism.

The second point in regard to the Korean "pure" patrilineality
is the system of succession. In Japan, a monopolized succession by
one person, usually the first son, was normal before World War II.
According this rule, "Kasan," or the property of the family, was
maintained. Property which was given to other sons was donated
property, not divided property, conceptually. On the contrary, to

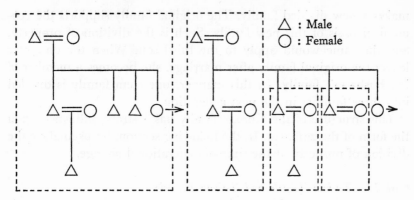

Fig. 6.

Table 4.

| Family structure | | 76 | 77 | 78 | 79 | 80 | 81.6 |
|---|---|---|---|---|---|---|---|
| Sol Wong-Sik | Textile | 38.2% | 38.2% | 33.5% | 32.3% | 32.3% | 32.3% |
| Wong-Chol | | | | | | | |
| Wong-Ryang | Electric | 13.1 | 13.1 | 12.8 | 12.1 | 11.7 | 11.7 |
| | Sugar | 13.0 | 13.0 | 12.6 | 12.1 | 11.8 | 11.8 |
| | Construction | | | 22.5 | 13.4 | 13.4 | ? |
| Wong-Pong | Construction | | | 7.1 | 4.2 | 4.2 | ? |
| | Sugar | | | | 5.3 | 5.3 | 5.1 |
| | Electric | | | | | | 1.0 |

Data: "Sang-jang Ju-sik," each year.

divide property among sons is the general rule in Korean society, because all sons are also blood relatives of the father, not only the first son. In Korea, all sons, except the successor of the father, always make a "Bunka," or a new divided family, and this economical base comes from "ponka," or the original family. It is not a donation, it is conceptually divided property. Under these conditions, the property of a family is not maintained. The property of a family is divided among the sons of the following generation.[6]

Figure 6 shows a model division of a Korean family by generation. The original family, occupying the big square on the left, has father, mother, three sons, one daughter, wife of the eldest son and grandson. When the second son marries, he leaves the original family and makes a new divided family. The original family supports the economical basis of this new family. Such is the division of property, and the same would apply to the third son. When the daughter leaves the original family after marriage, she becomes a member of her husband's family. In this manner, one stem family is divided into three families in the next generation.

This structure of the Korean family has a strong influence upon the form of the zaibatsu. In the following section, let us analyze the division of property at the time of generational change.

*Case 1: Taihan Textile and Taihan Electric*

Taihan Textile and Taihan Electric Wire were formally one zaibatsu founded by Mr. Sol Ke-Dong, father of Wong-Sik and Wong-Ryang. Before the death of Mr. Sol, *Taihan* zaibatsu was divided in two. The Taihan Textile zaibatsu was organized with the first son, Wong-Sik, as owner; the other, Taihan Electric Wire, was formed with the third son, Wong-Ryang, as owner. The fourth son, Wong-Pong, assisted his next eldest brother. As Table 4 shows, there is no relation between Textile and Electric, either in stockholding or management.

A case such as *Taihan* is not rare in Korea. The owners of *Kukjae* and *Chinyang* (companies who were formally one zaibatsu) are brothers. In the case of *Taewha* zaibatsu and *Taedong* zaibatsu, *Samsung* zaibatsu and *Hyosung* zaibatsu are not problems of family ties, but these cases show that non-family partner relationships are separated at the time of a family succession. A non-family partner relationship cannot be maintained after the death of the family head.

*Case 2: Kumho*

This zaibatsu was founded by Mr. Park In-Chon and his younger brother Tong-Bok, who assisted in the business. Figures 7–1 and 7–2 show the structure of stockholding in *Kumho*, dated December 1979, and June 1981. During that year and a half period, the stockholding structure changed rapidly.

Figure 7–1 shows that *Kumho* fell into the Pattern II type. At that time, *Kumho* had Kumho Co. as central, and Kwangju Highway

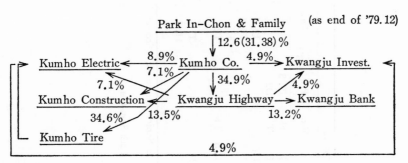

Fɪɢ. 7-1.

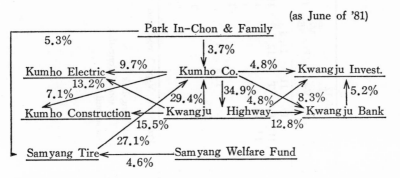

Fɪɢ. 7-2.

Lines as sub-central. But one and a half years later the pattern changed from II to III. The main differences between Figs 7-1 and 7-2 are, (1) a drastic decrease in the family's stockholdings, and (2) a deepening of the "reciprocal" relationship among affiliated companies.

But a more important thing to note is that during the time gap between Fig. 7-1 (Dec. 1979) and Fig. 7-2 (June 1981), Kumho Tire was separated from *Kumho*. At that time, the stock of Kumho Tire was held by Tong-Bok and his sons except for Mr. Park Sam-Gu, the son of In-Chon's elder brother. It is impossible to know precisely why Mr. Park Sam-Gu joined with his uncle. According to theory, the main part of the zaibatsu should be taken over by the

| | '78.12 | | | | | '80.12 | | | | | '81.12 | | | | |
|---|---|---|---|---|---|---|---|---|---|---|---|---|---|---|---|
| | Ch | V-c | Pre | V-p SED | Dr. | Ch | V-c | Pre | V-p SED | Dr. | Ch | V-c | Pre | V-c SED | Dr. |
| Kumho Co. | I | T | I1, 2 | T1, I3 | S | I | I1 | I2, 3 | | I1, 2 | I | I1 | I2, 3 | | I2, 3 |
| Kwangju Highway | I | T | I2 | | S, I1 | I | T | I2 | | I1, 2 | I | T | D2 | | I1, 2 |
| Construction | I1 | | | | S, T1 | I1 | | | | I1, 2 | I1 | | | | 3 |
| Electric | | | | | I1, S / T1 | | | | | T | | | | | |
| Tire | I | T | S | | I1, 2 / T2 | | T, S | T1 | | T, S | T, S | T1 | | | T2 |
| Kwangju Invest. | I | | | | T, I1 | I | | | T, I1 | I1, 2 | I | | | T | I1, 2 |
| Kwangju Bank | | | | | | | | | | | | | | | |

Note:  Ch: Chairman, V-c: Vice-Chairman, Pre: President, V-p: Vice-President, SED: Senior Executive Director, Dr.: Director.

I:  Park In-Chon              T:  Park Tong-Bok              S:  Park Sam-Gu
I1: The first son of In-Chon   T1: The first son of Tong-Bok
I2: The second                 T2: The second
I3: The third

Fig. 8.

sons of Mr. Park In-chon, the founder, in line with the principle of the Korean family system. The *Meil Kyeong-jae Sinmun*, the Daily Economic News, reported that Mr. Park In-Chon and his son hold only the stock of *Kumho*, while Mr. Park Tong-Bok and his family hold the stock of Tire only.

From the aspect of management, *Kumho* and Tire were not completely separated. For instance, Tire's management class was monopolized by the Tong-Bok family and Sam-Gu. But Tong-Bok and Sam-Gu also participated in Highway, Electric and Investment. Comparing this participation with that in December 1978, the differences are very clear. Figure 8 shows the participation of the two families and Sam-Gu.

Despite of this initial separation of *Kumho* and Tire, the two were reunified in 1981. By reorganizing in this way, *Kumho* has changed its pattern from type II to type III.

A separation similar to *Kumho*'s occurred in *Hyundai* as well. Mr. Chung Ju-Young's younger brother, In-Young went independent, but shortly after opted for reunification. In these instances, we can see that the credibility of a company is supported by the fact it is an affiliated company of a zaibatsu.

Thus, maintaining zaibatsu scale is a major issue in retaining leading status.

Regarding the traditional Korean family structure, zaibatsu are also divided among sons. Contrary to this tendency, there is another mechanism existing to prevent the dividing or reorganizing of a zaibatsu. In the following section I will analyze cases in which zaibatsu have tried to maintain their unity. These are the *Samsung* and *Doosan* zaibatsu.

*Case 3:  Samsung*

Mr. Lee Byung-Chol, the founder of *Samsung*, has three sons. According to the principle of succession for Korean families the first son must succeed his father's status. Unfortunately, the eldest is an invalid, and therefore Mr. Lee chose Gon-Hi, his third son, as successor. Mr. Lee announced that Gon-Hi would become successor in 1977. Because the structure of stockholding in *Samsung* has already been analyzed in Fig. 4, let us try here to analyze the change to come in the stockholding of the family and the Foundation.

TABLE 5.

| | | 1976 | 1977 | 1978 | 1979 | 1980 | 1981 |
|---|---|---|---|---|---|---|---|
| | | (%) | (%) | (%) | (%) | (%) | (%) |
| Lee Byung-Chol | Samsung Co. | 10.7 | 10.7 | 6.8 | 3.4 | ? | 3.4 |
| | Wool Textile | 8.9 | 8.8 | 8.1 | ? | 2.9 | 2.9 |
| | Synthetic | | | 10.4 | ? | 8.1 | ? |
| | Papers | 9.3 | 9.0 | 9.3 | 9.3 | 9.3 | 9.3 |
| U-Hi | | | | | | | |
| Chang-Hi | Synthetic | | | | | | 14.2 |
| Gon-Hi | Samsung Co. | | | 6.3 | 6.0 | 6.0 | 6.2 |
| | Wool Textile | | 5.7 | 5.4 | 5.4 | 7.6 | 7.9 |
| | Synthetic | | | | 5.4 | | |
| | Electronics | | | | | | 2.2 |
| Myung-Hi | Sugar | 3.0 | ? | 2.9 | 2.9 | 2.8 | ? |
| | Electronics | | | | | 1.8 | |
| Sun-Hi | Sugar | 2.4 | ? | 2.3 | ? | ? | 2.2 |
| In-Hi | | | | | | | |
| Foundation | Samsung Co. | 4.6 | 4.6 | 2.3 | ? | ? | ? |
| | Wool Textile | 21.9 | 21.9 | 14.2 | 14.2 | 9.3 | 9.9 |
| | Sugar | 29.1 | 15.5 | 9.0 | 9.6 | 6.9 | 6.9 |
| | Electronic Devices | | | | 16.9 | ? | ? |
| Mutual Aid | Samsung Co. | 4.9 | 4.9 | ? | ? | ? | ? |
| | Wool Textile | 5.1 | 5.1 | ? | ? | ? | ? |
| | Sugar | 11.1 | 7.9 | 4.8 | 3.6 | 2.6 | 2.6 |

Source:   "Sang-jang Ju-sik," each year.

Table 5 shows the changes that took place in the stockholdings of Mr. Lee's family and Foundation. It indicates some interesting points. One is that the first and second sons did not hold any stock, except for Chang-Hi's considerable share in Synthetic, in 1981. The second point is that the father's share of stock was transferred to the third son from 1978, just after the announcement of succession was made. In June 1981, Gon-Hi had a prominent stockholding position. An exception is the second son's stockholding in 1981. The third point regards the roles of the Foundation and Mutual Aid. Before the announcement of an intended successor, these two institutions held huge shares of stock. The shares of these organizations decreased with the beginning of devolution from father to Gon-Hi.

From these facts, it is possible to formulate the explanation that

TABLE 6.

|  |  | 1976 | 1977 | 1978 | 1979 | 1980 | 1981 |
|---|---|---|---|---|---|---|---|
| Park Yong-Gon | Beer | 13.4% | 13.2% | 13.1% | 12.7% | 10.1% | 9.8% |
|  | Food | 10.1 | 10.1 | 8.9 | 8.9 | 8.7 | 8.7 |
|  | Construction | 11.2 | ? | 8.5 | 8.1 | 6.1 | 5.7 |
| Yong-Oh | Food | 6.7 | 6.7 | 6.7 | ? | 5.8 | 5.8 |
|  | Construction | 5.0 | ? | 4.2 | 4.1 | 4.0 | 3.8 |
| Yong-Sung | Beer | 6.7 | 6.6 | 6.4 | 6.5 | 5.6 | 5.7 |
|  | Food | ? | 6.7 | 6.6 | 6.9 | 5.9 | 5.9 |
|  | Construction | 5.0 | 5.0 | 4.2 | 4.1 | 4.0 | 3.8 |
| Yong-Hyun | Beer | 6.7 | 6.6 | 6.4 | 6.5 | 5.9 | 5.7 |
|  | Food | 6.8 | 6.8 | 6.8 | ? | 5.8 | 5.8 |
|  | Construction | 5.0 | ? | ? | ? | ? | 3.8 |

Mr. Lee Byung-Chol was intent upon *not* dividing his zaibatsu. To realize his intention, he tried to choose one of his sons as successor to his position. But under the atmosphere of Korean familism, deciding upon only one of several sons as successor causes social friction. To minimize the friction, the two institutions, not Mr. Lee's family, held a huge share of stock and played the symbolic role of a united *Samsung*. After choosing the successor to *Sam-sung*, the two institutions' main function decreased. In line with this, their stockholdings were also decreased. It is impossible to say for certain, but I would guess that Mr. Lee's educational background influenced his decision he had been educated in Japan before World War II.

*Case 4: Doosan*

*Doosan* is another case in which the avoidance of a division of a zaibatsu was attempted. *Doosan* is not a big zaibatsu; its ranking is about 15th on the national scale. But this zaibatsu's history is longer than any of the others', dating from the end of the nineteenth century. The present owner of *Doosan*, Mr. Park Yong-Gon, is the grandson of the founder. The eldest son of the founder reorganized the Oriental Beer Company, which is the mother company of this zaibatsu.

Table 6 shows the stockholding structure in this family. It indicates that the sharing of stockholding among the brothers is very fair and in keeping with Korean principles of succession, except for the fifth and sixth brothers, who are now students in high school and university, respectively. But there is another way to ensure fair treatment among sons in family stockholding. This is to divide the zaibatsu by 4 or 6. *Doosan* has 4 big companies: Oriental Beer, Dongsan Construction, Hangyang Food and Doosan Industrial (unlisted), which could have been divided among the brothers. But they did not choose this way. They chose the method of sharing the main companies' stocks.

The reasoning behind the stock sharing here is to prevent division of the unit.

There are at least two methods of preventing division of a zaibatsu. *Samsung* used the method of choosing only one son, among three, as successor. To attain this purpose, Mr. Lee tried to exclude the other sons from stockholding and management. Foundation and Mutual Aid played the role of an invisible mantle or screen. *Doosan* chose the method of sharing the stock of each company and, in this way, prevented any one brother from obtaining a special interest with a certain company in the zaibatsu.

From the aspect of management Mr. Lee and his third son, and Mr. Park and his brothers naturally still have strong influence upon the management of their respective zaibatsu, but in comparison with others, these two have a relatively large number of professional managers in the top management class. Why has this occurred within these two zaibatsu? It is only my guess, but the top management of these two seem to think that maintaining the unity of the zaibatsu is inevitably necessary for development. And to achieve this purpose, professional managers and methods are necessary, whether desired or not.

For instance, in *Doosan*, from the death of the formal Chairman in 1971, until 1981, Mr. Chung Chang-Su (a professional manager), took over the chairmanship of *Doosan*. And when Mr. Park took office as Chairman instead of Mr. Chung in 1981, Mr. Park said in his announcement, "I shall not try to control both stockholding and management. Neither will I try to have a strong influence upon the management of *Doosan*. Because Mr. Chung was chosen as the Chairman of the Chamber of Commerce and Industry of Korea,

I took office as Chairman in his stead so as to free him for activities in public office."

## Conclusion

According to the preceding discussion, we can make the following tentative conclusion.

First, it is possible to formulate three patterns of stockholding in the zaibatsu. Pattern I is monopolized by a proprietor, Pattern II is controlled by a stockholding company and Pattern III is a reciprocal stockholding by affiliated companies. Accompanying a zaibatsu's growth in scale, the pattern of stockholding transfers from I to II and from II to III. The former transformation pattern is relatively easy, but the latter is not, because the traditional Korean family structure, especially the principle of succession, prevents a smooth transfer from II to III. Almost all Korean family businesses adhere to the structure of Pattern I. The reasons why they have this pattern is not simply explained, but undoubtedly the Korean family structure has a strong influence upon the structure of family businesses.

Second, the Korean principle of succession requires a division of property among sons. Sons must be treated fairly. Under this principle, it is natural that the zaibatsu will be divided, as *Taihan* and *Kukje* were divided. There is only one alternative if each son wishes to succeed to his father's status as both proprietor and top manager. The only answer is to divide the zaibatsu when their generation comes into control of the business.

Third, under these stated circumstances, there are some cases which were not subsumed in the above categories. In such cases, to prevent the disorganization of a zaibatsu, it was necessary to create some sort of mechanism. One was to select a son as successor and to exclude other sons from the zaibatsu as *Samsung* did. This is very similar to the Japanese custom of succession. Utilizing this method takes a very long time and requires a cautious attitude. Another mechanism involved sharing of the stockholding to prevent a descendant from holding too much interest in a certain company within the zaibatsu. In either case, a large number of professional managers are needed. As the scale of a zaibatsu increases, more and more managers are required, and the number of family members is limited. Someone must fill the gap. Because of this progression, the necessity of professional manager will increase.

The results of this analysis point to the conclusion that Korean zaibatsu seem to fall into two groups. One group maintains unity by untraditional methods, and in this case, the separation of capital and management will be increased slowly but steadily. The other group is to repeat a disorganization, generation by generation, as a cell divides over and over again.

## NOTES

1.  Sa-Gong, Il., "Economic Growth and Chaebol", *Chosun*, Sept. 1980. (in Korean)
2.  Tamio Hattori, "On the Concept of 'Dōzoku' in Japan and Korea: A Comparison", *Ajia Keizai*, Vol. 16, No. 2, Feb. 1975. (in Japanese)
3.  According to "*The Dong-A-Ilbo*" (Aug. 16, 1982), 35 among 50 large gross sales companies in the first half of 1982 are zaibatsu affiliated companies (5 among the 50 are banks).
4.  In detail, please see Tamio Hattori, "The Stockholding Patterns of Korean 'Zaibatsu'—with special reference to stockholding and family structure—", *The Social Science*, Doshisha University, March 1982. (in Japanese)
5.  This is based on late sociologist Dr. Eitarō Suzuki's "The Principles of Japanese Rural Sociology." (in Japanese)
6.  Hattori, ibid., 1975.
7.  "Doosan" (House Organ of Doosan Chaebol), March 1981. (in Korean)

# COMMENTS

Seishi Nakamura
*Tokyo Keizai University*

The purpose of this international conference on business history is to make clear the roles and characteristics of family business in the course of economic development in each country. I am convinced that this paper, dealing with Korean family business, will give us many useful materials and ideas for discussion at this conference.

I am a nonprofessional concerning the Korean economy and her business, but am presently researching a history of Japanese zaibatsu. Zaibatsu is an important subject in the realm of Japanese business history studies, and not a few business historians in Japan have been studying Japanese zaibatsu history from various viewpoints. As a result, the structure and characteristics of Japanese zaibatsu have been analyzed and made rather clear. Some of these main points have been presented by Professor Yasuoka and Professor Asajima in their papers. But now we are not sure whether these characteristics are peculiar to Japan or not. In order to inquire into this problem, international comparative studies of zaibatsu and family business are inevitable.

In many present-day developing countries, large business groups under family ownership and control are fast emerging and developing. They are the most important leaders of economic development in their countries and they appear to share common features with Japanese zaibatsu prior to the last World War. In particular, Korean Chaebol is supposed to be the most typical among them. Therefore, I think, it is worthwhile to compare existing Korean Chaebol with Japanese zaibatsu of the past.

Although Korea is a neighboring country, we Japanese have little knowledge about Korea's economy, business or society. So this paper gives us valuable information about the present state of Korean Chaebol. In this paper, Professor Hattori tries to analyze the relation between the formation of Korean Chaebol and the traditional structure of the Korean family. He presents the following three tentative conclusions:

## 1. Pattern of Stockholding

There are three patterns of stockholding in the Chaebol: ① Monopolized by a proprietor, ② Controlled by a stockholding company, ③ Reciprocal stockholding by an affiliated company.

## 2. Inheritance System

The Korean principle of succession requires a division among sons, so there is no concept of family property in Korea, traditionally. Therefore, in the case of succession, it is possible that the Chaebol will be dissolved.

## 3. Case of Preventing Dissolution

In spite of Korean traditional custom law, some Chaebols such as Sam-sung and Doosan tried to prevent division by untraditional methods.

These arguments are, I think, very clear and persuasive, and they can provide us with many hints when researching Japanese zaibatsu. I understand that the biggest difference between Japanese zaibatsu and Korean Chaebol results from the family structure, especially the inheritance system and family property management. However, I would like to ask some questions with regard to this paper to understand the Korean Chaebol more fully.

(1) It is certain that the structure of the Korean family has a strong effect on the structure of Korean Chaebol. But I think the pattern of fund raising has also influenced the Chaebol structure during the process of formation and development. Such cases could be found in the development process of Japanese zaibatsu, as was shown by Professor Miyamoto in his paper. What are the characteristics of fund raising by Korean Chaebol? What does professor Hattori think about the relation between fund raising and the structure of Chaebol?

(2)   Most Japanese zaibatsu had a pure holding company which exercised a general controlling function over the affiliated companies, as the headquarters. Are pure holding companies forbidden in Korea? Is there any head office where owners deal with business such as personnel and financial management?

(3)   The third question is concerned with the compatibility between the diversification strategy and family ownership. Generally speaking, the advance of diversification weakens the closed family ownership, in the long run. In the future, which will Chaebol owners select, diversification or closed family ownership?

# Ownership and Management of Indian Zaibatsu

Shoji Ito
*Institute of Developing Economies*

## Introduction

It is already more than a century since the most progressive among the adventurous merchants of India established modern cotton textile mills in Bombay in the 1850s. Until roughly the close of the nineteenth century, Indian modern enterprises in various fields, including cotton textiles, were more advanced than contemporary Japanese counterparts. Jamsetji Nusserwanji Tata (1839–1904) adopted one of the newly invented devices of ring spinning for the first time in the world. Even at the beginning of the present century, the history of Indian entrepreneurship got another feather in its cap: establishment of an integrated iron and steel mill (TISCO) solely with indigenous funds (but with the help of foreign technical experts).

The development of entrepreneurship in India, however, had been slow and lopsided, particularly because the colonial government was hostile to balanced industrial development in India, especially by the Indians. The circumstances in which the Indian entrepreneurs developed were in sharp contrast to the Japanese ones which were created by strong nationalist government.

On the other hand, India shared two common features with Japan. Firstly, both countries were latecomers, in terms of industrialization, compared with the Western countries, and the industrialists of both countries had to face stiff competition from the developed industrialists of the world. Secondly, both countries observed traditional customs of cohesion among family members or groups of families, though different in nature.

*147*

The first factor caused, at least partially, the early emergence of large-size enterprises and corporate groups, which after the Indian Independence were often called "finance capital," "empire" or "monopoly capital." The second factor partially explains the continuing hold by particular families over the undivided, expanding corporate groups.

This paper attempts to highlight the salient features of ownership and management of Indian "zaibatsu" today. The reason why the present paper limits its concern to the zaibatsu of India, even though the framework (i.e., 'family firms') of this conference is a much wider one, is mainly that, while family firms are the dominant form of enterprise in the Indian private sector, the zaibatsu assume a dominant position among them. In a way, it is representative of all the Indian family firms.

In Section I, general features of the Indian zaibatsu are described. Section II is devoted to a study of how a family's hold over a large group of companies is maintained in an unchallenged manner regardless of their relatively small amounts of capital ownership. In Section III and IV, a few characteristics of the moves toward professionalization of management in India will be highlighted. Firstly, the ultimate decision making power of the group of companies rests in the hands of the zaibatsu family's members. Secondly, as managerial work has expanded and become complicated, more and more responsible tasks have tended to be gradually entrusted to the salaried managers who were brought up through in-service training, but the families appear to have preferred men of their own caste/ community. Thirdly, a rational system of recruiting bright young men to be promoted to the top managerial rank is being tried by a few zaibatsu groups.

In the concluding section, the validity of the theorem[1] put forward by Professor Yasuoka, relating to the interrelationship between the nature of ownership and that of management, is tested in the light of the above analyses.

## I.  A Bird's-Eye View of Indian Zaibatsu

The public sector assumes a leading role in India's economic

development. Its share in the whole of gross domestic capital formation and gross fixed capital formation are 41 and 53%, respectively
(1977/78). Moreover its share in the total paid-up capital of the
limited companies is as much as 76% (1978).

However its productivity is so low that it has no inherent capacity
of its own for expansion, and it requires extra-economic forces for
extended reproduction. The private sector is much more dynamic.
Take for instance the ratio of gross profit to total capital employed
in Indian factories: the ratio for the public sector is 0.06 while that
for the private sector is 0.30.[2]

The Indian factory sector is characterized by its high concentration in large-size enterprises. Factories that employ 1,000 or more
workers are 1.2%, but they employ no less than 43.8% of all factory
workers (1974). The corresponding figures for Japan are 4.5 and
36.8%, respectively. The high concentration of large-size factories
in India was caused by the establishment of huge factories by the
public and private sectors, which in turn reflects the availability of
scale-merit technologies in the world.

As of 1977/78, 67 companies out of the top 200 limited companies
of India belong to the public sector. Of the remaining 133 companies, 31 companies are considered to be substantially controlled
by foreign capital. Some of them are under the control of MNCs
such as the Lever Group of Netherlands-Britain (one company),
Imperial Chemical (three companies), and the Inchicapes (two
companies). Many of the remaining 102 Indian companies are under
the control of the dominant business groups of India. The Tatas,
one of the two largest groups, control 10 companies including the
TISCO, which is the largest company in the Indian private sector,
and the Tata Engineering & Locomotives Co., Ltd. (TELCO),
which is the second largest. The Birlas, another of the largest groups,
control 16 companies including Gwalior Rayon Co., Ltd., their
largest company. And among the remaining companies are 4
companies under the Mafatlals, 2 companies under the Walchands,
2 companies under the Singhanias, 1 company under the Shri Rams,
3 companies under the Thapars and 2 companies each under the
Modis and the Mahindras.[3]

According to a census of public limited companies in the private

TABLE 1  List of the Larger Zaibatsu of India (1966).

| | Name (1) | Community (2) | No. of Cos. (3) | Total Net Assets (4) | Main Business Interests (5) |
|---|---|---|---|---|---|
| 1. | Tata | Parsi | 74 | 585 | Various |
| 2. | Birla | Marwari Maheshwari | 265 | 576 | Various |
| 3. | Mafatlal | Gujerati Kunbi | 21 | 136 | Textiles, Chemicals, Petro-chemicals, Sugar |
| 4. | Bangur | Marwari | 85 | 125 | Finance, Textiles, Cement, Paper, Cable |
| 5. | Bajoria-Jalan | Marwari Agarwal | 105 | 107 | Eng., Textiles, Sugar, Railway |
| 6. | Shri Ram | Agarwal | 36 | 107 | Textiles, Chemicals, Electricals, Eng., Ceramics |
| 7. | Thapar | Punjabi Khatri | 53 | 103 | Electrical, Paper, Coal, Sugar, Textiles, Eng., Vanaspathi |
| 8. | Walchand | Gujerati Jaina | 27 | 80 | Car, Industrial Machinery, Sugar, Construction |
| 9. | Sahu-Jain | Marwari Jaina | 27 | 80 | Cement, Textiles, Paper, Sugar, Plywood, Printing & Publishing, Eng. |
| 10. | J. K. Shinghania | Marwari Agarwal | 47 | 79 | Textiles, Paper, Sugar, Metals, Chemicals |
| 11. | Goenka | Marwari Agarwal | 54 | 65 | Textiles, Tea, Generation |

Source: Government of India, *Report of the Monopoly Inquiry Commission, 1965*, 1965, pp. 373–414 for Column (5) and Govt. of India, *Report of the Industrial Licensing Policies Inquiry Committee*, Appendices Volume II, pp. 1–45 for Columns (3) and (4).

Note: Column (4); in Rs. 10 million (US$1≒Rs. 9).

sector,[4] the larger the companies are, the higher the net profit ratios are: the companies whose net assets were below Rupees 2.5 million showed a negative profit rate, and those with assets between Rs. 2.5 million and 5 million had a net profit rate of 1.3%. These rates increased steadily to 26.5% for the largest companies with net assets over Rs. 200 million (1971/72).

It is estimated that, while the "foreign capital controlled companies" accounted for 30% of the total turnover of the private companies in 1971/72, the 20 largest Indian groups accounted for 35% in 1975.[5]

All of these facts taken together indicate that the large national and foreign groups of companies have fostered giant and profitable concerns.

Professor Shigeaki Yasuoka defines the term 'zaibatsu' as a group of companies that is owned by a family (or a group of families) and is controlled through a holding company as an appex with some of its larger members enjoying oligopolistic positions. When this definition is applied to the Indian model, some 10 or 20 of India's largest groups can be called zaibatsu as well.

Except for the Associated Cement Company groups (A.C.C.), they have been controlled by particular families. The groups' nomenclature is often suggestive of this: they usually adopt the family names.

Having passed through the initial stage, almost all the private enterprises have been essentially family business. Groups like the Birlas or the Tatas are two cases in point; they employ no less than 300 thousand people and account for more than one tenth of the assets of the companies in the private sector.

Table 1 shows some salient features of the 11 largest zaibatsu.

## II.  Family Ownership of Group Companies

The zaibatsu in India are the outcome of expansion of the once small family business. The expansion was both through creation of new enterprises and takeover of ongoing or bankrupt concerns. Therefore, there are normally no two public opinions as to who owns an enterprise. In the rare case where the takeover bid is being disputed, the noisy 'proxy war' occurs at the time of the general meeting of the company concerned.

But more often than not, the family's shareholding is much less than a majority, particularly in the case of large manufacturing companies. Take for instance Hindustan Motors Ltd., the then largest company of the Birla Group; the members of the Birla families owned less than 2% of the paid-up ordinary shares as of December 1971.[6]

According to Dr. Hazari's thoroughgoing study, assisted by Professor A. N. Oza, the zaibatsu family members owned less than 12%, in face value, of the total ordinary share capital of the 888 companies belonging to the 20 "corporate groups" as of 1958.[7] Even if the shareholdings of the charitable trusts (endowments) established by the families are also taken into account, the picture does not change much (15%).

The main reason why family ownership is not challenged by outsiders, in spite of such minority shareholding is due to, according to Dr. Hazari, the extensive networks of intercorporate investments among group companies: the group companies held 33% of the total ordinary shares issued by the group companies as of 1958.

Further, he found in the Tatas case:

1)  the family and their trusts owned, rather exclusively, an appex company (Tata Sons Private Ltd.),

2)  the family, the trusts and the appex company owned an investment company, and then

3)  all the above four institutions jointly owned many of the large industrial companies of the group, which in turn jointly or singly owned other minor companies.

This pyramidal structure reminds us of the structure of the old Japanese zaibatsu.

However, he found many a circular chain of investments in the cases of the Birlas and the Bangurs, in which company A held some shares in company B, company B in company C, C in D, D in E and E, in turn, in A. Chains of this sort were especially observed among investment companies. He concluded that it was not clear just where the chain started.

While this appears to be a labyrinth, the puzzle is not a difficult one to solve in light of the pyramidal order observed in the Tatas or Japanese zaibatsu of large size. According to a study by the present author, a few of these investment companies are very closely held by the zaibatsu family members. These companies can, therefore, be regarded as the starting points of the chain. All the so-called investment companies are not investment companies in the usual sense of the term. They are in practice joint holding companies, from any point of view. Thus, the zaibatsu of India, with numerous companies under a common authority, have holding companies in disguise which play the role of keeping the family's claim of ownership over group companies intact.[8]

## III.  Family System and Control over Management

### 1.  Family System

Unlike the traditional system in Japan, all the sons (not daughters in traditional India) had equal rights over the father's property. Adoption was not common practice. And rigid conditions restricting the manner of adoption have been established and observed.

However, many of the richer families have maintained the custom of an extended family—the Hindu joint family. The ancestral properties tended to be kept undivided in joint ownership (coparcenary) among the members (coparceners). According to Hindu Law, joint ownership was to be presupposed unless expressed otherwise. And management of the property used to be entrusted to the family head, called *karta*, usually the most senior and able male member of the family. It was  the duty of *karta* to properly maintain the property for the sake of all the members, and it was a virtue for the juniors to obey whatever the *karta* did: The latter was not accountable to the former for his conduct, though he had to be *bona fide* and show, through account books, the net results of his conduct when so demanded by any member. In the case of traditional trading castes/communities, they used to keep the ancestral family business as a "joint family firm."

These traditions of coherence among the extended family members must have contributed to the tendency of maintaining an undivided family business even after the death of its head.

TABLE 2　Common Directorship with Tata Sons Pvt., Ltd. (1972).

| Name of Company | Name of Common Director |
|---|---|
| TISCO | J.R.D. Tata (Ch), S. Moolgaokar (Vice-ch), M.A. Wadud Khan. |
| TELCO | J.R.D. Tata (Ch), S. Moolgaokar (Vice-ch), N.H. Tata |
| Indian Tube | None |
| Tata Power | N.H. Tata (Ch), J.D. Choksi |
| Tata Hydro | N.H. Tata (Ch), N.A. Palkhivala |
| Andhra V. Power | N.H. Tata (Ch) |
| Tata Chemicals | J.R.D. Tata (Ch), N.A. Palkhivala |
| TOMCO (Tata Oil Mills) | J.R.D. Tata (Ch), N.H. Tata (Vice-ch), M.A. Wadud Khan (Mg. Dr) |
| Voltas | J.D. Choksi, A.B. Bilimoria |

Source:　Data available at the office of the Registrar of Companies, Bombay.
Note:　Ch stands for chairman of the board of directors, Vice-ch for vice-chairman, and Mg. Dr for Managing Director. The nine largest companies of the Tatas are included.

However, individualism among family members has been rapidly developing because of British influence. It should be noted that the traditional Hindu law had inherent elements for "individualism" such as equitable rights over property among brothers, right of co-parcener to ask at liberty for separation of his own share of property from joint ownership, etc. The Hindu family laws enacted during the 1950s gave a further impetus to division and recently, increasing feuds among brothers in quite a few zaibatsu families are reportedly leading to division of the group companies after the head's death.

The family system in the zaibatsu of India appears to be at a crossroad. However, in view of the scale-merits of larger groups consisting of multiple activities, as well as the traditional cordial relationship between brothers in India, the process for division is slow.

The Birlas' case is suggestive of it. In terms of management, they have divided responsibility, but they maintain cordiality as well as networks of intercorporate investments, both leading to a federation of group companies.

TABLE 3 Community Distribution of Directorships for the Birlas' 14 Largest Companies (1972).

| Community | No. of Directors | No. of Directorships Held by the Directors |
|---|---|---|
| The Birlas | 9 | 15 |
| Other Marwaris | 44 (2) | 55 (2) |
| Parsis | 1 | 1 |
| Gujaratis | 8 (6) | 9 (7) |
| Bengalees | 7 | 8 |
| Tamilians | 4 | 4 |
| U.P.-Kayastha | 1 | 1 |
| Muslim | 1 | 1 |
| Punjabi | 1 | 1 |
| Foreigners & Unidentifiable | 9 | 10 |
| Total | 85 (8) | 105 (9) |

Notes: 1. The names of directors were compiled with the help of Kothari & Sons ed., *Kothari's Economic & Industrial Guide of India, 1973–74* (n.d.) and the data available at the offices of the Registrars of Companies in Bombay and Calcutta. Then they were classified by community, often with the names themselves.
2. The figures in brackets show the number of directors that belong to other zaibatsu including the Sahu-Jains, Kanorias, Mafatlals, Kasturbhai-Lalbhais and Thackerseys, and that of the directorships held by them.

## 2. Indian Ways of Maintaining Family Control over Group Companies

In the case of typical pre-war Japanese zaibatsu, the zaibatsu families tended to entrust loyal and brilliant salaried managers with management of enterprises *en bloc*.

In the case of India, the zaibatsu family members have been active leaders of management. All the important decisions have been made by themselves with the help and advice of loyal salaried managers.

Their hold over the management of the group companies has been maintained by various arrangements. The managing agency system had been the most important one until its abolition in 1970.[9] Multiple directorship is another one, with members of the zaibatsu family occupying the key management positions in the various companies. Table 2 illustrates the case of the Tatas.

Special attention should be paid to the nature of Indian society and to its bearings on the continuing managerial control by a par-

TABLE 4    Community Distribution of Directorships for the Tatas' 10 Largest
Companies (1972).

| Community | No. of Directors | No. of Directorships Held by the Directors |
|---|---|---|
| The Tatas | 3 | 12 |
| Other Parsis | 14 | 25 |
| Marwari | 1 (1) | 1 (1) |
| Gujaratis | 11 (4) | 14 (4) |
| Bengalees | 6 | 7 |
| Marathis | 3 | 5 |
| Punjabis | 3 (1) | 4 (2) |
| Muslim | 3 | 6 |
| Tamilians | 2 | 2 |
| Mysorian | 1 | 3 |
| Malayalees | 2 | 2 |
| Foreigners & Unidentifiable | 24 | 27 |
| Total | 73 (6) | 108 (7) |

Notes:   Cf. the preceding table. The figures in brackets relate to the Mafatlals,
Mahindras, Kilachands, Thackerseys, Bajajs, and Khataus.

ticular family. Indian society is divided into a large number of communities which are either minor religious communities, such as the
Parsis, or sub-castes of the Hindus. Each community has exclusivity,
particularly in the matter of marriage and adoption, as well as
cohesion. It is only natural, under these circumstances, that a man
in business could trust, and has trusted, the members of his own
community.

Resort, in various manners, to the traditional community ties
in business management has been one of the conspicuous characteristics of Indian business. It was in fact the most important factor
behind the successful emergence of the Marwari community as
India's dominant trading firm during the last century.[10]

An analysis of community distribution of the company directors belonging to India's two representative zaibatsu would indicate the extent to which community ties are utilized by the zaibatsu families. Tables 3 and 4 show the community-wise distribution
of the directors of the companies, belonging to the Birlas and the
Tatas, respectively, whose net assets were over Rs. 100 million,
around 1972. The Birlas' companies are considered by the general

TABLE 5    The Birlas, Marwaris and Non-Marwari Directors in 76 Companies Belonging to the Birla Group, and Percentage of Directorships Held by Them in the Birlas' Companies (1972).

| | | Number of Directorships | | | |
|---|---|---|---|---|---|
| | | Number of Directors (1) | Total (2) | Of which, Directorships in the Birlas' Companies (3) | Directorships in the Second Tier (4) | $\frac{3+4(\%)}{2}$ (5) |
| The Birlas | A | 0 | 0 | 0 | 0 | — |
| | B | 18 | 106 | 104 | 0 | 98 |
| Other Marwaris | A | 28 | 272 | 73 | 9 | 30 |
| | B | 83 | 382 | 286 | 20 | 80 |
| Of which, Other | A | (5) | (61) | (8) | (0) | (13) |
| Groups | B | (0) | (0) | (0) | (0) | (—) |
| Others (including | A | 16 | 133 | 41 | 2 | 32 |
| Unidentifiable) | B | 17 | 79 | 63 | 0 | 80 |
| Total | A | 44 | 405 | 114 | 11 | 31 |
| | B | 118 | 567 | 453 | 20 | 83 |

Note:   Those directors whose communities were not identifiable constitute about half of the "Others." The identifiable ones include the Bengalees, Gujaratis, U.P. Banias, etc.

public to be managed exclusively by the family members or their "henchmen." On the contrary, the Tatas are considered to be the most modern and open minded of the Indian zaibatsu, relying on salaried professional managers to a great extent.

As Table 3 shows, two-thirds of the directorships (at least 70 out of 105, i.e., 67%) were held by the Marwaris, the Birlas' own community. In the Tatas' case, it is surprising to see, Table 4, that the Parsi directors occupied an unduly large percentage of directorships (37 out of 108, i.e., 34%) in lieu of the community's rather small size; its population was hardly 100,000. Particularly in the case of the appex company, Tata Sons Pvt. Ltd., the Parsis accounted for 6 of the 7 directors in 1968 and 8 of the 10 in 1972.

As regards the Birlas, Birla Brothers Pvt. Ltd. had been the most important managing agent. The directors of this company mainly consisted of members of the Birla family.

As mentioned before, the Birlas hold a number of investment

companies. Table 5 shows those directors who held directorships in any of the Birlas' investment, trading or financial companies. These directors were singled out because they can be regarded as those persons most trusted by the Birlas in view of the nature of the business.

The figures in lines B of Table 5 show that out of 118 such directors, no less than 101 persons (86%) were the Marwaris.

The directors of some 20 companies belonging to the Birlas but working in other activities were also studied, the results are shown in lines A of the Table. Those having no directorships in any company in the fields of investment, finance and trade numbered 44. They held as many as 405 directorships. However, only 125 directorships (31%) were held in the companies belonging to the Birlas. The corresponding percentage figure for the 118 directors was no less than 83%.[11]

Last, but not least, apart from the resort to community ties, Indian zaibatsu have established a variety of family charitable trusts. As Isamu Hirota points out, these trusts have a function of maintaining the family's controlling interests (i.e., vote-carrying shares) undivided among the individual members.[12]

The members of the zaibatsu family do not always hold the most powerful legal status in the management of the companies: a young member may be merely a general manager or president who is not legally responsible to the general meeting of the companies. Still, it is because of the above mentioned arrangements that they have unchallenged managerial power in the group companies.

## IV. Subtle Changes toward Professionalization of Management

Almost all of the zaibatsu families belong to some trading community. Even when examining exceptions, the founders of such groups have usually accumulated their initial capital by trading and speculation, as was the case with the Tatas. The family members have not lost their traders' acumen and traits, even today. The profitability of industrial enterprises depends to a good extent on factors other than productivity and quality of products. For instance,

TABLE 6   Increasing Importance of Salary Earners among Total Employees
(1951–70).

(in 1,000 persons)

| | Both Wage & Salary Earners (1) | Of which, Salary Earners (2) | $\frac{(2)}{(1)}$ % (3) |
|---|---|---|---|
| 1951 | 1,633 | 154 | 9.4 |
| 1955 | 1,784 | 195 | 11 |
| 1960 | 2,904 | 323 | 11 |
| 1965 | 3,986 | 641 | 16 |
| 1970* | 4,311 | 797 | 18 |

Sources:  For 1951 and 1955, *Tenth Census of Indian Manufactures, 1955*, Govt. of India;
for the later years, various issues of *Annual Survey of Industries*. Govt. of India.
Note:  * The figures for 1970 are in million man-hours.

the availability of raw materials, and hence their prices, fluctuate volatilely in India. Thus, shrewdness in speculative activities can be numbered as one of the more important qualifications of a successful entrepreneur.

However, given the favorable conditions created by the independent government's policies toward heavy industrialization in the 1950s, business groups started to increasingly diversify their manufacturing activities into more sophisticated fields. This necessitated employment of an increasing number of qualified engineers and other technicians. Table 6 suggests this tendency.

A series of fiscal incentives, many governmental financial institutions and licensing systems such as Industrial Licensing and Capital Goods Import Licensing, have been created in order to guide private business activities into priority fields, as defined by the government from time to time. Both incentive and prohibitive measures accompanied increasing administrative and accounting burdens in all the large companies, which in turn required the zaibatsu to employ legal specialists, accountants (including Chartered Accountants), and other experts, including those who had undergone rigorous training in post-graduate courses at MIT or Harvard Business School.

The qualitative and quantitative expansion of managerial responsibility has led to employment of unrelated personnel for not only middle management but also upper management, though at a much slower pace in the latter case. The Tatas were in the forefront in this matter even before the Independence. In the case of the British groups which emerged in colonial India, the partners used to be selected from among the British who served the group well, but toward the end of British rule, they started recruiting some Indian staff as junior or even senior partners. Dr. R.N. Mukherji, a Bengalee engineer in Indian Iron & Steel (Burn Group) was perhaps the first such case. Mahindra, in the Burn Group, and Ananthramakrishnan, in the Simpson Group, are other conspicuous examples.

On the contrary, most of the Indian zaibatsu groups, particularly those belonging to the Marwaris, were much slower to introduce unrelated persons into top management personnel. When the ownership of British firms was taken over, senior officers were sometimes dismissed and replaced by the new Indian owner's "henchmen," who were often connected with the owner through blood ties, community ties or at least village ties.

However, the members and relatives of the family, even if its size was large, could not continue to handle the expanding tasks of top management. Hence, there emerged various measures to employ unrelated persons in top managerial positions. In the following subsections, new measures are described, including references to in-service training which retained a somewhat traditional nature.

### 1. In-service Training and Promotion to Upper Echelons

It is more than one hundred years since modern university education was introduced in India. But merchants of India, even the richest of them, rarely sent their children to formal educational institutions for middle and higher education. They used to train the young boys in their own firms until they became competent enough to join as partners in the family business or start new firms of their own. This type of in-service training was the predominant form of education up until the 1950s.

Most of the elderly bosses of the present-day zaibatsu received primary education only. This does not necessarily mean that they are dull, rough and uncivilized; to the contrary, they are highly intelligent, paying attention to worldwide news relating to politics, economy, commerce and technology. G. D. Birla, the founder of the Birla group, was a typical example.

As business interests widened, the family started depending on unrelated, but in-service-trained, persons for daily matters and, in course of time, even for more responsible matters.

The case of the Birla zaibatsu is illustrative of fostering and promoting unrelated, in-service-trained persons to upper echelon position.

D. P. Mandelia, T. C. Saboo, G. D. Thirani, M. D. Dalmia, S. N. Hada, M. L. Bagrodia and R. K. Birla are important topmost salaried managers in the Birla zaibatsu.

According to a lawyer, "M. L. Bagrodia started his life as a clerk in a Birla concern drawing less than Rs. 100 per month. He proved himself very useful to Birlas as he brought fortune to Birlas and to himself by his magic wand."[13]

As regards S. N. Hada (born in 1924), he "started his life in Birla concern as a lowest paid mill-hand and had no technical or university qualification or experience. It is a mystery as to how he paved his way to the top-most position in a Birla concern and how he amassed more than Rs. 5 lakhs (100,000) to buy shares in Hada Textiles after honouring heavy Income Tax Liabilities."[14] He has come to assume very important positions in the Birla zaibatsu in the course of time; as of 1972, he acted as the Managing Director of New Swadeshi Mills of Ahmedabad, and Director in Indore Exporting & Importing Co., Ltd., which is an important holding company, Bharat General & Textile Industries Ltd. and six other important companies, including two Birlas' companies which were working in Ethiopia and Nigeria.[15]

The most important of them all is perhaps D. P. Mandelia (born in 1907). He started his life as a warehouse keeper of a Birla concern. By 1950 he had directorships in 14 Birla companies including the Birla Brothers (Gwalior) Private Ltd. which was an important managing agent of the Birlas, Gwalior Rayon Co., Ltd. and Textile Machineries Corporation (Gwalior) Ltd. Today he is advisor to the head of the Birlas, G. D. Birla. As of 1971, he had directorships in 10 companies; these included Pilani Investment Co., Ltd., the most important holding company of the Birlas, and Zuari Agro-Chemicals

Ltd. which was then the latest and huge chemical fertilizer manufacturer.[16] He drew remunerations from various Birla companies
amounting to Rs. 30,000 per month, and resided in "a palatial
house" at Gwalior City, paying as rent Rs. 2,100 per annum (which
the Income Tax department estimated at Rs. 6,000 per annum).[17]

When the present author of this paper interviewed such an important manager in 1973, he said categorically that "family background, capability and loyalty" were the very conditions requisite
to promotion to higher positions. This is reminiscent of the old
Japanese custom.

Though further details have yet to be explored, it may not be out
of context to refer to a college professor who has been on good terms
with the Birlas and is being well looked after by them as well. He
told me that the Birlas have continued to be quite sympathetic and
generous to those who had contributed to them whole-heartedly.

There is, however, a conspicuous difference between the positions
of Indian and Japanese employed managers: the Indian ones are
often allowed to start and run their own business enterprises separately while serving the masters.

The in-service training mentioned above is not sufficient for
bringing up engineers and other specialists in particular fields who
become immediately necessary when any zaibatsu ventures into
any new activities in big way. In such cases, the necessary specialists
are taken on from any firms within the country (and even from
abroad). Thus the turnover of specialists is fairly high in India.

According to the present author's impression, the in-service
trained persons are weak in technological aspects, but they are much
more "loyal" to the particular firm or group to which they belong.

### 2.  "Tata Administrative Service"

In order to assure both the merits of in-service training and those
of obtaining brilliant persons with high qualifications, the Tatas
have introduced a modern system called "Tata Administrative
Service" (TAS).

The TAS was started in 1956.[18] Dr. Fredy Mehta (1928–), a
London-educated economist who has been a director in Tata Sons
Pvt. Ltd. since 1972, is the first person to be recruited by TAS. While

only a few persons were recruited at the initial stages, 12 persons were recruited last year (1981–82), and the total strength of the TAS has reached over one hundred. It is of interest that they are recruited through a central body called the TAS Committee for all of the Tata companies. Its influence is such that quite a few of those persons who passed the most prestigious examinations for the Indian Administrative Service or Indian Foreign Service joined TAS instead.

It should be added that the TAS is not likely to undermine the authority of the Tata family in the near future. One should not be astonished by the news that a young member of the family, 45-year old Ratan Tata, was appointed Chairman of Tata Industries Ltd. in spite of the availability of more senior and "competent" persons within the company. This is taken as a gesture signifying his likely appointment as the leader of the Tatas in the future.[19]

### 3.  Professionalization of Family Members Themselves

Zaibatsu families' excessive power has been severely criticized by various kinds of people, not only by the leftist or egalitarian intellectuals but also by wide varieties of officials and liberal professionals.

In the 1950s, the zaibatsu families started sending their young children to formal higher educational institutions in India, and sometimes abroad, for scientific as well as managerial study. Today, those members in their 30s or below are mostly college graduates. They often go abroad (especially to the U.S.A.) for short-term training courses.

This is a response to the above mentioned criticism as well as their own need to become capable of executing scientific management and exercising leadership over their highly qualified experts who are often much older and abler. A young, college-educated member of one of largest zaibatsu families reportedly said that, without first becoming highly professionalized himself, he could not direct his specialists properly or with authority.

## V.  Concluding Remarks

Though the zaibatsu families' holds over both ownership and

management have been diluted quantitatively in the process of growth among the groups, control over their companies has been maintained by resorting to various means which are either of universal nature or those very peculiar to Indian nature.

Though professionalization of management has started and is a welcome development, it is still within the overall framework of maintaining the families' firm control. One of the TAS's functions is to integrate the group, as we have seen. In the case of the Birlas, in which many companies are managed by employed managers, the performances of these companies are closely monitored by the family.

However, relationships among the family members are elastic and opportunistic. While many a zaibatsu extended family enjoy amicable internal relationships, quite a few, such as the Mafatlals, Singhanias and Jaipurias, are suffering from family feuds. This is perhaps because the norms of family members have not been rigidly defined. Further, the basic reason behind this is perhaps that all the individual members, at least male members, of the family have traditionally had equal ownership rights over ancestoral property.

This is in sharp contrast to Japanese traditional merchant families which were based on primogeniture and collective ownership of property.

Professor Yasuoka presumes that, as against the case of collective ownership, families based on individual ownership tend to actively manage their businesses themselves while making efforts to exclude undesirable members.[20] Such tendencies have also been observed in the Indian cases where all the members have been expected to be active leaders of the family business. Moreover, there have been a few cases of ousting undesirable members, such as the late G. Birla.

However, the individualistic attitude is a fairly new phenomenon in India, and efforts to consolidate the ownerships dispersed through equal succession have been continuously made by way of establishing, from time to time, a series of "charitable" family trusts, holding companies and chains of intercorporate investments. It may be that careful studies are necessary in order to see whether these efforts are due to traditional ideas favoring extended family or the scale merits of business. The present author of this paper presumes that the latter is the major, albeit not the sole, factor.

*Acknowledgements*

Professor P. N. Agarwala, New Delhi, and particularly Professor A. N. Oza, Bombay University, kindly made many comments on a rough draft of this article, many of which have been incorporated in the present edition. But whatever bias or mistakes that remain are wholly the author's.

NOTES

1. Shigeaki Yasuoka, "Ownership and Management of Family Business: An International Comparison," (HSDRJE-63/UNUP-414), The U.N. Univ., Tokyo, 1982, 29p.
2. Government of India, *Annual Survey of Industries; 1977–78, Summary Results for Factory Sector*, New Delhi, 1980, pp. 26, 30.
3. According to the present author's own classification of the 200 largest companies listed in *The Times of India Directory & Year-book 1980/81*, Bombay, 1981.
4. "Census of public limited companies, 1971–72," *Reserve Bank of India Bulletin* (June 1978), p. 447.
5. Nirmal K. Chandra, "Role of foreign capital in India," *Social Scientist* (April 1977), pp. 3–20; S. K. Goyal, *Monopoly Capital and Public Policy*, Allied Publishers Pvt. Ltd., New Delhi, 1979, pp. 52–53.
6. Shoji Ito, "Indo no aru dai-kigyō no kabunushi-kōsei" [An analysis of the share-holders' list of a large public limited company in India], *Ajia Keizai* (Oct., 1974), pp. 84–90.
7. R. K. Hazari, *The Structure of the Corporate Private Sector, A Study of Concentration, Ownership and Control*, Bombay, 1966, 400p.
8. For further details, cf. Shoji Ito, "On the basic nature of the investment company in India," in *The Developing Economies*, XVI-3 (Sept. 1978), pp. 223–238; Ito, "Studies in Indian zaibatsu; roles of intercorporate investment," in *The Journal of Intercultural Studies*, No. 2 (1975), pp. 51–56.
9. P. S. Lokanathan's Study (*Industrial Organization in India*, London, 1935, 413p.) is the classical work on the Managing Agency System. Many studies have been made since. Kenji Koike's study (*Keiei Dairi Seido Ron* [*On the Managing Agency System*], Tokyo, 1979) puts forward a novel idea that the system's aim was to basically preempt industrial profit by corrupt entrepreneurs, while Shin'ichi Yone-

kawa in one of his articles ("Indo boseki kabushiki kaisha ni okeru keiei dairi seido no teichaku katei" [The settlement process of the managing agency system in Indian textile companies], *Hitotsubashi Roso*, Vol. 85, No. 1, 1980) proved that the mercantile approach of the ealier entrepreneurs was its origin.

10. Tomas A. Thimberg, *The Marwaris; From Traders to Industrialists*, New Delhi, 1978, 268p. The community ties were important also for the Nattukottai Chettiars, Parsis, Gujerati Banias at the time when they started expansion of their networks of transaction in remote places.; Shoji Ito, "A note on the 'business combine' in India—with special reference to the Nattukottai Chettiars," in *The Developing Economies*, IV-3 (Sep. 1966), pp. 370–372; Ito, "Indo ni okeru zaibatsu no shutsuji ni tsuite; 19-seiki–dai-ichiji-taisen" [On the origins of Indian zaibatsu; from the 19th century to World War I] in *Shakai Keizai Shi-gaku*, Vol. 45, No. 5 (1980), pp. 29–54. These remind us of a similarity shared by the Ōmi merchants of Japan who used village ties for building up wide networks; Eiichiro Ogura, *Ōmi Shōnin no Keifu [Genera of Merchants from Ōmi Region]* Tokyo, 1980.

11. For more details, cf. Shoji Ito, "Indo ni okeru dai-zaibatsu no dōzoku-teki seikaku no sai-kentō" [A reexamination of family characteristics of large Indian zaibatsu], in *Keizai to Keizaigaku* (Mar. 1978), pp. 35–46.

12. Isamu Hirota, "Indo ni okeru kazoku-teki keiei no seiritsu jijō" [Circumstances pertaining to the establishment of family management], in *Shōgaku Ronshū*, No. 14 (1979), pp. 1–27.

13. N. C. Roy, *Mystery of Bajoria-Jalan House*, Calcutta, 1972, p. 208.

14. Ibid., p. 208.

15. From the "List of Directorships" available in "D" files at the office of Registrar of Companies, Calcutta.

16. Ibid.

17. Roy, op. cit., pp. 204–205.

18. The following information was collected from the Tatas' office in Bombay, Sept. 1982.

19. "The Tatas: changing of the guard," *India Today*, Dec. 31, 1981, p. 96ff.

20. Shigeaki Yasuoka, *op. cit.*, pp. 23–24.

# COMMENTS

Hisashi Watanabe
*Kyoto University*

First of all I would like to express my best thanks to Mr. Ito because I, a layman in Indology, learned many things from his very instructive paper and have been informed of basic problems in the contemporary stand of studies of the Indian economic and business history.

As for the synthesis of typology of "family enterprise," which should be one of the principal concerns of our conference, the Indian type of family enterprise seems to present a unique way of combining a social institution (i.e. "family") and an economic one (i.e. "enterprise") in comparison with the Euro-American and the East Asian types. For historical analysis of such a complex institution it may be necessary to make distinctions among various aspects of the phenomenon to be examined, i.e.,

1) aspect due to the traditional system of the Indian family (especially the joint family) and of business activities (especially commerce within the Indian subcontinent and along the coasts of the Arabian Sea and the Bay of Bengal);

2) aspect due to the British ruling and exploitation of the colonial India,

3) aspect due to the system of modern capitalistic economy in general which was partially introduced into India parallel with the process of colonization, and

4) aspect due to characteristics which are common to the early stage of capitalistic development in a country.

In consideration of these different aspects I would like to make remarks which consist of five points.

First, Mr. Ito emphasizes that the individualistic tendency of family members in India is a relatively new phenomenon, and he attributes it to British influence. Thus it must be related to the second aspect I have listed. I got another impression, however, from his paper: that the principle of the family system in traditional India had been much more individualistic than that of the modern Japanese system. On the whole, so I think, we could not interpret "individualistic" tendency in India today as a byproduct of the British rule. It might be better to interpret this tendency in such a way that potential individualism hidden in the traditional social system was only stimulated through contact with modern British individualism. So far the "new" tendency should concern rather the first aspect.

Secondly, if I understood Mr. Ito correctly, the family system in India—especially in joint families—has been rather functional, or even opportunistic, in spite of its structural solidity in appearance. As far as all male family members have equal ownership right over ancestoral property, individualism in family system may be inevitable. Economic individualism is, however, unfavorable to rapid accumulation and optimum allocation of capital during the early stage of industrialization. Therefore it must be somehow effectively restrained also in India. Coparcenery functioned, so I suppose, as a counterbalance against economic individualism. In this sense the family system in the Indian enterprises is related to the fourth aspect.

Thirdly, according to Mr. Ito's description, the reservoirs for formation of Indian family enterprises have been "communities" or "sub-castes." I wish Mr. Ito would kindly explain to us this very key term for Indology in more detail. I got the impression from his paper that the relationship between "community" and "family enterprise" has some similarity with that between "resolvent" and "crystal." It means that a family enterprise is built up under certain conditions out of a certain "community." If conditions have become inadequate for maintenance of the family enterprise it resolves into the community to become personal enterprises. If this analogy has a certain validity we could then better understand so-called "family enterprise" in India by using the term "community enterprise" or "community-family enterprise." In any case "community" is one of the given conditions for formation of family enterprise. So far this factor must be related to the first aspect.

Fourthly, as far as "community" or "sub-caste" is not only a religious unit but also a *marriage area*, this concept has a certain similarity with "sect" in Protestant societies. In Germany, for instance, communities (*Gemeinden*) established by Protestant sects have not only been local units of religion, but also of marriage areas, and therefore they are very often bases of capital combination and recruitment of managers through the relationships established by marriage. I would like to show one example which may be instructive for a comparison between the Indian and the European family enterprise. Essen and Remscheid belong to representative Lutheran communities in Rhineland, one of the largest centers of German industrialization. Gustav Bohlen und Harbach, from a famous steel manufacturer family in Müngsten near Remscheid, in 1906 married the daughter of Friedrich Alfred Krupp in Essen and became the successor of the Krupp concern as Gustav Krupp von Bohlen und Harbach. (I believe Dr. Brockstedt will be discussing the case of the Krupps in detail.) It is not only in India that the religious element has played a decisive role for the formation of family enterprise.

Lastly, generally speaking, the two institutions "family" and "enterprise" can be connected with each other in different ways, in different regions, in different periods. Although each institution is a given condition for the other, it is important for us to understand the familiar element of family enterprise through the logic of enterprise, and not the reverse. From this viewpoint, I agree totally with Mr. Ito when he presumes in the last part of his paper that efforts to consolidate the ownership dispersed through equal succession have been continuously made in different ways mainly because of the scale merits of business, but not because of the traditional idea favoring the extended family.

# Family Business in Britain:
# An Historical and Analytical Survey

Peter L. Payne
*University of Aberdeen*

## I. The Tenacity of the Family Firm in Britain

Family firms have been an integral part of British business for centuries, and their preeminence in the nation's economic institutions undoubtedly reached its peak during the classic period of the Industrial Revolution. Even during the latter half of the nineteenth century, by which time a legal structure existed which made fundamental changes in the structure of the individual enterprise possible, few firms adopted the corporate form. In contrast with the expectations of those responsible for the early Company Acts, there developed the private company (legally unrecognized until 1907) and this, it is safe to say, was initially all but indistinguishable from the family partnerships or unlimited joint-stock companies which had preceded it, the object of private registration being to obtain limited liability while retaining both the original management and the privacy of the past. Thus, until the 1880s entrepreneurs operated within organizations which show little alteration from those of their pioneering forebears. Certainly there was little movement toward the differentiation of management from ownership; toward the elongation of organizational hierarchies; toward, in effect, the emergence of the corporate economy.[1]

Following his examination of the relevant Parliamentary Papers and the files of the *Economist*, Sir John Clapham outlined those branches of British industry and commerce that were still dominated by family business in 1886–87:

All, or nearly all, the wool firms; outside Oldham, nearly all the cotton firms; and the same in linen, silk, jute, lace and hosiery. Most of the smaller, and some of the largest, engineering firms, and nearly all the cutlery and pottery firms. Brewing was a family affair. So, with certain outstanding exceptions, were the Birmingham trades and the great, perhaps the major, part of the shipbuilding industry. In housebuilding and the associated trades there were very few limited companies; few in the clothing trades; few in the food trades. . . . Merchants of all kinds had rarely 'limited' their existing firms, and the flotation of a brand new mercantile company was not easy. Add the many scores of thousands of retail business, 'unlimited' almost to a shop.[2]

Clapham's observations have largely been confirmed by more recent studies; even in the ever increasing number of partnerships being transformed into joint-stock limited liability companies by registration under the Act of 1856, the direction, management and even ownership was virtually identical with those of the former firms. In the vast majority of cases, the adoption of corporate status initially did nothing to disrupt the familial nature of British business organization.[3] Only in the public utilities, particularly the provision of gas, light and water, and in transport (railways and, to a lesser extent, shipping) was family control either eroded or given little opportunity to develop. Of the major manufacturing sectors of the economy, perhaps only cotton witnessed a diminution of family dominance and even this appears to have been confined to certain geographical localities such as Oldham.[4]

Not until the great boom of the early 1870s can there be discerned any significant relaxation of the grip of the partnership. Companies involved in coal mining and iron making led the way. A need for fixed capital beyond the accumulated wealth of the founders and their successors, many of whom wished to withdraw from active participation in the firms that had been instrumental in creating their fortunes, coupled with a desire to reduce their financial responsibilities when the inevitable reaction to the boom set in, brought about the formation of a host of limited companies in coal and iron, shipbuilding and engineering, chemicals and textiles. With a number of important exceptions, most of these companies were "conversions"; that is, cases in which the original members of family partnerships sold their firms, as going concerns, to limited companies, and in payment received an overwhelming proportion of the ordinary share capital. Thus, as Cottrell has emphasized, "although the number of public companies grew, this development did not lead to 'outside' shareholders gaining control of the assets. The equity, which carried voting rights, remained in the hands of the vendors whereas extra funds were raised at the time of conversions, or subsequently, by the issues of either preference shares or debentures. . . By issuing such non-voting securities to 'outside' investors, the management group of a converted company [invariably the members of the original proprietorial family] . . . could continue to control it in an unfettered way and thus were in the same position as the shareholders of a private limited company."[5]

Even the very large mergers that took place in branches of the textile industry and in brewing, iron and steel, cement, wallpaper and tobacco at the close of the nineteenth century often failed greatly to weaken the hold of the founding families, so high a proportion of the issued share capital was retained by the vendors.[6] If to these important companies be added the enormous number of private companies being created at the turn of the century, in which there continued the *complete* marriage of ownership and control characteristic of earlier epochs,[7] the remarkable tenacity of the family firm in Britain's economy is revealed.

Superficially, little change took place in the inter-war period. As the work of Professor Hannah has shown, although there was a perceptible increase in the separation of ownership and control in the largest companies in the decades following the end of the First World War, this had "not progressed far enough to displace founding or family directors from company boards; 110 of the 200 largest firms in 1919, or 55 per cent, had family board members, as did 140, or 70 per cent, in 1930 and 119, or 59.5 per cent, in 1948."[8] Although it should be emphasized that the mere persistence of family names on the board does not *necessarily* mean that they exercised a dominant role in direction and management, there is little doubt that in several sectors, particularly in brewing, shipbuilding and food, founding families retained much power.[9] And if this was so in the case of the *largest* firms, how much more is it true of what the late Professor P.

TABLE 1   Owner-managership and Controlling Interests in Small Firms.

(a)   Number of partners or shareholders having a controlling interest

|  | 1 | 2 | 3–5 | 6–10 | 11 and over | All |
|---|---|---|---|---|---|---|
|  | | | Percentage of small firms | | | |
| Manufacturing | 39.4 | 46.3 | 13.0 | 0.8 | 0.5 | 100.0 |
| Non-manufacturing | 42.0 | 46.6 | 10.0 | 0.5 | 1.0 | 100.0 |

(b)   Number of working partners or shareholders

|  | 1 | 2 | 3–5 | 6–10 | 11 and over | All |
|---|---|---|---|---|---|---|
|  | | | Percentage of small firms | | | |
| Manufacturing | 20.8 | 45.9 | 29.9 | 2.2 | 1.2 | 100.0 |
| Non-manufacturing | 25.2 | 44.8 | 27.4 | 1.3 | 1.3 | 100.0 |

Source:   *Bolton Report*, pp. 6–7, based on Bolton Committee Postal Questionnaire Survey, Research Report No. 17.

Sargant Florence called the medium and smaller large companies.[10] And below these were the thousands of small public companies and tens of thousands of companies which by 1938 had virtually superceded the sole proprietorship and the small partnership in manufacturing activity.[11]

Despite the profound changes in the British economy since the end of the Second World War, the family business continues to play an important role, though its relative significance is certainly diminishing.[12] A number of recent studies have shed considerable light on the *small* firm and it is apparent that many concerns so categorized are as much family businesses as their historical predecessors.[13] In their internal structures and control mechanisms they are almost identical to the archetypal firms of the Industrial Revolution. Those small firms[14] who responded to the Bolton Inquiry in 1969–70 were "almost exclusively under their proprietors' control and a large proportion of them were family businesses of one sort or another":

Over 85 per cent of respondent [firms] are controlled and almost certainly owned by one or two people; this was true for both manufacturing and non-manufacturing. A further 13 per cent (in manu-

TABLE 2   Family Ownership of Small Firms (By Percentages).

| Ownership Type | Manu-facturing | Con-struction | Wholesale | Motor Trade | Retail |
|---|---|---|---|---|---|
| First generation family | 18 ⎫ 38 | 11 ⎫ 44 | 46 ⎫ 69 | 35 ⎫ 49 | 49 ⎫ 68 |
| Second or greater generation family | 20 ⎭ | 33 ⎭ | 23 ⎭ | 14 ⎭ | 19 ⎭ |
| Non-family and family/ non-family shared | 62 | 56 | 31 | 51 | 32 |
| Total | 100 | 100 | 100 | 100 | 100 |
| Number of Firms | 126 | 36 | 113 | 109 | 128 |

Source:   Merrett Cyriax Associates, *Dynamics of Small Firms*, Research Report for the Bolton Committee, No. 12, p. 11.

facturing) are controlled by three, four or five people. Generally speaking the larger the firm the more dispersed the ownership. As a result, although in manufacturing only about a fifth of firms are wholly owned by one person, in the retail trades proprietorship predominates . . . . The majority [of small firms] are managed by those having a controlling interest, usually the founder or members of his family. In 81 per cent of small firms in manufacturing the 'boss' was the founder of the business or a member of the founder's family and over a third of all small manufacturing businesses and over two thirds in the distributive trades are wholly owned by first, second or third generations of the same family [See Tables 1 and 2].[15]

But it is not these saplings in the forest, as the economist Alfred Marshall might have described them, that are our principal concern on this occasion;[16] our attention has been explicitly directed to the larger organizational units. In this category, although family businesses have survived they are now powerful in very few sectors of economic activity. In 1951 Florence indicated that perhaps a third of Britain's very large companies (those with issued capitals of £3 million and more) were still owner-controlled and thus capable, to varying degrees, of being designated family business. But within little more than a decade several of these giant concerns ceased to qualify as such. Among them were Associated Electrical Industries, the Bristol Aeroplane Company, J. & J. Colman Ltd. and Bovril. Furthermore, the trend against familial ownership evident in the largest firms is equally apparent in Florence's next size

TABLE 3    Percentage Distribution of Family and Non-family Companies by Degree of Diversification.

| Category | 1950 No. of Companies F (Percent) | 1950 No. of Companies Non-F (Percent) | 1960 No. of Companies F (Percent) | 1960 No. of Companies Non-F (Percent) | 1970 No. of Companies F (Percent) | 1970 No. of Companies Non-F (Percent) |
|---|---|---|---|---|---|---|
| Single Product | 36 | 31 | 24 | 15 | 7 | 6 |
| Dominant Product | 44 | 36 | 41 | 33 | 40 | 31 |
| Related Product | 18 | 31 | 33 | 45 | 50 | 56 |
| Unrelated Product | 2 | 2 | 2 | 7 | 3 | 7 |
| Total | 100 | 100 | 100 | 100 | 100 | 100 |
| Sample Size | 50 | 42 | 42 | 54 | 30* | 70 |

Notes:    * See Table 3a.
Source:    Channon, *Strategy and Structure*, p. 76.


TABLE 3a    The Companies Exhibiting "Significant Elements of Family Control" Included the Following:

| | Structure | | |
|---|---|---|---|
| *Single Product Companies*[1] : | | | |
| International Distillers and Vintners | F/HC | (M) | Wines and spirits, manufacture and distribution. |
| Watney Mann | F | | Brewing, public houses, hotels, entertainment. |
| *Dominant Product Companies:* | | | |
| Pilkington Brothers* | M.D. | (M) | Glass |
| Ford Motor | M.D. | (M) | Automobiles |
| Swan Hunter* | M.D. | | Shipbuilding |
| I.B.M. | M.D. | (M) | Computers |
| *Related Product:* | | | |
| *Food* | | | |
| Associated British Foods | M.D. | | |
| Brooke Bond Liebig | M.G. | (M) | |
| Cadbury/Schweppes* | M.D. | (M) | |
| J. Lyons* | M.D. | | |
| Mars | M.D. | (F) | |
| Rank Hovis McDougall* | M.D. | (M) | |
| Spillers | M.D. | | |
| *Materials and Glass* | | | |
| Marley Tile* | F | (M) | |
| *Engineering* | | | |
| John Brown | H.C. | | |

*Electrical and Electronic Engineering*

| | | |
|---|---|---|
| Plessey* | M.D. | (M) |
| Phillips (U.K.) | M.D. | (F)(M) |
| Thorn Electric* | M.D. | (M) |

*Textiles and Clothing*

| | | |
|---|---|---|
| Coats Patons* | H.C. | (M) |

*Paper and Packaging*

| | | |
|---|---|---|
| Dickinson Robinson* | M.D. | (M) |
| Thomson Organization* | M.D. | (M) |

*Unrelated Product:*

| | | |
|---|---|---|
| Reckitt & Coleman | M.D. | (M) |

Key:    F = Functional
    M.D. = Multidivisional
    H.C. = Holding Company
    (M) = Multinational
    (F) = Subsidiary company controlled by a non-British parent company.
    * = Classified as owner-controlled by Nyman and Silberston in 1976 because of shareholdings of "directors and their families" or by the Chairman or Managing Director being either the founder, his family or descendants.

Notes:  1  Shortly after Derek F. Channon compiled his list, I.D.V. was acquired by Watney Mann, which in turn was acquired by Grand Metropolitan Hotels, itself "owner-controlled."

Sources:  Derek F. Channon, *The Strategy and Structure of British Enterprise*, pp. 52–63, supplemented by a personal communication to the author, 18 November, 1982.

S. Nyman and A. Silberston, "The Ownership and Control of Industry," *Oxford Economic Papers*, N. S. Vol. XXX (1978), pp. 74–101, supplemented by additional data referred to on p. 84, note 2.

category—the "medium large" concerns with capitals between £1 million and £3 million. Only among companies smaller still was control by the owner still characteristic of the majority of enterprises.[17]

Yet Channon, in perhaps the most penetrating of recent inquiries into the structure of British enterprise, was still able to discern a substantial number of "family" companies within his sample population of the largest British manufacturing firms in 1969/70. Finding, as others have done both before and after his analysis, that "the pattern of share ownership was not in reality an entirely meaningful measure of family control," he deemed it necessary to adopt a more rigorous definition:

A company was . . . termed family controlled if a family member
was the chief executive officer, if there had been at least two generations of family control, and if a minimum of 5 per cent of the voting stock was still held by the family or trust interests associated
with it.[18]

Using these criteria, Channon found that no less than fifty out of 92
companies in his sample had been controlled by families in 1950
and that even by 1970 thirty of the 100 companies "still contained
*significant elements* of family control" (See Table 3). And, in a study
completed six years after Channon's investigation, Steve Nyman
and Aubrey Silberston identified 126 companies among the largest
250 enterprises in the United Kingdom as being "owner controlled,"
of which 77 (or, say, 30 per cent of the total) exhibited significant
elements of family control either by virtue of the shareholdings of
the "directors and their families" (62) or because the company
chairman or managing director was a relation of the firm's founder
or his family (15).[19] In such firms, men bearing the family name
continued to occupy directoral seats and to wield considerable
power however diluted their personal ownership of the company had
become.[20] Furthermore, among the ranks of the unquoted private
companies in 1970 were to be found a number of very large businesses in which entrepreneurial power remained almost totally with
the owner-managers: with the Ferrantis in electrical engineering,
the McAlpines in construction, the Moores (Littlewoods) and the
Sainsburys in retailing, the Lithgows in shipbuilding, the Brintons
in carpets, the Clarks in footwear and the Vesteys in the meat trade.[21]

  But are these *large* firms which display, in varying degrees, elements of family control the last of their kind? Are they the survivors
of a once numerous and powerful species doomed, if not to extinction,
to play an ever decreasing role in the British economy? I suspect so.
My reason is this. The large-scale business organization which now
dominate so many sectors of the economy operate within an environment fundamentally different from that which existed even as
recently as 1945.[22] The degree of industrial concentration is remarkably high in Britain: the large firms are very large.[23] Furthermore, since it would appear that large, medium and small firms
grow on average by the same proportionate amount (Gibrat's Law),

the concentration of output in the larger firms will doubtless increase.[24] But in this growth process those firms which retain significant elements of family control and management will be at a disadvantage compared with their more "corporate" counterparts, for family firms are increasingly unlikely to be able to grow at the same rate as the latter unless they increase diversification, permit "outside" capital to come into the firm and relax "leadership by inheritance." Hence, only by divesting themselves of those very characteristics which distinguish "family firms" from giant "public" firms will the former be able to successfully compete in the growth race.[25] The conclusion must be that if a family firm chooses to remain of this category, its relative importance within its own industrial or commercial sector must decline; if it chooses to grow, it has little option but to cease to be a "family" firm.[26] Either way, the family firm in the British economy seems destined to be relegated or confined to the medium or even small size range.[27]

Despite their declining relative significance in the British economy as a whole—not least because of the spread of the multinational company and the nationalization of the coal industry (1947) and much of the iron and steel (1967) and shipbuilding (1977) industries—it is apparent that a number of "family firms" are still to be found among the largest individual enterprises in certain fields of activity. How have these firms managed to survive and grow when it is arguable that, generally speaking, the familial character of firms seems to be inversely correlated with the size of the unit (measured by total assets or by sales)? Is it possible to be more specific in outlining the process of change from the family firm to the large-scale corporate concern? Is this transformation to be explained in terms of efforts to overcome the managerial constraints to the growth of the firm? Has the persistence of the family firm been prejudicial to the nation's economic growth? It is to questions such as this that we must turn, but first it is imperative to survey the timing of the separation of ownership from control in British business and the nature of the different control systems exhibited by firms of different size.

## II.  The Management Structure and Changing Nature of the British Family Firm

The *small* firms to which we have already alluded—be they those which characterized business organizations in the period of early industrialization or those which still form the majority of British firms—rarely possessed a formal management structure. To employ the words of the Bolton Committee: "small firms [were and] are simply run by their owners" (p. 6). In the family firm there was for decades rarely any need to evolve a sophisticated bureaucratic hierarchy. If growth in size necessitated some degree of functional specialization, members of the founding family or a junior unrelated partner —perhaps originally a trusted foreman—would be assigned the responsibility.[28] Not until changing technology dictated an increase in size beyond their combined resources, was it necessary to devise a new structure for the firm. Meanwhile, as Marshall wrote: "The master's eye is everywhere; there is no shirking by his foreman, no divided responsibility, no sending half understood messages backwards and forwards from one department to another."[29]

Indeed, the maintenance and exercise of personal control was regarded as so vital that the growth of the family enterprise cannot but have been inhibited. In the shipbuilding industry, for example, Professor Slaven has shown that although the growing scale of operations in the Clyde yards involved the creation of a hierarchical organization in which "operating or tactical decisions required to implement policy were clearly delegated to departmental heads and then increasingly subdivided and delegated downward in a functional ladder through supervisors, foremen, under-foremen etc. to the shop floor," at these "lower levels the guidelines controlling action . . . were so detailed and precise that decision taking and action fused together to create the impression that the decision was almost automatic and unthinking." The small, management board at the top really exercised control and this meant that severe limits were imposed on the size of the enterprise. The words of Thomas Bell, managing director of John Brown & Co. at Clydebank, to the Board of Trade Committee on Shipping and Shipbuilding in 1916, quoted by Professor Slaven, certainly have a more general applicability. "Personally I may say I am very much against developing individual works too much. It is impossible to manage them if you do. It is the personal factor and I do not care how splendid the works are; the personal factor cannot spread itself out too much."[30]

It is this " 'mechanistic [management] system,' in which authority is concentrated at the top of the organization, work is functionally specialized and organized in sub-units, and interaction between members of the concern is vertical, between superior and subordinate,"[31] that is so often found in the family firm. And it is the adoption of this system that permitted the marriage of ownership and control to prevail for so long in the British economy: whether in the industrial sector, merchandising or in the service industries such as banking and insurance.

Even the establishment of giant firms produced by the multifirm mergers in the period 1885–1905 failed in perhaps the majority of cases to produce any fundamental internal organizational changes:

> The fact that the majority of them were single-product companies, involving little integration and even less diversification, and that they were inspired by defensive motives rather than by a desire for great efficiency meant that centralized management was still possible, if not appropriate. Thus those who came out on top during the course of the internecine wars of vendor-directors of the new combinations could continue to conduct the affairs of the merged companies as if all that had happened was that what had hitherto been their own particular firms had grown larger by the multiplication of units. . . .[32]

Thus, in iron and steel and in brewing, for example, the descendants and relations of the founders continued to dominate their companies. Many of the multi-unit enterprises emerging at the turn of the century adopted a loose holding company form and remained essentially federations of family firms.[33] Some families—those whose firms constituted a minor part of an amalgamation—undoubtedly experienced a certain diminution of power, it is true, but others— those whose share of the newly created equity capital essentially gave them ultimate control of their giant firms—enhanced their positions within their industries. Members of the Coats family, for example, dominated the board of J. & P. Coats, and hence the entire thread market.

But Coats, perhaps the most efficient of all the nineteenth-century combinations, clearly evolved a highly efficient bureaucratic structure. Apparently, the board concentrated on central direction; the creation of statistical departments made possible the interchange of fully comprehensive information for the formulation of policy; departments for buying, selling, and other basic functions were established; the lines of communications between branches and the central office made explicit, and detailed accounting procedures instituted.[34] All this meant that in time professional managers were recruited: accountants, lawyers and technicians (engineers and chemists, particularly) were increasingly placed in positions of authority. The genesis of the process whereby ownership and control became divorced can be perceived even in the very large family firm. A similar example is provided by Professor Hannah:

> Before World War I . . . the names of board members, the addresses of offices, and other information listed for the United Alkali Company imply that the firm was still owned by the family that founded it, was not administered by salaried managers, put out a single product, and was organized as a holding company. . . . More detailed research indicates, however, that the number of professional managers in the higher echelons was increasing and suggests that the company was developing a more diversified range of products, was vertically integrated, was organized according to functional departments, and was centrally administered.[35]

Three conclusions are inescapable. The first is that inferences based simply upon knowledge of the names of the board members of the larger family firms are potentially misleading if it be assumed that the continued unification of ownership and control meant little or no structural change. Second, only further case studies will provide the information necessary for a proper appreciation of the organizational changes that the growth of the firm demanded. And third, it would appear that if family firms were to grow, they had to evolve internal management systems that were similar to those of their corporate counterparts. If they did not do so, their growth was stunted, limited to a level lower than might otherwise have been possible and economically desirable.

Following his analysis of large British companies in 1936–51, Florence concluded that "it looks as though control by personal or family

TABLE 4 Distribution of Family and Non-family Companies and Number with Multidivisional Structures.

| Category | 1950 No. (M.D.No.) | | 1960 No. (M.D.No.) | | 1970 No. (M.D.No.) | |
|---|---|---|---|---|---|---|
| | F | Non-F | F | Non-F | F | Non-F |
| Single product | 18(0) | 13(2) | 10(0) | 8(3) | 2(0) | 4(1) |
| Dominant product | 22(2) | 15(2) | 17(2) | 18(6) | 12(8) | 22(17) |
| Unrelated and related product | 10(3) | 14(4) | 15(8) | 28(13) | 16(13) | 44(34) |
| Total | 50(5) | 42(8) | 42(10) | 54(22) | 30(21) | 70(52) |

Source: Channon, *Strategy and Structure*, p. 76.

ownership [is] not possible beyond a certain size of company."[36] If this observation proves to be correct, then the explanation for the diminishing importance of the family firm becomes clearer. With the growth of giant firms in twentieth century Britain—recently investigated by Dr. S. J. Prias and Professor Hannah[37]—the relative significance of those firms which retain elements of family control has inevitably declined. The evolution of their organizational structures has been slower than their corporate counterparts (see Table 4); their reluctance to go to the market for capital and their inability to raise the funds necessary for expansion from alternative sources (by profit retention, or by familial connections and contacts or by bank loans) has retarded growth. Only in certain, increasingly limited, sectors of activity can they retain some vestige of their previous predominance. Furthermore, I believe it would be accurate to say that even those large family firms that have survived are not really comparable with those of even a few decades ago. They may exhibit, as Channon has phrased it, "significant elements of family control,"[38] but among *large firms*, the family firm characteristic of the nineteenth century—even of the inter-war period—no longer exists. Family firms are essentially confined to the medium or small size categories, many of them having consciously decided not to expand.

Family firms, proud of their individualism, wary of outsiders both at board and senior management levels, and anxious to restrict their growth to the level made possible by the retention of profits, were reluctant to follow the lead of their corporate counterparts who, by

the adoption of the multidivisional form, were slowly pushing back
the barriers of the managerial diseconomies of scale. This issue has
been well surveyed by Professor Hannah in his study *The Rise of the
Corporate Economy*. Obsessed by a belief that potential mergers and a
larger scale of operations would lead to a loss of personal dominance
and control, many family-owned firms chose to spurn the opportunities implicit in enhanced size. Perhaps the best documented case
is that of Kenricks, the Midland hardware firm whose records have
been analyzed by Professor Roy Church.[39] Advised in 1937 by their
management consultants, Peat, Marwick, Mitchell & Co., to seek
a merger with their rivals and thoroughly to overhaul and strengthen
the company's management and administration, the recommendations were rejected because to have implemented them would have
"change[d] entirely the character of the business as one controlled
and managed by the principal owners, which had been its constitution from the beginning."[40]

Even without the goad of a management consultant's report, there
must have been many family firms who were forced to acknowledge
the deficiencies of their own organizations but who chose not to
embark on structural change because it was so repugnant to the
boards whose families had for generations owned and controlled the
business and who viewed "with disfavour the [idea] of appointing
from outside the family a stranger [to] an important position of
control."[41] How else can the slower diversification of family-controlled companies and their obvious reluctance to adopt the multidivisional structure, even in the recent past,[42] be explained?

Frequently, some traumatic experience (such as the death or
retirement of a family leader or the dying out of a branch of a dominant family because of a failure to produce male heirs) was required
to induce structural reorganization,[43] though even here it would
appear that unless some widening of the firm's product range by diversification had already taken place(or was necessary for continued
survival) it was likely that fundamental change would be resisted.[44]
And not the least reason for this refusal to change and to cling on to
their own little businesses was "the feudal idea of handing it on to
their family."[45] In such cases can be perceived manifestations of
Chandler's original dictum that strategy dictates structure, and fur-

ther illustrations of the fact that the more family concerns grow, the more they are forced to divest themselves of the characteristics of the true family firm, in which "the whole of the capital . . . is privately held, practically all the important and administrative posts are filled by members of the family, and in which there are no employees in positions of real authority."[46]

With this caveat in mind, a number of large "family businesses" continue to survive in Britain today. They are to be found in the food and drink industries, glass, electrical and electronics components, publishing and printing, construction, carpets, shipping, retailing and other service industries. But, where the details are known, the majority of them increasingly resemble their corporate counterparts. Pilkingtons, until only recently Britain's largest private company in which authority was highly concentrated within a small family caucus, was forced to go to the market to raise the funds necessary for expansion and diversification in 1970 and become a public company. Much of the stock remained in family hands and members of the Pilkington family continued to play a highly important role in the firm, but the adoption of a multidivisional structure in 1969 and the increasing introduction of non-family directors from the mid-1960's, "seem likely to result in an eventual loss of family control."[47]

At Guiness, the brewers, the company may be family-owned and controlled at board level, but there is apparently little family intervention in management. For well over fifty years the running of the business has been left largely to carefully chosen outsiders. Indeed, "the last member of the Guiness family who was managing director of the company . . . retired in 1902." The internal structure retains a holding company form and the pursuit of the maximum profit does not appear to be a major policy objective.[48] Nor does it at Brintons carpets, John Laings, the second largest construction company in Britain, or Ferrantis, the electronics firm, if the utterances of the chairmen of these companies are anything to go by.[49]

Although some of the major family businesses have grown rapidly in size in recent years (e.g. Marks and Spencer,[50] Marley Tiles), others have chosen to eschew the maximum rate of growth rather than go to the stock market or to open their board rooms to outsiders. Sebastian de Ferranti would "sooner become smaller than raise public money," and at Wates and at McAlpines, the building and construction firms, there is evidence that expansion has been restricted until family partners were available to supervise new contracts or take on new responsibilities.[51]

Such examples could be multiplied, though really hard information is difficult to obtain. They would merely illustrate, I suspect, some of the generalizations made earlier in this paper and would tend to confirm explanations of a continuing relative decline of family power in British industry and commerce. Even in merchant banking, a series of mergers in the early 1960's has lessened the family sovereignty once so apparent in this sector.[52] "Financial conglomerates" have emerged offering a wide range of financial services and this has necessitated structural changes, sometimes the adoption of the multidivisional form. More surprisingly perhaps, this was the organizational form favored by the new thrusting property, retailing and hotel companies which were founded only in the late 1950's and mid-1960's by men such as Charles Clore, Max Joseph, John Collier, Isaac Wolfson and Jim Slater, men who were masters at seeking the potential of a deal rather than becoming concerned with day to day operations and who therefore found a variant of the multidivisional system ideal for their purposes.[53] Thus, even in the service industries, where numerous large firms—particularly those involved with the property market—are still led by their original founding entrepreneurs (so recent is their creation), the family business is declining in relative importance and it is difficult to foresee any reversal of this powerful trend.

## III. The Family Firm and Economic Development

### 1. The Charge against the Family Firm

Perhaps the neatest summary of the role of the family firm in a nation's economic development is that provided by Kindleberger, published nearly two decades ago in his *Economic Growth in France and Britain, 1851–1950*. Drawing on the pioneering work of David Landes, John Sawyer and Jesse Pitts, the French family firm, Kindleberger comments:

is said to have sinned against economic efficiency, and hence against growth, by limiting expansion—failing both to extend into new markets when finance was available from internal funds and to seek outside funds when these were required for expansion. Mergers were shunned so as not to get involved with 'others.' Public sale of stock was avoided. When expansion was possible through inside funds, it frequently took the form of purchase of discrete units of limited size, with their markets, to provide an outlet for the energies of other scions of the family; or there would be vertical integration but without the cost accounting that might enable effective control of the verious units. Recruiting was undertaken from within the family, except for faithful retainers who assisted the firm against the revolutionary working force.[54]

This general thesis was not without its critics. Alexander Gerschenkron was perhaps the most penetrating, and one cannot but agree with him that to accept its validity one is forced "to overlook vast and significant fields of French entrepreneurial endeavour, such as railroads, mines, iron and steel industry, automobile production, banks and department stores."[55] Taking a comparative view, Habakkuk argued that the family firm in Britain was in fact not only compatible with rapid economic progress but its main agent.[56] The importance of this argument warrants further investigation over a longer time span.

The foremost difficulty encountered in such an examination is that of accurate generalization. Is the typical family firm in textiles during the Industrial Revolution, for example, to be found among those founded by M'Connel and Kennedy, Robert Peel, Jedidiah Strutt, Benjamin Gott and John Marshall, all of whom were thrusting, highly successful and innovative, or among the Needhams of Litton, the Austins of Wotton-under-Edge, John Cartwright of Retford or William Lupton of Leeds, all of whose concerns suffered from serious entrepreneurial failings coupled with gross management?[57] Later, in the mid-nineteenth century, very different conclusions might be drawn concerning the role of the family firm in, for example, the iron industry if these findings were to be based on a collection of firms that included Joshua Walker & Co., John Darwin, Lloyd, Foster & Co. and the Crawshays of Cyfarthfa, all of whose businesses were either wound up or suffered significant decline,[58] or based upon such infinitely more successful firms as those owned and controlled by the Guests of Dowlais, J. P. Budd of Ynyscedwyn, the Dixons of Calder and Govan and the Wrights of Butterley.[59] It is unnecessary to labor this point. It does, however, illustrate the dangers involved in "arguing by example" and raises the crucial question of whether an enterprise whose existence is essentially confined to the tenure of the founding proprietor is in any real sense a *family* firm.

## 2. The Family Firm and the British Economy since 1870: The Third Generation Argument

Nevertheless, there can be little doubt that the family firm was the vehicle whereby the Industrial Revolution was accomplished. To that extent Habakkuk's belief that the British family firm has been an important engine of economic progress is incontrovertible. The issue that deserves further discussion and, for its resolution, much more intensive research[60] is whether the persistence of the family firm had some causal connection with the apparent loss of economic vitality and retardation in economic growth during the closing decades of the nineteenth century.[61] The verdict of David Landes will be familiar:

> In many [family] firms, the grandfather who started the business and built it by unremitting application and by thrift bordering on miserliness had long since died; the father who took over a solid enterprise and, starting with larger ambitions, raised it to undreamed-of heights, had passed on the reins; now it was the turn of the third generation, the children of affluence, tired of the tedium of trade and flushed with the bucolic aspirations of the country gentlemen. . . Many of them retired and forced the conversion of their firms into joint-stock companies. Others stayed on and went through the motions of entrepreneurship between the long weekends; they worked at play and played at work. . . . Nor were corporate enterprises significantly better. For one thing, family considerations often determined the selection of managing personnel.[62]

In discussing this resounding passage elsewhere,[63] I was concerned to draw attention to what I believed were the weaknesses of Landes' condemnation of British entrepreneurship. My argument on that occasion need not be repeated, but one fundamental issue raised by Landes is highly germane to the subject of this conference. It is whether the typical British family firm did, in fact, exhibit the cycle depicted by Landes: an energetic, aggressive and dedicated founder, followed by a son who expanded the thriving business he had inherited and who in turn was succeeded by the founder's grandchildren, the "children of affluence," who let the business decline. It is highly improbable.

The fact *seems* to be that very few family firms survived long enough to permit a member of the third generation to wreck such havoc upon a hitherto successful enterprise. True, there are examples; the best known being the Marshalls of Leeds, a firm which had been the world's leading concern in flax-spinning in the opening decades of the nineteenth century but which, by the 1880s, had passed into receivership, after the founder's sons had neglected the business and their own sons in turn despised it.[64] Other cases undoubtedly exist—one such was the business established by Benjamin Gott[65]—but firms conforming to the Landes model are suspiciously hard to find. Furthermore, there are notable exceptions to what has been called the "Buddenbrook syndrome." The Pilkington family in glass, the Yarrows in shipbuilding, the Stewarts in steel, the Coats in textiles, are examples of families who continued successfully to play a major role in their firms beyond the third generation.[66]

But these too are almost certainly exceptional. Much more numerous and representative are, I suspect, firms in which the founders' *sons*, not grandsons, choose not to follow in their father's footsteps. Witness a Hawick minister castigating the local tweedmakers in 1909:

> We [have] had many men chiefly in the founders of our businessmen not afraid of very hard work, keeping pleasure in its place, sticking fast to their posts. In the *second generation*, however, we have often seen a different spirit; sometimes contempt for trades, an aping of the fine gentleman, an aspiring to be what they were not . . . love of ease, self indulgence and lack of grit and backbone. They must work in the spirit of their fathers . . . study the technique of their business, bend their energies and talents in one direction.[67]

Such examples are legion, as are cases in which the very founders of highly successful firms display waning entrepreneurial energies as soon as sufficient wealth has been amassed to permit them to participate in local or national politics, to assume largely ceremonial public duties, to purchase and enjoy a country estate, and to indulge in manifold sporting activities: the turf, hunting, shooting and fishing, and yachting were all pursuits of the gentleman.[68]

## 3.  Age and Ownership Statistics

However inconclusive, discussion of the third-generation argument does emphasize the desirability of discovering just how many firms remained under the control of the same family for three generations and what proportion of the total number of firms in any industrial, commercial or service sector they constituted. Indeed, just how many firms—even in the early nineteenth century—would qualify as "family companies" under Channon's definition if it were to be applied to periods earlier than that (1950–1970) with which he was concerned?

The partnership in the early period of British industrialization was an infinitely adaptable organizational form. Partnerships appear to have been created, supplemented, remodelled and frequently terminated when conditions called for change. Partnership agreements rarely lasted their full term, which was in any case, frequently only about seven years in duration. Thus, a partnership created in 1825 to establish an iron foundry called, say, Smith, Campbell & Co., with John Smith as the senior partner, might within a decade or so (and after several intermediate transformations) be owned and controlled by the nephew of the original junior partner, Bruce Campbell, and his cousin Forbes McRae, in company with two new men who had earlier been trusted employees in the casting shop and the cash room. Furthermore, by 1845 the business could well have integrated backwards and come to own two blast furnaces. The reason for providing this hypothetical example is to ask whether Campbell, McRae & Co., iron masters, is the same firm as Smith, Campbell & Co., foundrymen? Or has the changing nature of the firm's principal activities and the different composition of the firm's ownership and management created an entirely new enterprise? Problems such as this are often encountered in British business history and bedevil quantitative analysis.

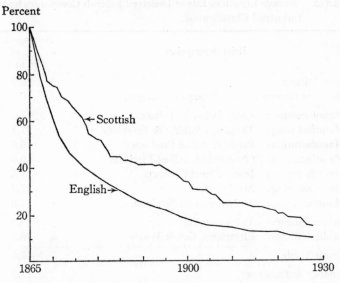

Fig. 1 Percentage Survival of English and Scottish Companies Incorporated between 1956 and 1865.
Source: Payne, *The Early Scottish Limited Companies*, p. 38.

The fact is that we do not possess an age pyramid for nineteenth century firms. All that we know is that the mortality rate of firms was remarkably high[69] and one cannot help suspecting that only a very small proportion of firms created and continued by deed of partnership survived more than thirty years, a period insufficiently long to sustain more than two generations of a founding family. But what of the incorporated company: the company registered with limited liability under the Joint Stock Act of 1856? Could it be that the benefits bestowed by such legislation, particularly the advantage that an incorporated company need not be wound up following the death of a partner, resulted in a more lengthy life span and thus facilitated the establishment and continuance of family dynasties? An analysis of the early Scottish joint-stock companies points to a positive answer to this question.[70] Although the *average* length of life of the first three thousand companies registered under the Act of 1856 was only sixteen years, the use of the mean conceals a wide distribution. Despite the high infant mortality of Scottish companies, about

TABLE 5   Average Length of Life of Dissolved Scottish Companies by Selected Industrial Classification.

| Brief description | | Average length of life in years |
|---|---|---|
| Coal Mining | | 20.9 |
| Overseas Companies in Mining & Quarrying | | 6.4 |
| Manufacturing: | Food, Drink & Tobacco | 17.2 |
| Manufacturing: | Textiles, Clothing & Footwear | 21.1 |
| Manufacturing: | Paper & Allied Products | 16.6 |
| Manufacturing: | Chemicals & Allied Products | 10.0 |
| Manufacturing: | Iron & Steel Products | 14.8 |
| Manufacturing: | Machinery | 12.7 |
| Manufacturing: | Transportation Equipment | 11.9 |
| Public Utilities: | Transportation | 13.4 |
| Public Utilities: | Electricity, Gas & Water | 36.1 |
| Retail Trade | | 13.6 |
| Finance & Insurance | | 17.7 |
| Real Estate | | 24.9 |
| Agricultural, Forestry & Fishing | | 13.6 |
| All Dissolved Companies | | 16.4 |

Source:   Payne, *The Early Scottish Limited Companies*, p. 101.

25 per cent of those formed between 1856 and 1865 were still in existence on the eve of the First World War and about 12.5 per cent on the eve of the Second World War. For London-registered companies the figures are approximately 13 per cent and 8 per cent, respectively[71] (see Fig. 1). Although a disproportionate number of the long lived companies were public utility companies, a number of important firms in manufacturing and the service industries did enjoy a relatively long life (see Table 5) and it is almost certain that among them were a few family firms. What the information contained in the company files at West Register House, Edinburgh, did not reveal was just how many could accurately be so described. I would *guess* that of those companies surviving forty years or more, family firms constituted less than one per cent of the total. It is to be hoped that the data being collected by the Company Archives Survey being conducted by the Business Archives Council in London may provide more information on this subject.

TABLE 6   Number of Generations in which Founding or Investing Families Hold Top Offices in Steel Firms.

| Number of generations of family control | Number of cases | Percentage of cases |
|---|---|---|
| No family managing and owning | 14 | 18 |
| One generation | 9 | 11 |
| Two generations | 38 | 47 |
| Three generations | 12 | 15 |
| Four or more generations | 7 | 9 |
| Total | 80 | 100 |

Source:   Erickson, *British Industrialists*, p. 53.

Meanwhile, we still have Professor Charlotte Erickson's very interesting data on the steel industry. In her pioneering study in the 1950s (i.e. before the nationalization of the industry) she found that it was possible to trace the duration of family control in eighty firms. "The founding families were still represented at Butterley, John Summers, Stewart and Lloyds, United Steel, Dorman Long, and Partridge, Jones." She also discovered that "frequently the family which [continued] into the third and fourth generation is not that of the founder of founders of the firms but a family of later investors" and that a number of "what might be called 'bureaucratic dynasties' [had] been established in a number of public companies in the industry. The father, having worked his way up within the firm, was able to ease his son's career within the same firm . . . . Thus the establishment of a family dynasty in the steel industry was not always the result of founding or investing in the firm. Two generations of the same family, whose role was primarily managerial rather than proprietary, have controlled some companies and, in part, account for the continued presence of 'family careers' in the industry." Table 6 shows that in thirty-eight of Professor Erickson's cases, a founding or investing family lost or gave up control after two generations. "The mean duration of family influence was 66.4 ±40 years."[72]

It will be appreciated that Professor Erickson was concerned with an industry notorious for its family control.[73] It would therefore be unwise and illegitimate to extend her findings to other sectors of the British economy.[74] Nevertheless, Erickson's work does suggest the question that if family influence in steel lasted but two generations,

TABLE 7   Average Ages (in years) of Small Firms in 1963.

|  | Oldest Quartile | Median | Youngest Quartile |
|---|---|---|---|
| Manufacturing | 51 | 22 | 10 |
| Construction | 93 | 69 | 44 |
| Wholesale Trades | 66 | 29 | 10 |
| Motor Trades | 35 | 19 | 9 |
| Retail Trades | 47 | 19 | 7 |

Source:   Merrett Cyriax Associates, *Dynamics of Small Firms*, Research Report for the
Bolton Committee, No. 12, p. 12; amended by the Bolton Committee, whose
figures are cited (*Report*, p. 7).

how much shorter must have been the domination of the family in
large public companies in other spheres of activity? At the other
end of the age spectrum, the period of family ownership and control,
which was probably relatively short during early industrialization,
*may* have lengthened during the course of the twentieth century. It is
conceivable that the adoption of corporate status coupled with a
rate of growth slow enough to permit continued management by
members of the founding family, has enhanced the prospects for
survival of individual small family firms. Certainly, the information
collected for the Bolton Committee indicates this possibility. The
admittedly fragile data are given in Tables 2 and 7. These show that
half of those small firms that are wholly owned by one family are in
the hands of the second or third generation. In manufacturing
industries, half of small firms in 1963 were over 22 years old; in non-
manufacturing the median ages ranged from 69 years in construction to 19 in motor trades. The authors of the Bolton Report do note,
however, that "the age of a company may be misleading in this
context since it may change hands after its foundation."[75]

   Certainly, the average ages given in Table 7 could well have
been appreciably lower had the firms founded between 1963 and
1970 been included and those that had ceased to operate during
these seven years been omitted. What is disappointing is that we
have no similar statistics for an earlier period with which to compare
these figures. However, we do have a detailed study by Jonathan
Boswell, again of *small* firms, which is somewhat more detailed than
that of the research associates reporting to the Bolton Committee.
Boswell's "Companies House Study"[76] found, *inter alia*, that (i)

TABLE 8   The Performance of Independent Firms:   Medians by Age of Firm, 1967 and 1968 (Figures in Percentages).

| Measures of performance | Year | Firms Founded | | | | |
|---|---|---|---|---|---|---|
| | | Pre-1870 | 1870–99 | 1900–18 | 1914–44 | Post-1945 |
| Asset Growth | 1967 | 1.7 | 2.4 | 3.9 | 4.3 | 8.4 |
| | 1968 | 0.8 | 1.2 | 3.7 | 5.9 | 15.3 |
| Sales Growth | 1968 | 3.1 | 10.1 | 3.5 | 7.3 | 8.0 |
| Gross Profitability | 1967 | 13.2 | 18.4 | 15.4 | 20.1 | 21.8 |
| | 1968 | 11.8 | 17.2 | 15.9 | 19.8 | 25.5 |
| Net Profitability | 1967 | 7.4 | 9.5 | 7.9 | 15.7 | 15.2 |
| | 1968 | 6.9 | 8.7 | 10.8 | 13.1 | 15.5 |

Source:   Boswell, *Small Firms*, p. 245.

founder-run firms were above average in nearly every measure of performance; (ii) the firms run by late inheritors (i.e. third and subsequent generations) performed worst; (iii) in terms of age, the younger firms appeared to perform better in every way (see Table 8).

Taken in conjunction with the earlier discussion, these scattered data suggest that the founders of firms, whether they are partnerships, private joint-stock companies or public companies, are perhaps generally more thrusting and efficient than their successors in managing their businesses. This is not a startling conclusion but it may be vital in evaluating the role of family firms in promoting economic growth, for if it proves to be valid for all time periods, then it indicates that what is of the greatest significance for the promotion of growth is not so much the *form* of company structure as the ability of the founder,[77] the quality of the management, the number of firms coming into existence in any time period and the nature of their activities. Since nearly all founders of firms inevitably start on a relatively small scale, what is important for economic growth is that a legal and financial environment favorable for the *birth* of firms be encouraged. This is because small firms—which almost by definition are *initially* family firms—"provide the means of entry into business for new entrepreneurial talent and the seedbed from which new large companies will grow to challenge and stimulate the established leaders of industry."[78]

## IV.  Conclusions

Any conclusions that may be drawn from this brief, exploratory survey must be regarded as highly tentative. Greater confidence can only come with the collection and analysis of more data, but even this will fail to clarify the role of the family firm in the development of the British economy unless the "family firm" is carefully defined. If nothing else emerges from this study it will at least be apparent that the family firm today is, except in the small size range, a very different creature from the family firm in the decades preceding the First World War.

Nevertheless, I would agree with Professor Habakkuk that the family firm in Britain has been, and has the potential to continue to be (albeit on a somewhat lesser scale), an engine of economic growth, but paradoxically this is largely because the overwhelming majority of individual family firms in Britain did not and do not enjoy a particularly great longevity. Their importance was and is to serve as a vehicle for the exercise of entrepreneurial energies of the founder and frequently his sons. After this there would on balance appear to have been a marked diminution of drive and business ability. Now this does not seem to have had any markedly deleterious effect in the nineteenth century since very few firms passed into the hands of the third and subsequent generations. Only with the coming of the joint-stock company with limited liability did the life span of firms tend to increase sufficiently to make this possible on an appreciable scale, but since this change in the legal form of the company coincided with the steady advance of professional management recruited from outside the existing firm, its harmful effect was minimized.

It is true that in several branches of activity—steel, coal, pottery, carpets, boots and shoes, cocoa, brewing, sugar and certain types of engineering—"leadership by inheritance" has been discerned,[79] but even here it was by no means as prevalent and stultifying as once was believed.[80] I would argue that if there was any causal connection between the family firm and a loss of economic vitality, it occurred not in the closing decades of the nineteenth century but in the inter-war years when a number of holding companies were still sufficiently familial in nature, being essentially federations of family firms, to be reluctant to adopt a centralized structure and to create a managerial staff that would have permitted them more easily to overcome the diseconomies of size.[81] Indeed, even after 1945 those companies which contained significant elements of family control have been less willing to diversify and more reluctant to adopt a multidivisional organization structure.[82] Put very crudely, the *large* public company which retains elements of family control may retard economic growth; whereas, on balance, the *small* family business positively promotes economic growth.

Lastly, bearing in mind the exceptions to the idea that family management constituted a brake on economic development, it is necessary to emphasize the strong possibility, put forward by Hannah, that in Britain "there is as much variation, if not more, within the two groups of firms—those still controlled by family and those run by salaried managers—as there is between them."[83]

## NOTES

1. These issues have been discussed by the author elsewhere. See Payne, *British Entrepreneurship in the Nineteenth Century* (London: Macmillan, 1974), pp. 17–23, and "Industrial Entrepreneurship and Management—Britain, c. 1760–1770," in P. Mathias and M. M. Postan (eds.), *The Cambridge Economic History of Europe*, Vol. VII, *The Industrial Economies: Capital, Labour and Enterprise* (Cambridge: Cambridge University Press, 1978), Part I, pp. 191–93.

2. Sir John Clapham, *An Economic History of Modern Britain* (Cambridge: Cambridge University Press, 1951), Vol. III, p. 203.

3. Clapham, *op. cit.*, Vol. II, pp. 138–40; J.B. Jeffreys, *Business Organization in Great Britain, 1856–1914* (Ph. D. Thesis, University of London, 1938, published in its original form by Arno Press, New York, 1977), pp. 116, 118, 403; P. L. Payne, *The Early Scottish Limited Companies, 1856–1895* (Edinburgh: Scottish Academic Press, 1980), p. 56; P. L. Cottrell, *Industrial Finance, 1830–1914* (London: Methuen, 1980), pp. 104–5.

4. Jeffreys, *op. cit.*, p. 117; D. A. Farnie, *The English Cotton Industry and the World Market, 1815–1896* (Oxford: Clarendon Press, 1979), pp. 244–76.

5. Cottrell, *op. cit.*, p. 164.

6. P. L. Payne, "The Emergence of the Large-Scale Company in Great Britain," *Economic History Review*, 2nd series, XX (1967), Section 2; H. W. Macrosty, "Business Aspects of British Trusts," *Economic Journal*, XII (1902), p. 354; Jeffreys, *op. cit.*, p. 451.

7. It was reported by the Registrar of Joint Stock Companies in 1895, that of the 1,328 companies limited by shares registered in London during the first six months of 1890, "415 [were] more or less of a private character." These were listed and analyzed. It is apparent that of the "private or family companies" (which, incidentally included Bradbury, Wilkinson's, William Hollins, Abram Lyle, Lever Brothers and Reeves & Sons), the bulk of the shares in over a third of them was held by three shareholders or less and well over 80 per cent of the companies had fewer than 15 members. *Report of the Departmental Committee of the Board of Trade on the Company Acts*, C. 7779 (1895), pp. 54–63. Ten years later, in 1906, the Company Law Amendment Committee found that "a *large and increasing proportion* of the companies [formed] under the [Companies] Acts are classed . . . as private companies [in which] the number of members generally does not exceed twenty, and very commonly is not above seven." Of the "well-known concerns . . . carried on as private companies" were listed Harland & Wolff, Huntley & Palmers, Crosse & Blackwell and J. & J. Colman. In the early years of the twentieth century well over 80 per cent of all companies registered were private. *Report of the Company Law Amendment Committee*, Cd. 3052 (1906), pp. 2–3, 17. Emphasis supplied.

8. Leslie Hannah, "Visible and Invisible Hands in Great Britain," in A. D. Chandler and H. Daems (eds.), *Managerial Hierarchies* (Cambridge, Mass: Harvard University Press, 1980), p. 53.

9. Ibid., p. 55. For shipbuilding, see A. Slaven, "Growth and Stagnation in British/Scottish Shipbuilding, 1913–1977," in Jan Kuuse and A. Slaven (eds.), *Scottish and Scandinavian Shipbuilding Seminar: Development Problems in Historical Perspective* (Glasgow, 1980), pp. 19–20.

10. P. Sargant Florence, *Ownership, Control and Success of Large Companies* (London: Sweet & Maxwell, 1961).

11. A. B. Levy, *Private Corporations and Their Control*, 2 vols. (London, 1950), I, pp. 224–29, gives the number of British public companies in 1938 as 14,355 (paid-up capital £4,097m); the private companies numbered 135,221 (paid-up capital £1,894m).

12. Just how much it was diminishing depends partly on the importance attached to the respective *roles* of the large and small firm in the economy.

13. Perhaps the most important recent British inquiry has been that conducted by the Bolton Committee. Its own Report and the associated research reports constitute a remarkably rich quarry of detailed information on the small firm in Britain. See the *Report of the Committee of Inquiry on Small Firms* [*The Bolton Report*]. Cmd. 4811 (London: HMSO, 1971). No less than eighteen research reports were published simultaneously. See also Johnathan Boswell, *The Rise and Decline of Small Firms* (London: Allen & Unwin, 1973). A number of interesting case studies are provided by Philip Clarke, *Small Businesses: How They Survive and Succeed* (Newton Abbot: David & Charles, 1972).

14. The definition of small firms adopted by the Bolton Inquiry is carefully set down in Chapter 1 of the Report, p. 3. For "manufacturing" the statistical definition was that the small firm possessed 200 employees or less and for "retailing," a turnover of £50,000 per annum or less. These definitions covered 94 per cent and 96 per cent of all firms in the respective industries.

15. *Bolton Report*, p. 6.

16. See the recent very interesting article by R. Lloyd-Jones and A. A. Le Roux, "Marshall and the Birth and Death of Firms: The Growth and Size Distribution of Firms in the Early Nineteenth-Century Cotton Industry," *Business History*, XXIV (1982), pp. 141–55.

17. P. S. Florence, *Ownership, Control and Success*, pp. 71–73, Appendix B, pp. 222–65. Although it is legitimate to argue with Florence's definitions and his tests of concentrated ownership, the case he makes is convincing. Only for those companies which were wholly or mainly owned by other (mainly overseas) companies, themselves manager-controlled (such as the British Match Corporation and F.W. Woolworth) would one seriously dispute his figures. See the discussion by M. M. Postan, *An Economic History of Western Europe, 1945–1964* (London: Methuen, 1967), p. 252.

18. Derek F. Channon, *The Strategy and Structure of British Enterprise* (London: Macmillan, 1971), p. 161; cf. P. S. Florence, *op. cit.*, pp. 70–73, 136, and Hannah, *op. cit.*, p. 53.

19. Channon, *op. cit.*, p. 75. Emphasis supplied; Steve Nyman and A. Silberston, "The Ownership and Control of Industry," *Oxford Economic Papers*, N. S., Vol. XXX (1978), pp. 84–5.

20. William Mennell, *Takeover: The Growth of Monopoly in Britain, 1951–1961* (London, 1962), pp. 173ff.

21. A. J. Merrett & M. E. Lehr, *The Private Company Today* (London: Gower Press, 1971), pp. 15, 67–71. Since 1970, a number of these large private companies have gone public. Sainsburys did so in 1973, although in 1981, 45 per cent of the ordinary shares were still owned or controlled by the directors and their families; Ferrantis is now also a public company, a large proportion of its voting stock being held by the National Enterprise Board; the shipbuilding activities of Lithgows was taken into public ownership under the Aircraft and Shipbuilding Act of 1977.

22. Leslie Hannah, *The Rise of the Corporate Economy* (London: Methuen, 1976); S. J. Prais, *The Evolution of Giant Firms in Britain* (Cambridge: C. U. P., 1976).

23. See, for example, Prais, *op. cit.*, p. 5.

24. See the prediction made by G. D. Newbould & A. S. Jackson, *The Receding Ideal* (Liverpool: Guthstead, 1972). On Gibrat's Law, see P. E. Hart, *Studies in Profit, Business Saving and Investment in the United Kingdom, 1920–1962* (London: Allen & Unwin, 1965), pp. 150–51; L. Hannah & J. A. Kay, *Concentration in Modern Industry* (London: Macmillan, 1977), pp. 98–101; S. J. Prais, *op. cit.*, pp. 27–8; Payne, *The Early Scottish Limited Companies*, pp. 102–4.

25. Some issues raised in this paragraph are further considered below, pp. 184–87.

26. It is interesting to note that in one of the most important recent studies of company law, the author observes that for business concerns the "normal rule is to expand or die." Tom Hadden, *Company Law and Capitalism* (London: Weidenfeld & Nicolson, 1972), p. 98.

27. Channon, *op. cit.*, p. 77, indicates that "as the product-market scope of a company increases [i.e. as a company chooses to grow by diversification], it becomes more difficult for a family to maintain managerial control by the family." Professor Channon's most recent work, *The Service Industries: Strategy, Structure and Financial Performance* (London: Macmillan, 1977) and his continuing researches lerd support to this view. Derek F. Channon in a personal communication to the author, November, 1982.

28. See S. Pollard, *The Genesis of Modern Management* (London: Arnold, 1965), pp. 150–51; S. D. Chapman, "The Peels in the English Cotton Industry," *Business History*, XI (July 1969); J. C. Logan, "The Dumbarton Glass Works Company: A Study in Entrepreneurship," *Business History*, XIV (January 1972), pp. 71–81.

29. Quoted by H. J. Habakkuk, "Industrial Organization since the Industrial Revolution," *The Fifteenth Fawley Foundation Lecture* in the University of Southampton, 1968, p. 8.

30. A. Slaven, "Management and Shipbuilding, 1890–1938: Structure and Strategy in the Shipbuilding Firm on the Clyde," in A. Slaven and D. H. Aldcroft (eds.), *Business, Banking and Urban History* (Edinburgh: Donald, 1982), pp. 43–5.

31. *Ibid.*, p. 44. Professor Slaven refers the reader to the paper by T. Burns and G. Stalker, "Mechanistic and Organistic Systems of Management," in *Management of Innovation* (1961), pp. 110–25.

32. Payne, in Mathias and Postan, *op. cit.*, p. 206.

33. Hannah, *op. cit.*, pp. 53, 55; and see the same author's *The Rise of the Corporate Economy*, pp. 96–99. See also Payne, "The Emergence of the Large-Scale Company," pp. 528–29, 533–35.

34. Payne, "The Emergence of the Large-Scale Company," p. 530.

35. Hannah, "Visible and Invisible Hands," p. 52.

36. Florence, *Ownership Control and Success*, p. 192.

37. S. J. Prais, *The Evolution of Giant Firms in Britain* and L. Hannah, *The Rise of the Corporate Economy*.

38. Channon, *op. cit.*, p. 75.

39. R. A. Church, *Kenricks in Hardware. A Family Business. 1791–1966* (Newton Abbot: David & Charles, 1969).

40. *Ibid.*, p. 217, see also p. 213.

41. The words used in the Report by Peat, Marwick, Mitchell & Co. on Kenricks, 1937, quoted Church, *op. cit.*, p. 212.

42. Channon, *op. cit.*, pp. 75–76. Channon's detailed investigation covered the period 1950–1970.

43. *Ibid.*, p. 141; for case studies, see P. L. Payne, *Rubber and Railways in the Nineteenth Century* (Liverpool: Liverpool University Press, 1961), pp. 48–52, and see Stanley Chapman, "Strategy and Structure at Boots the Chemists," in L. Hannah (ed.), *Management Strategy and Business Development* (London: Macmillan, 1976), pp. 95–107.

44. Channon, *op. cit.*, p. 77.

45. P. S. Florence, "Problems of Rationalization" in a discussion reported in the *Economic Journal*, Vol. XL (1930), p. 365, quoted by Hannah, *The Rise of the Corporate Economy*, p. 148.

46. Once again, the words of the Report by Peat, Marwick, Mitchell & Co. on Kenricks, have been adopted. Church, *op. cit.*, p. 211.

47. Channon, *op. cit.*, p. 123; T. C. Barker, *The Glassmakers. Pilkington: the Rise of an International Company, 1826–1976* (London: Weidenfeld and Nicolson, 1977), pp. 406–25. See also T. C. Barker, "A Family

Firm becomes a Public Company: Changes at Pilkington Brothers Limited in the Interwar Years," in L. Hannah (ed.), *Management Strategy and Business Development* (London: Macmillan, 1976), pp. 85–94, and P. L. Cook, *Effects of Mergers* (London: Allen & Unwin, 1958), pp. 242–43.

48. Channon, *op. cit.*, pp. 96–7; Graham Turner, *Business in Britain* (London: Eyre & Spottiswood, 1969), pp. 222, 226–27.

49. Turner, *op. cit.*, pp. 231, 339–41. Professor Edith Penrose has made the point that "family firms" tend to be "content with a comfortable profit." E. T. Penrose, *The Theory of the Growth of the Firm* (Oxford: Blackwell, 1959), p. 34.

50. For Marks & Spencer, see Goronwy Rees, *St. Michael. A History of Marks & Spencer* (London: Weidenfeld & Nicolson, 1969), particularly, pp. 70–78, and Stephen Aris, *The Jews in Business* (London: Johnathan Cape, 1970), pp. 137–54. Until the death of Lord Marks in 1964, only a few of Marks & Spencer's hundreds of thousands of shareholders had the right to vote at the company's meetings: all the voting shares were held by members of the founding family and the Prudential Assurance Co.

51. Turner, *op. cit.*, p. 230.

52. In 1970 even Rothschilds became a private limited company, some years after bringing in much outside talent to the previous private partnership. See Aris, *op. cit.*, pp. 60–63.

53. For these service industries, see D. F. Channon, "Corporate Evolution in the Service Industries," in L. Hannah (ed.), *op. cit.*, pp. 213–34. For a more detailed study of those whose rapid rise was essentially based on the exploitation of rising property values and/or the real as opposed to the balance sheet values of properties owned by businesses engaged in brewing, hotels or retailing, see Oliver Marriott, *The Property Boom* (London: Hamish Hamilton, 1967).

54. Charles P. Kindleberger, *Economic Growth in France and Britain, 1851–1950* (London: Oxford University Press, 1964), p. 115.

55. A. Gerschenkron, "Social Attitudes, Entrepreneurship and Economic Development," *Explorations in Entrepreneurial History*, VI (October 1953), p. 10.

56. H. J. Habakkuk, "The Historical Experience on the Basic Conditions of Economic Progress," in L. H. Dupriez (ed.), *Economic Progress* (Louvain: Institut de Recherches Economiques et Sociales, 1955), p. 159.

57. Payne, *British Entrepreneurship*, pp. 33–34, where references may be found.

58. *Ibid.*, pp. 37–38.

59. For the Guests and J. P. Budd, see T. Boyns, Dennis Thomas and Colin Baber, "The Iron, Steel and Tinplate Industries, 1750–1914," in A. H. John and G. Williams (eds.), *Industrial Glamorgan* (Cardiff, 1980), pp. 112–17; for the Dixons, see I. F. Gibson, "The Economic History of the Scottish Iron and Steel Industry, 1830–1880" (University of London, thesis for the degree of Ph. D., 1955), pp. 117 ff, 168–85; for the Wrights, see R. H. Mottram & C. Coote, *Through Five Generations: The History of the Butterley Company* (London: Faber, 1950), pp. 77–84.

60. It is hoped and expected that two extensive inquiries currently being conducted by the Business History Unit at London University under the direction of Professor Leslie Hannah and the Scottish Business History Project under the direction of Professor A. Slaven at Glasgow University, will produce data sufficient to permit more confident generalizations about the family firm.

61. Kindleberger, *op. cit.*, p. 114.

62. David Landes, "Technological Change and Development in Western Europe, 1750–1914," In H. J. Habakkuk and M. Postan (eds.) *Cambridge Economic History of Europe*, Vol. VI; *The Industrial Revolution and After* (Cambridge: C.U.P., 1965), pp. 563–64.

63. Payne, "Industrial Entrepreneurship," pp. 202–5.

64. W. G. Rimmer, *Marshalls of Leeds, Flax Spinners, 1788–1886* (Cambridge: C.U.P., 1960).

65. H. Heaton, "Benjamin Gott and the Industrial Revolution in Yorkshire," *Economic History Review*, III (1931–2), pp. 15–16.

66. For the Pilkingtons, see T. C. Barker, *op. cit.*, and the Stewarts, *Stewarts and Lloyds Limited, 1903–1953* (Privately printed for Stewarts and Lloyds, n.d. [c. 1954]), p. 7. Information on the Yarrow and Coats families were collected by the author during his tenure of the Colquhoun Lectureship in Business History at the University of Glasgow, 1959–69.

67. C. Gulvin, *The Tweedmakers: A History of the Scottish Fancy Woollen Industry, 1600–1914* (Newton Abbot: David & Charles, 1973), p. 150. Alfred Marshall also criticized the founder's "*sons* who had been brought up to think life easy." A. Marshall, *Industry and Trade* (London: Macmillan, 1923), pp. 91–92. Emphasis supplied.

68. M. J. Weiner, *English Culture and the Decline of the Industrial Spirit, 1850–1980* (Cambridge: C.U.P., 1981) represents a recent examination of this phenomenon; see also D. C. Coleman, "Gentlemen and Players," *Economic History Review*, 2nd series, XXVI (1973), pp. 95–96.

69. Research into this subject is currently being conducted by M. S. Moss and J. R. Hume who are indexing and analyzing the Scottish sequestration (bankruptcy) processes for the period 1839 to 1913. I am indebted to them for permitting me to read their unpublished paper "Business Failure in Scotland, 1839–1913." The Merrett Cyriax Report for the Bolton Committee found that the proportion of *small* firms existing in 1963 that had gone into liquidation, ceased to trade or been taken over by 1970 was very high, ranging from 19 per cent in the motor trade to 32.5 per cent in wholesaling. Of the firms in "manufacturing and construction," 23.1 per cent ceased to exist. *Loc. cit.*, p. 18.

70. P. L. Payne, *The Early Scottish Limited Companies, 1856–1895.*

71. H. A. Shannon, "The First Five Thousand Companies and their Duration," *Economic History*, II (1931).

72. Charlotte Erickson, *British Industrialists: Steel and Hosiery, 1850–1950* (Cambridge: C.U.P., 1959), pp. 52–53.

73. See, for example, Duncan Burn, *The Economic History of Steel Making, 1867–1939* (Cambridge: C.U.P., 1940), pp. 296–305; J. H. Burnham and G. O. Hoskins, *Iron and Steel in Britain* (London: Allen & Unwin, 1943), p. 248; J. E. Vaizey, *The History of British Steel* (London: Weidenfeld & Nicolson, 1974), p. 10.

74. In carpets, where until nearly the end of the nineteenth century most firms were owned and controlled either by one person or more often by a partnership, of 31 firms founded in Kidderminster and Stourport, no less than 12 survived less than 11 years and an other ten had closed down within fifteen years; five still existed in 1970 but at least two of them had lost their original independence. See J. N. Bartlett, *Carpeting The Millions: The Growth of Britain's Carpet Industry* (Edinburgh: John Donald, 1978), pp. 111, 157–58.

75. *Bolton Report*, p. 7.

76. Boswell's "Companies House Study" constitutes Appendix 4 of his study, *The Rise and Decline of Small Firms*, pp. 232–53; see also *Bolton Report*, p. 17.

77. It is, I believe, worth emphasizing that when Charles Wilson, in his defense of British entrepreneurship in late Victorian Britain, drew

attention to the vigor and ingenuity of "the Levers, the Boots, the Harrods, the Whiteleys and Lewises," he was referring to individual founders of what were to become famous firms irrespective of the precise legal nature of such firms. Charles Wilson, "Economy and Society in Late Victorian Britain," *Economic History Review*, 2nd series, XVIII (1965–66), p. 189. The Merrett Cyriax Report for the Bolton Committee found that "Management ability, as evidenced by new markets and products, is the main factor differentiating the fast and slow growers [among small firms], while the founder managed firms showed outstanding growth despite the total absence of formal qualifications and in many cases no direct prior experiences of the industry concerned." Merrett Cyriax Associates, *The Dynamics of Small Firms* (1971), p. 4.

78. Bolton Report, p. 84. Examples of small firms which have "started from nothing and grown to substantial size, even since World War II," are Kenwood, Letraset, Nu-Swift Industries and Racal Electronics. *Ibid.*, pp. 30–31.

79. P. S. Florence, *The Logic of British and American Industry*, pp. 295, 303–4, 320.

80. The only way in which it is possible even to begin to discover just how much influence "a member of the family" had on company policy is to examine the records of the company in question (cf. Nyman & Silberston, *op. cit.*, p. 78). The majority of the shares of Colvilles Ltd., for example, were held by trustees of the Colville family, yet from 1916 control was firmly in the hands of professional managers, and it was made plain that members of the third generation of the Colville family could not expect even to be considered for positions of responsibility within the firm until they had thoroughly learned the trade. See P. L. Payne, *Colvilles and the Scottish Steel Industry* (Oxford: Clarendon Press, 1979), p. 356 and *passim*. To speak, as Florence does (and his argument is cited approvingly by Kindleberger, *op. cit.*, p. 124) of the existence of "leadership by inheritance" in a number of major sectors is apt to be misleading. Were *all* the major units within such sectors similarly affected? Or was it only a small proportion? And, even so, did "amateur" family members on the board really have much influence, or were their views politely received and ignored by the salaried managers on the board? Furthermore, there is a growing body of evidence that in recent years possession of the family name may have eased the way to the boardroom but was insufficient in itself to secure election. The name has to be supported

by professional expertise (see, for example, Mennell, *Takeover*, pp. 137–40; T. C. Barker, "A Family Firm," p. 91; Aris, *The Jews*, pp. 62, 140–1). We need to know more about such matters but my guess would be that the importance of "leadership by inheritance" is declining and from the 1930's was perhaps never as significant as the mere presence of family names on the board would imply.

As for Florence's point (*Logic*, p. 304) that large share holdings in family businesses by distant members of the family—whose interests are often fiercely protected by trustees—are likely to result in a dividend policy prejudicial to the accumulation of reserves and the reinvestment of profits, the evidence is inconclusive. Sir John Craig, the managing director of Colvilles, begrudged paying a penny to the ordinary shareholders, overwhelmingly Colville trustees, during his tenure of office (Payne, *Colvilles*, p. 317), and William Lyons, chairman and managing director of SS Cars Ltd., later Jaguar Cars Ltd., made sure that the profit available for distribution remained low: "I never let them get above £300,000 a year. I thought that was quite enough . . . ." (*Sunday Times*, 29 August, 1982). It is arguable that managing directors in family firms (whether they were salaried managers or members of the family) are in a stronger position to resist appeals for generous dividends than the chairman of public companies.

81. The point made by Hannah, "Visible and Invisible Hands," p. 56.
82. Channon, *op. cit.*, pp. 75–76.
83. Hannah, "Visible and Invisible Hands," p. 55. For the similar findings of an American survey, see R. G. Donnelley, "The Family Business," *Harvard Business Review*, Vol. 42, No. 4 (July–August 1964), pp. 93–105.

# COMMENTS

Terushi Hara
*Waseda University*

## I.

Professor Payne's paper consists of three parts. In the first part he describes the tenacity of the family firm in Britain where the family firm has been very important since the Industrial Revolution. Even after World War II, the family firm continued to exist in many industries, but its relative importance has been diminishing.

In the second part, Professor Payne analyzes the management structure and changing nature of the British Family firm, primarily from the business historian's viewpoint. According to him, the mechanistic management system was especially popular in the British family firm. Under such a system, authority is concentrated at the top of the organization, work is functionally specialized and organized in sub-units, and interaction between members of the concern is vertical. Professor Payne concludes that it was the adoption of this system that permitted the marriage of ownership and control to prevail for so long in the British economy. Since 1945 British family firms have been obliged to choose between rapid growth with outside capital and maintenance of the status quo.

In the last part he discusses the family firm and economic development from the economic historian's viewpoint. He speaks about the charge against the family firm, the third generation argument, giving age and ownership statistics. His conclusion shows that the family firm has been an engine of economic growth and will continue to be such in the future.

## II.

Having given this brief summary of his paper, I would like to ask him the following three questions.

First, Professor Payne did not speak about relationships between the types of ownership and management styles. This is one of the main points which the project leader mentioned. I hope Professor Payne will explain this to us.

Second, Professor Payne writes about two kinds of family firms. One is the firm which chooses growth with outside capital and outside managerial talents, the other decides to retain its physical proportion. What factors bring about this difference?

Last, I hope that Professor Payne will explain the recruitment of managerial staff within the family firm. How does the family firm attract or create managerial talent?

# The Large Family Firm in the French Manufacturing Industry

Maurice Lévy-Leboyer
*University of Paris X-Nanterre*

Even though there is a general tendency to look upon all family firms as very much alike—and so they probably are in terms of lifetime employment, career opportunities, zeal and loyalty of their officers to the company—one should keep in mind that historical factors in France, more specifically the great depression that held down industry in the latter part of the 19th century, have contributed to shape its business institutions in ways that may have proved detrimental in the long run. Quite apart from technological change and market development which no doubt had an immediate impact on policies and structures, the fact that growth had been deficient for some twenty years or so meant that, in the many sectors which they came to dominate, the large corporations based on family ownership and management did not make up a group of homogeneous and mature enterprises. All these firms had been launched over a long period of time, before and after the beginning of the depression, and they reacted therefore to its adverse effects in two opposite ways. Most of the older concerns that had managed to survive the period of difficulties were prevented from expanding and diversifying their production; very few among them, even after the 1914–18 war, were able to adopt the multi-line, multi-market strategies that were characteristic in other industrial countries of modern corporations branching out into new ventures.[1] While the more recent ones, having often started their operations at the turn of the century, in what were years of slow revival, hence from a narrow basis and with limited outside finance, were still striving in the 1920s to establish themselves. The paradox of French large family

firms, in the early part of the 20th century, is that the great majority
were considered as having had long years of experience and capital
accumulation—some textile mills and ironworks, in fact, had been
under the control of the same families for six or seven generations
and sometimes even longer in the North and Eastern France—
although only a limited number, as a few instances will show, had
reached a position of financial autonomy and a secure basis.

A. The *older group*, dating back for many of its members from
Napoleon's days, included in its formative years large mercantile
houses that had entered industry. It is an original feature of the
country that Swiss, German and of course French merchant bankers,
located in the out-ports and in Paris, were among the prime movers of
the first industrial revolution, supplying them with capital, information, managing partners and even correspondents to develop the
works they had contributed to create. However, in spite of these past
achievements and of their long standing position among the French
business elite—some of their descendants were still holding directorships by the 1920s in railroad companies, banks and leading industrial firms—their influence had been on the wane all through the
19th century, for reasons that may be perceived by examining
briefly the example of the Rothschilds as a case in point.

The house, originating from Frankfurt in the 18th century, included five brothers and five banks spread over the main European
cities, though with business centered first in London, up to the 1840s,
and then in Paris, until the death of James de Rothschild in 1868.
Their success, exemplified by their multiple business initiatives and
accumulated wealth,[2] may be partly ascribed to the constraints that
a strongly knit family could assign to its members. According to the
deeds of settlement, revised every three years or so from 1818, there
was to be among them a community of capital: balance sheets had
to be consolidated each year into one single account, all profits being
retained and cumulated, after deduction of fixed family expenses,
interest charges, etc.; all books were to remain secret and closed to
the children after the death of a partner; no arbitration was allowed,
out of the family circle, in case of litigation between members, etc.
There was also to be a community in ways of life and ideas regulated

by written rules (each partner being required to give all his time to the house, to circulate information by weekly letters, to make frequent visits to his parents); and it was further strengthened by family customs that were then traditional in Jewish communities (James de Rothschild, for instance, married one of his nieces in 1824, and marriages between cousins were to follow in the third and fourth generations).

But these were abstract principles easy to apply only up to the second generation. With the passage of time, there was a risk that the family's initial cohesion might be undermined because of the unequal success of the different houses, and further because of a change in business orientation, the firm having moved from bills of exchange and specie (the main Frankfurt and London trade), first, into the financing of post-war indemnities and government debts, and then—at least so far as the continental houses are concerned— into railroad building and industrial investment, that made them more dependent on local economic conditions. Of course equality had been very much on the mind of the founder and his sons; they had devised schemes that entitled each of the partners to a share in profits that was adjusted periodically to their capital (in the consolidated balance sheet) and to their own responsibilities (in each of the individual houses). But the system, quite complex, tended in practice to reduce the share of the London partners, who withdrew from the association when the third generation came of age, and it was finally given up in the 1850s with the decline of the Vienna and Naples houses, the latter being liquidated in 1860–63. Solidarity was upheld, but between what had become *de facto* independent firms, endowed with great prestige, but having no more resources than the big deposit banks of the day: the Paris house, still the most powerful, had a capital of 40 million francs in 1868 (50 million in 1880 divided equally between James' three sons), so that, with the partners accounts (assessed to 30 or 40 million) and those of the public, the house's total liabilities were of the order of 280–300 million francs, that is, one-half the total held by the other private bankers, but only one-fourth of those of the four big deposit banks in Paris.[3]

This could not maintain the Rothschilds in the lead, overcommitted as they were with capital invested and to a certain extent frozen in steel plants and coal mines (in Belgium) and in railroads (in France, Northern Italy and Spain). They had given up a project, studied in 1849 by a junior partner, of enlarging their foreign trade operations and of opening a sixth house in New York; they renewed their attempt in the 1860s, then giving precedence to the oil and metals trades. But they had to wait until the pre-1914 war recovery in the stock market and in raw material prices to have enough funds released and reassert themselves. And the outcome was not dissimilar with the other merchant bankers in Paris: they had to cope with the country's territorial dismemberment and monetary inconvertibility in the 1870s, and later with the displacement of railroad traffic to the Gothard and with the industrial slowdown; some succeeded in protecting the name of their family, but they did not regain much of their former influence.

B.   *New developments*, though, became possible with the reform of company laws (limited liability being instituted in 1863–67), with the rise in stock market operations (and a shift in savers' demand from bonds to equities after the 1890s), and with the entry of a new generation of entrepreneurs and engineers eager to use new technologies and market opportunities to build what became for the first time large-scale production units. Major increases in business' annual turnover were reported after the beginning of the century. Earlier in the past a 100 million francs sales per year was a limit that had been seldom achieved except by the big department stores and textile chains; it had remained out of reach among manufacturing firms before 1900: 15–20 million F was the range that pioneers had set in chemicals, when successful; 20–30 million was not unfrequent in the steel industry, 40–55 in coal mining and in the automobile sector. But with the revival of activity in the pre-war years and with the war orders, the whole economy was set in motion: the 100 million F mark was passed by Saint-Gobain (the leading chemicals and glass manufacturer) as early as 1910, 200–300 million by firms in the mechanical industries (Renault reached 350 million turnover in 1918, almost seven times the firm's pre-war figure); 400–450 million were often registered in steel, metals and engineering—one billion at the Schneiders' works in 1918; and the trend was to con-

TABLE 1  Securities Issued by Private Corporations on the Stock Exchange, 1900–1939 (average annual value in millions of 1913 francs).

|         | Shares | Bonds | Total | Percentage shares | Share Bonds |
|---------|--------|-------|-------|-------------------|-------------|
| 1904–13 | 650    | 460   | 1,110 | 58%               | 42%         |
| 1920–29 | 1,700  | 615   | 2,315 | 73                | 27          |
| 1930–34 | 840    | 610   | 1,450 | 58                | 42          |
| 1935–39 | 300    | 210   | 510   | 59                | 41          |
| 1900–39 | 935    | 490   | 1,425 | 66                | 34          |

Source: *Annuaire statistique de la France* (Paris, 1966), pp. 352–53. The railroad companies are not included in the table.

tinue with the 1920s inflation that multiplied prices by a factor of five: although they tried to rationalize their production and hold down costs to bolster their sales, the three leaders in the automobile sector were heading for 740 million at Peugeot, and 1.4 and 1.8 billion at Renault and Citroën, respectively, in 1929–1930.

This major increase in the level of business operations caused acute financial problems: firms had to build up new plants in their own product line; some moved back from the assembly of parts to that of their manufacturing and into more basic sectors, to overcome supply shortages. Further, since industries could no longer rely on the assistance of old-established trade houses and on that of the State (as during the war), many entered marketing or enlarged their commercial operations, all steps that were even more demanding both in capital and credit facilities. A shortage of liquid funds therefore developed that was most serious in the automobile industry: an old and experienced firm like Peugeot kept on the average 100–120 million francs of net cash assets through the 1920s, i.e. the equivalent of one year's sales immediately after the war; but the ratio very soon fell to much lower levels—to one-fifth in 1927—as a consequence of the company's rising activity; at André Citroën's, who had started his car plant only after the war, the firm reported in 1927 a short-term liability position of 100 million francs against a turnover that had passed one billion. It is this imbalance between cash funds and the flow of current operations that became the concern of all the large industrial companies and made it necessary for them to appoint bankers on the board (sometimes for a few months) and to call on the securities market, first, to issue new shares—bonds being unsaleable in the 1920s, since people had lost four-fifths in real value on their past bond holdings (Table 1)—and, second, to do so on a scale that had never been registered before: in 1913, capital stocks had seldom reached 30 million francs per firm (coming from 0.6–0.8 million in the mid-1890s for new firms in the modern sectors); but they increased by five and even ten times in the 1920s: Edouard Michelin, the tire manufacturer, was able to raise his capital, in two issues, up to 150 million by 1924; Robert Peugeot to 250 million, in four steps, by 1930; André Citroën was already at 400 million in 1928 (against 50 million in 1924 when his firm had become a public company), etc. Some of the older firms that were carrying on a policy of diversification, for instance in the chemicals industry, were heading for half a billion F capital, sometimes after twelve or thirteen stock issues.

If bonds had been still in use—and firms frequently turned back to them after 1930—the danger would have been minimal. But with the fall in the level of equities that individuals or families could hope to keep in industrial companies, it was to be doubted that family firms would last very long. In point of fact, two waves of mergers in the 1920s brought to the fore a new generation of engineers who had access to the Paris financial market, to State orders, and so were able to take over large sectors of production in the more capital-intensive parts of industry. The threat of a separation between ownership and management thus had become an actual issue. Some family firms, though, held on to their past structures, through one of three main devices.

(1) *Financial holdings:* In a few sectors, where manufacturers had to carry on their usual production, and at the same time finance and often conduct the operations of a customer or a subsidiary company—e.g. when some industrial plant had been erected by an engineering firm, or when streetcars, generating power stations or other public utility companies were set up by a more specialized concern—it had become customary, even before the war, to incorporate a holding company that would act as a financial intermediary, i.e. to issue, buy, hold or sell stocks for the account of the mother firm, using as cash reserves the spare funds held by the

sub-companies and co-partners. The *Centrale de Dynamite* had acted in such capacity for the Nobel trust from 1887, the *Société parisienne pour l'industrie électrique* in 1900 for the group headed by Edouard Empain, the *Union européenne industrielle et financière* in 1920 for that of Eugène Schneider II, etc. Their primary aim had been to procure external funds and allocate them between the members of the industrial group. And they were later used in practice by its founder (who maintained a majority share in the holding) to keep some influence over the affiliated companies: indirect financial controls were thus being used to protect individuals' or families' interests.

(2) *Family trusts:* Many firms in the 19th century were managed under the influence of some inside group having a substantial, but not always a majority, share in the capital: Eugène Schneider I, for instance, who built the country's largest industrial company, had started his career at the Creusot plants with a small capital share limited to 5%, but with the backing of two substantial shareholders whose descendants were still present a century later in the company's executive committee. In a similar way, members of the board at St-Gobain, who were recruited for some four generations in the same narrow circle of ten old families, held together 4% or 5% of the equities as an outside limit but enjoyed throughout the confidence of two or three parties whose influence was decisive in the 19th century when the company had a limited number of shareholders (375 in 1862, less than 1,400 in 1907), and after the war, thanks to the wide dissemination of the stock. In the 1920s, however, with the massive sales of equities by companies which were then only medium-sized family firms, some of the directors felt that they were at the mercy of bankers, collecting blank votes in the public at large, and that they could no longer be content with tacit and informal pacts. They organized new trust companies on a family basis—such as *Progil* (1919) in the man-made textile industries, *Filor* (1924) in the foundry and metals sector, etc.: they were in charge of holding the shares individual members had transferred to them, of raising the extra funds necessary to subscribe to new issues and of protecting their position in the company.

(3) *Preference shares:* On the assumption that the public was more interested in cashing dividends than in having a say in a busi-

ness firm's policy, many companies had issued just before the war and in the mid-1920s passive shares (*parts de fondateur*), i.e. stocks with no stated value, no right to take part in the shareholders' general assemblies, but entitled to some 15 or 20% of the net profit; they were distributed as a kind of indemnity to their shareholders by Dollfus-Mieg and other Alsatian cotton firms, Michelin, Peugeot, Citroën and many others, when the capital of these companies was opened to outside subscribers. The same proceeding was adopted in a slightly amended form, again in the 1920s, to market further stock issues: shares labelled "A", with a plural vote, were assigned to the older members of the company, while shares "B", with a one vote each, were being issued to the public at large. This gave rise to a wide variety of schemes: some firms, like Michelin in 1928, had the passive shares listed on the stock exchange to the exclusion of the active ones—probably for arbitrage purposes; others tried to hold on to those that had a greater voting power—all the 20,000 "A" shares that had been issued in 1928 were back into the hands of the Peugeot family by March 1931—they amounted to a fraction of the 500,000 shares then in circulation, but to 29% of the votes; André Citroën in 1934 also held 50,000 "A" shares in his company (with six votes each) and 104,000 "B" shares and was entitled to 22% of the votes, against a lesser portion of the capital stock, etc. All these and other measures, such as a right of preemption that some firms had reserved for themselves over their own shares, were devised in a pragmatic way to strengthen the authority of managers having to supervise the activities and coordinate the resources of what had become, probably in too short a time, large-scale organizations.

These, however, were but temporary devices that could not stop the slow erosion of families' influence over business activity: new company laws, destructive of artificial majorities, were passed in 1933–35—they brought to a par all types of equities in terms of voting power; freedom of sale was claimed in courts by shareholders; economic setbacks and fiscal reforms seriously curtailed individuals' incomes, contracting further the means that could be allocated to holding companies, etc. Still, the large family firms held their sway in the 1930s, keeping a real power of attraction and a true resilience through the depression, in contrast with many overgrown enterprises that had captured the public's attention but had made wrong market forecasts. This was no doubt because of the major success they had achieved in the earlier part of the century, and also because of the social environment they were able to maintain, financial and majority problems being only a minor factor compared to the human relations some of these firms had built and preserved. It is therefore logical, first, to determine the factors that may explain their performance up to the 1930s depression, their contribution to the country's economic growth, and, second, to ascertain the forces that made their decline foreseeable in the near future.

## I. Hierarchical Structures and Personnel Management

French large corporations did not differ in their institutional setting from those one finds in most European countries: with a large labor force per firm and with closely integrated production units to service the market, they had to be managed under elaborate hierarchies, strongly structured, made up of two different sets of personel and objectives, one for general management and external relations, and one for more routine and concrete duties. These two were to be found as early as the 1850s in the six railroad companies which had built the great trunk lines and kept henceforth the task of their management. At the Compagnie du Nord, the Rothschilds' main line, the board of directors was made up of men of finance (including members of that family) and officials from the State, Chambers of Commerce and other local authorities; their office was to negotiate with outside parties (including the State) and to review the whole operation at regular intervals, while the actual task of operating the lines was left to the care of a staff of engineers who had an organization of their own within the company and enjoyed a fair measure of autonomy. This dual system was extended to new sectors in the latter part of the 19th century for the reason that big manufacturing firms like St-Gobain, the Schneiders' works, the main machine and repair shops, as well as iron-works in Eastern and Central France, ran across serious difficulties: they met falling markets in the 1880s and faced serious competition from firms having access to superior technology and cheaper resources; and their pro-

prietors were therefore compelled to transfer much of the business
duties to engineers and high ranking officers who took it upon themselves to enter new markets and to experiment with new products
that proved successful (fertilizers at St-Gobain, ordnance and
engineering at the Schneiders' works, more elaborate products in
the Lorraine works, etc.).[7] The same dual structures applied in
many of the new family firms after the turn of the century, even
though they had taken initially single-product lines that did not
require extensive planning and supervision. But growth in their
case was achieved rapidly and, given the constraints of modern
industries, they had to depend on the close cooperation of an active
staff—teams of three, five or even ten people from the start, and not
one single entrepreneur working in isolation were to be found
running most firms[8]—and also on the assistance of personalities
recruited from the public and the private sectors who entered the
board (and sometimes assumed its presidency) to hasten its social
and financial establishment. All large-scale enterprises thus had
central executive offices working in a highly cohesive way with the
board of directors, a system in keeping with the idea of authoritarian
command that was a key to the management of all French companies, family and non-family alike.

These two sets of authority did not remain closed to each other.
In the past century, it is true, the recruitment of directors tended
to be rather restricted because the boards were limited to a few
members and also because family nominees belonged to a small
elite. At St-Gobain, according to an analysis of the pre-1870s
personnel, they were all men of distinction, by birth or through
scientific achievements; many had served as civil servants or members of the government before entering the board. And so, they were
fully prepared to run the affairs of the company and to keep aside
the officers in the staff who had the training, the experience and
often the revenues of high-ranking officials—with much higher
salaries than those allocated to the board—but who remained in a
subordinate position, in particular because they could be dismissed
and had never (except two in a century) the opportunity of being
called to the board.[9] But with the change in the scale of operations
that new technologies and the integration of production had brought

about, barriers to mobility were partly removed, first, because the personnel in the central offices assumed a new dimension: staff members at St-Gobain who had been in the order of 65–100 in the 1880s were to reach 350 in 1910, and their numbers trebled in the inter-war years, their increase in number and greater specialization opening new ways to career mobility. Second, the mere experience gained in business life became a decisive element: as has been shown by various studies of corporations, officers unrelated to business families or influential circles who had followed ordinary business careers and who were called to a board of directors secured a significant proportion among managers; they accounted over the 1912–1973 period for one fourth of the larger corporations' executives.[10] These are general trends that apply to all companies. While there is no sample study restricted to family firms that might help to differentiate their case, on the basis of a number of historical records, two further points may be worth mentioning.

1.  In conformity with a tradition firmly rooted in the eastern and some of the more central regions of calico printing, clock and machine manufacturing industries, firms under family control had always been attentive to the problem of training their work force. This attitude had mixed origins, partly religious (a minimal level of literacy being the concern of Protestant minorities in the North-East), and partly technical (mills being opened in rural areas where labor had to acquire new skills and be upgraded). Eugène Schneider, for instance, on the very first year of his appointment to le Creusot in 1837, had set up an elementary school for his workers' children. That was followed within ten years by a second, more technical "école spéciale préparatoire," to train foremen, mechanics, drawers and accountants, and prepare the better ones to enter a provincial engineering school. These local institutions that existed in many plants all through the country were eventually transferred to the State for political reasons, and also because of the increased attendance of pupils that gratuity had brought to the educational system in the 1870s: at le Creusot, the student body jumped from 600 to 2,200 in 1873, and had trebled by 1878, the schools being made public in 1882. But the Schneiders still maintained control over the special preparatory classes with 400–500 students in the 1890s, to

prepare middle ranking personnel as in the past and to help the most eligible who wished to complete their studies in one of the engineering schools, including those in Paris, and return to the works fully equipped with higher degrees.

This policy which was duplicated by many companies answered two purposes: to raise the technical ability of the staff and to strengthen its authority. (1) After an ill-fated attempt in the 1870s and 1880s at intensifying work, capturing markets by sales-drives or simply sharing them through cartels, manufacturers had turned to new sectors that required centralized offices, research divisions, as well as a network of plants and subsidiary companies. Hence the sharp increase of engineers working for industry: some 13,000 in the 1870s, 28–30,000 at the turn of the century and easily twice that number in 1930, the old family firms taking the lead, because of their past traditions, in calling on their services.[11] (2) All firms in allocating young people when they entered industry had a well-known bias in favor of graduates from the higher engineering schools ("les grandes écoles"); they were given precedence and quicker promotions irrespective of their age and experience; the heads of classes from Polytechnique, for instance, held one-fifth of the presidencies of the large corporations in the 1912–1973 period, although they accounted for less than one percent of the engineering profession. This policy expressed on the part of employers a true respect for fundamental sciences, but even more so their will to give a new spur to authority by having business responsibilities entrusted to individuals whose qualifications were undisputed. Wrongly or not it was felt that the hierarchical structure would be better accepted if ranks and merits were made to coincide.

2.   School facilities were only one part of the services that manufacturers, when located in remote areas, had been induced to offer. There were many in the 19th century who had set up—leaving aside wage schedules which were more or less regulated by regional customs—elaborate systems of social benefits, i.e. cheap housing facilities, family allowances on a per-child basis, health care at the shop floor (and in hospital at le Creusot), accident and old age pensions; and, as additional incentives, to ensure the stability of the work force, bonuses that were awarded on a fixed rate (a thirteenth

month after five years or service at the de Wendel's works, in Lorraine), or in a more flexible and personal way at St-Gobain, where such indemnities amounted to 5–7% of the nominal wages in the 1870s but almost ten per cent in 1912 (for a total wage bill that increased in that period from 8 to 20 million F).[12] These highly paternalistic measures, which were clearly aimed at fixing and disciplining the work force, explain that few employees were tempted or enticed away: to take a job with a family firm in the country was something of a lifetime decision; according to samples taken in the 1860s and 1880s, laborers entered rural mills at less than 20 years of age and remained on the average for 33 to 37 years at work with the same company.

But, once urbanization had opened up new job opportunities, the lifetime employment system came to an end, labor turnover developing in proportion to wage competition and loss of involvement in work: in Paris, the ratio for semi-skilled workers was of 100:23 per year (one hundred hands to be taken in to keep 23 at work) at the *Bon Marché* in the 1870s; and it increased to 100:17 during the 1914-war at the Renault plants; in the country, the same outflow was reported, but at the level of trained personnel (two out of five engineers leaving the company, at St-Gobain, every ten years in the pre-war period). Against this turnover, the response of manufacturers was of course to broaden up the range of social services, join building societies, press for reductions in the price of public utilities for the benefit of their employees, and also to devise more specific measures. The most simple one, when vacancies could be filled by promotions from the ranks, was to structure the careers of individuals so that they would perceive their future through the company; this induced firms to create intermediate levels in the first line staff, broaden the dispersion of wages, reward seniority especially during periods of full employment, etc.[13] But the most pressing problem for provincial companies was that of the drift of engineers to Paris and the northern industrial region. This was due to low salaries (young graduates who had just come out of school were being paid the equivalent of an overseer's wage), the absence of self-fulfillment in work (during the transition period from school to work), and to uncertain career prospects. These were questions that family firms, given their concern for their employees, could handle efficiently. From 1891, after a review of their alumni's position by provincial engineering schools, new rules were applied at le Creusot and extended to other companies: young engineers were offered standard wage rates that were to be steeply increased during their first years of tenure (by fifty per cent in four years), to impose a true penalty if they left the company; wage structures were revised upward to bridge the gap between middle and higher ranking management; reasearch divisions were instituted as intermediary stages between school and practical work; new rules for promotions were introduced, etc. Beyond these individual measures, quite in line with 19th century paternalism, it should be kept in mind that the absence of information, lack of the personal relationship that exists in human-sized enterprises and loss in the quality of life, which are the penalties of size, could be better obviated in large family firms, for they offered some participation in decisions and rewards, a true concern for the quality of products and pride in the name and repute of the company. It is not surprising that an old engineer at the Schneiders' works still remembered in the 1970s the firm as "a magnificent instrument for social promotion."[14]

## II.   Two Limits to Business Families' Influence

Large firms that had been under family control for a number of generations remained somewhat immune to the social strife that plagued the 1930s: no strikes were reported in the major provincial works, in particular at le Creusot (in contrast with the mass movements that had cost the company some 15% of its labor force who had left the city in 1899–1900); unemployment was contained, in part because firms were situated in progressive sectors that were among the first to recover (Peugeot in 1935–37 reported substantial increases in its work force and wage rates); and, although the drying up of profits meant that investments were halted, very few casualties were registered in their ranks. This might lead one to imagine that these firms still had the power to ward off outside difficulties and that they would later revive unchanged. But a closer analysis of their social and financial structures shows that their position was precarious and their future uncertain.

First, the legitimacy of family leadership was unquestioned in the 1920s. This was due not only to the family element that pervaded all businesses, but also to the prestige of some key business families. According to traditions that had been laid down during the first industrial revolution, their members had been submitted, before entering practical life, to a formal training, at school and in business, that had made them equal—leaving aside all questions of ownership, experience and personal character—to any member on their staff. This had been true of the generation of founders in the early part of the 19th century (Eugène Schneider, for instance, had graduated as an engineer, together with a great many Alsatian manufacturers); it was so of the heirs to older family firms, dating back from the 18th century, who were educated at Polytechnique or at the Ecole Centrale and held prominent positions, such as the de Wendels who developed the Thomas steel patent in the 1880s, or the Peugeots and Bréguets who pioneered the automobile and aircraft industries. After the turn of the century, the same constraints were reinforced; and it was only logical that, among the large corporations' executives who had business family ties over the 1913–1972 period, one finds 58% were engineers, 15% lawyers, 10% university graduates, etc.

Still, leadership tended to depend much more upon the institutional framework and less upon individual characteristics and kinship. The broadening of functions assumed by large corporations meant that new lines of authority, new decision centers—and so counter-forces—were created that would limit in time the power formerly held by business families. Changes, of course, were slight in the textile and metal industries, since low technology, single-product lines and mutual trust were still of paramount importance: Pont-à-Mousson in the 1920s, to take the case of a prosperous family firm in the foundry business, had only two managers, both of the family in control, two main departments (for sales and production), and standing committees to maintain contacts with the personnel and initiate research. Many firms in Alsace and northern France divided their operations between smaller independent units to maintain this simple functional organization, in keeping with family means. But in the chemicals, engineering and other growth sectors, where sizable firms were accumulating profits (during the recovery

TABLE 2  Four Family Firms: Main Items from the Balance Sheets, 1899–1938 (millions of current francs).

| | Assets | | | | | Liabilities | | | | | Total | Annual sales |
|---|---|---|---|---|---|---|---|---|---|---|---|---|
| | Buildings and plants | Stocks | Cash, bills | Other credits | Shares[a] held | Capital reserves | Bonds | Cash debts | Other debts | Balance | | |
| *Michelin* (Clermont-Ferrand)—rubber | | | | | | | | | | | | |
| 1899 | 1.1 | 2.9 | 0.1 | 0.6 | — | 2.2 | 0.7 | 0.2 | 1.2 | 0.3 | 4.6 | — |
| 1919 | 20 | 1 | 174 | — | — | 107 | — | 71 | — | 17 | 195 | — |
| 1928 | 78 | 253 | 360 | 174 | 343 | 427 | 75 | 256 | 172 | 119 | 1050 | 3250[b] |
| 1931 | 123 | 164 | 547 | 360 | 303 | 586 | 296 | 101 | 138 | 32 | 1153 | — |
| 1934 | 113 | 201 | 385 | 36 | 229 | 457 | 279 | 57 | 144 | 6 | 942 | — |
| 1935 | 120 | 171 | 109 | 234 | 325 | 459 | 273 | 69 | 141 | 31 | 973 | — |
| *Peugeot* (Sochaux)—automobiles | | | | | | | | | | | | |
| 1899 | 1.1 | 2.9 | 0.1 | 0.5 | — | 2.9 | — | 0.1 | 1.2 | 0.3 | 3.7 | 2.9 |
| 1919 | 45 | 47 | 29 | 52 | — | 93 | 9 | 64 | — | 6 | 172 | 120 |
| 1924 | 62 | 163 | 19 | 63 | — | 116 | 53 | 136 | — | 5 | 310 | 295 |
| 1930 | 235 | 223 | 86 | 154 | 68 | 394 | 181 | 199 | 50 | 44 | 867 | 740 |
| 1934 | 431 | 144 | 41 | 36 | 50 | 448 | 174 | 26 | 23 | 51 | 722 | 606 |
| 1935 | 420 | 146 | 41 | 49 | 44 | 460 | 160 | 19 | — | 60 | 699 | 668 |
| *Dolfus-Mieg* (Mulhouse)—cotton | | | | | | | | | | | | |
| 1919 | 5 | 50 | 10 | 5 | 2 | 43 | 10 | 18 | — | 3 | 73 | — |
| 1929 | 16 | 52 | 221 | 25 | 6 | 172 | — | 118 | — | 29 | 319 | — |
| 1935 | 11 | 30 | 237 | 14 | 29 | 180 | — | 99 | — | 48 | 322 | — |
| 1938 | 10 | 36 | 104 | 144 | 32 | 180 | — | 99 | — | 44 | 326 | — |
| *A. Prouvost* (Roubaix)—wool | | | | | | | | | | | | |
| 1920 | 4 | 17 | 1 | 21 | 3 | 10 | 4 | 21 | 11 | — | 46 | — |
| 1931 | 78 | 68 | 37 | 29 | 17 | 85 | 25 | 89 | 23 | 7 | 210 | — |
| 1938 | 31 | 78 | 60 | 27 | 26 | 85 | 25 | 77 | 30 | 6 | 222 | 280 |

Source:  *Bilans annuels, présentés aux Assemblées générales d'actionnaires.*

On the asset side, buildings and plants are presented in gross value at Peugeot (the depreciation charges being added to the capital and reserve accounts), and net of depreciation at Michelin, Dollfus-Mieg and A. Prouvost. The item "shares held" (a) includes securities and participations in subsidiary firms. The balancing items are not detailed Separately in the assets. Sales at Michelin (b) are a press estimate.

period) and had started raising capital in the stock market from about 1905, the scale of operations of the parent firm and the management of its subsidiary companies—Schneider and St-Gobain had accumulated each 170–180 such companies by 1930–brought new problems that could not be solved without a true reallocation of authority between branches, departments and the central office. The tendency, in practice, for the larger corporations still under family influence or control—e.g. Kulhmann, les Aciéries de la Marine, those of Longwy, the Schneiders' group, etc.—was to let the company transform itself into a loose federation of semi-independent units with a holding organization at the top, probably for the reason that it answered two purposes: one, to maintain in function the board of directors or the supervisory committees, as in the past, with their family element; and, two, to appoint a general director, who was brought in at first as representative or advisor to the shareholding families, but who had assumed by the 1920s a position of real autonomy, being recruited in one of the State engineers' corps and being as such acceptable to the staff.

The case of St-Gobain, then the largest corporation in the country, was somewhat different. It had followed policies similar to those of other firms, entering foreign markets through branches and subsidiaries, and steadily diversifying its production through the 1920s under the lead of its departments' directors. Perhaps to too great an extent, for the company found itself with falling sales and uncompleted investments in 1932–33, when the boom came to an end. This made its reorganization a more urgent matter. One obvious solution, in line with past policies, was to strengthen the authority of the board by calling in new recruits and setting up a new executive sub-committee, restricted in number and reinforced by a consultant engineer, to review current policies and offer new lines for action. But, in the mid-1930s, as the depression was deepening, an alternative solution was taken up: an officer, who had set in order one of the subsidiary companies was called to the presidency, with the task of building up a central executive office and a divisional organization that were to supercede the functions formerly held by the board. This reform—which did not do away with family tradition in the company[15]—was a further sign of the greater weight inside officers had won in large corporations and of the need to find a new balance between inside officers and family representatives.

The second limit was financial. There was a general feeling that the wealth of business families made their firms safe and secure, whatever the state of the market. This belief came from a wrong assessment the public had made of the amount of funds all firms had accumulated in the 1920s inflationary period, price rises relieving them for a while of the necessity of clearing up their debts, and again in 1928–30, once inflation had abated, when active, but obviously exaggerated campaigns were organized in the press to prepare their introduction on the stock market and to float new issues. Further, most family firms, especially in the provinces, had kept to the same old amortization rules that were used in the 19th century—they still depreciated their capital investment as fully as possible each year—so that their rise in market value, when they were first quoted on the stock exchange, uncovered what appeared at the time as hidden resources, but amounted simply to the substitution of inflated replacement costs for old depreciated values. It may be recalled that fixed assets at the Michelins' company were entered in 1928 accounts for less than 80 million francs (Table 2), although they included sales agencies (at home and abroad), plants (with a capacity equal to 40% of the French tire production), workers housing facilities and rubber plantations (still unproductive); these two last items alone were valued in financial reports for half a billion F, six times more than all the company's depreciated assets taken together. In the same way, Dollfus-Mieg & Cie maintained at 12–15 million francs—the figure at which they had been appraised in the 1890 accounts—the net value of their plants, although some 225 million F, almost six million a year, had been invested in the intervening forty years, etc. When companies remained unlisted, as the majority were, State officials' interventions often brought about the same impression, for they had the power to revise upwards—for tax purposes—the companies' balance sheets. For instance, the gross value of the plants, at A. Prouvost's textile mills, in Roubaix, was raised in one stroke in the 1931 accounts from 100 to 150 million F, and other cases of similar magnitude were many. Besides the same conservative methods of valuation applied to inventories of imported

raw materials whenever the French currency fell on the foreign
exchanges, price rises were being under-reported in the accounts
for fear of a possible reversal of the market. In 1929–30, at the time
of the Wall Street crash, this procedure was extended further to other
items in certain firms' accounts to hedge against foreseeable losses.
As one could read in the late 1920s reports to the shareholders at
the Dollfus-Mieg company:

> all financial elements, bank accounts, in France and in foreign
> countries, debts to be cashed in, bills receivable and securities in
> the company's portfolio, have been entered with important depre-
> ciation charges to guard against any contingency.

But these and other measures were to prove defective under the
impact of the depression, because it was most severe in the modern
sectors where firms had built vertically integrated units, combining
production and marketing, highly vulnerable to changes in
demand; and because the length of the debt-deflation process,
once the collapse of the stock market had closed a major source of
capital, and the long deferment of replacement orders, meant that
no one could remain unscathed. Contemporary observers tended
to draw a distinction between the old conservative families, who
were supposed to hold financial reserves, and the more recent ones
who had built excess capacities with borrowed capital, more particularly in the automobile sector, where, in contrast to his competitors, André Citroën, who had redesigned his production lines
and made large investments in response to the crisis, was forced to
suspend his payments in December 1934, with more than 900
million in debts unprovided for. But this presentation is unacceptable
as it does not give a fair account of facts.

Two concrete cases may be recalled. First, that of the Peugeots.
They are said to have pursued a most uneventful course, keeping
their output equal to one-fifth of the market, extending and specializ-
ing their production and sales facilities, ear-marking each year
large sums for depreciation charges and issuing new stocks ahead of
the crash to keep out of debt. The firm, though, was unexpectedly
caught short in October 1930 when the two bankers who had been
admitted to the board to organize the company's financial operations

went bankrupt (the first in a long list), leaving unpaid the last of the company's capital issue and costing thereby three-fifths of its cash accounts. The accident was overcome by writing off the 1930 profit, deducting the balance from the reserves and drawing in almost all outstanding credits. But at a cost: sales were cut by a third in 1930–32, and remained for three years at 80–85% of their peak level, at half of what was technically the potential output.[16] The Michelins' firm was never in such a predicament, thanks to their large reserves and net short term assets; they remained all through the 1930s among the ten largest industrial firms listed on the exchange.[17] But they could not escape losses. These came from the depreciation of their raw materials' stocks (profits were already down by 30% in 1926–28); the contraction in sales turnover and bad debts—250 million F were written off in 1933 to cancel part of the credits left unpaid by Citroën, the firm's main customer, and last, from the fall of this firm, since the Michelins had to reduce the value of the shares they still held in the company and to subscribe most of the new stock that was issued in 1935 to absorb it, Citroën becoming a subsidiary that had to be kept running.[18] Inflation had produced fictitious profits, but the depression did cost large capital outlays to cover hidden, but genuine, losses.

This is not to say that family firms had no cards to play: they still had the power to command sacrifice from their shareholders in the shape of foregone dividends (through most of the 1930s); their affiliated companies were able to raise new credits from local banks, using the parent firm's old reputed name; they proved more sensitive to changes in consumer demand (market studies conducted in 1935–36, when demand at last revived, led Peugeot and Citroën, under its new direction, to start manufacturing economy cars).[19] But the new trends that have been examined—the greater autonomy of the firms' managerial structures and the loss of capital resources during the 1930s—were two adverse forces that could not be remedied.

To sum up the main points, the large family firm, i.e. a firm in partial control of a market, which had remained for two or three generations or more in the hands of the same family, did not play in France the role that might have been expected from the country's past technical achievements. As it was recalled, the great merchant banking houses did not regain after the 1860s their former position, and in 1929, family firms were few to have reached a scale of operations that would have made them competitive by international standards.[20] Economic factors—the sluggishness of the domestic market, a great vulnerability of the export trade, concentrated as it was on products with high skilled labor and technical content, and two sharp depressions in the late 19th century and in the 1930s—were among the causes of this disappointing performance. But it may well be that the family system as such was not economically viable. This is not to say that it did not deserve consideration and esteem. The idea that family capital could be substituted to outside finance, business responsibilities should be allocated according to school achievements and the building of a community based on the forbearance and dedication of the work-force, in short that family firms could ward off market forces, had much to commend in a country of small entrepreneurs who were still living by these principles. But this is no proof that they were well adapted to the requirements of large-scale production and mass markets, the priority given to the upgrading of the work force, the selection of high ranking engineers and paternalistic measures being no substitute for long-term planning and managerial efficiency.

## NOTES

1. M. Lévy-Leboyer, "The Large Corporation in Modern France," in A. D. Chandler, Jr., and H. Daems, ed., *Managerial Hierarchies. Comparative Perspectives on the Rise of Modern Industrial Enterprise* (Cambridge, Mass., 1980), pp. 118–ff.
2. High estimates of the capital that belonged to the five Rothschild houses have been made: £2–4 millions in 1818–25, 22 in 1863 and 35 million in 1875, i.e. equivalent to 900 million francs. Cf. B. Gille, *Histoire de la Maison Rothschild* (Genève, 1965–1966), t. I, pp. 450–1, and t. II, p. 571.
3. A. Plessis, *La Banque de France sous le Second Empire* (Université de Paris-I, unpubl. Pd. D. thesis, 1982), pp. 428–ff.

4. B. Gille, *Les Rothschild*, *op. cit.*, II, pp. 539–64 and 579–89.

5. On the role of the Neuflize and Seillière families at le Creusot, cf. J. A. Roy, *Histoire de la famille Schneider et du Creusot* (Paris, 1962). An analysis of the shareholders at St-Gobain—150 in 1830, and 60,000 in 1900—has been sketched by J. P. Daviet, "La direction des affaires de la Cie de St-Gobain, 1830–1872," paper presented at the 2nd Congrès national de l'Association française des Historiens économistes, Paris, 1980; and "Les problèmes de gestion et d'organization de St-Gobain entre les deux guerres mondiales" (unpubl. paper, 1981). Cf. also M. Lévy-Leboyer, "Hierarchical Structures and Incentives in a Large Corporation: the Early Managerial Experience of St-Gobain, 1872–1912," in N. Horn and J. Kocka, *Recht und Entwicklung der Grossunternehmen im 19. und frühen 20. Jahrhundert* (Göttingen, 1979), pp. 451–ff.

6. P. Cayez, "Une explosion du capitalism urbain: La naissance de la société Progil, 1918–25," in *Colloque franco-suisse d'histoire économique* (Lyons, 1977); A. Baudant, *Pont-à-Mousson, 1918–1930. Stratégies industrielles d'une dynastie lorraine* (Université de Paris-I, Unpubl. Ph. D. thesis, 1979), which presents an account of the Financière Lorraine, the holding trust of the Cavallier family, who dominated Pont-à-Mousson.

7. F. Caron, *Histoire de l'exploitation d'un grand réseau. La compagnie du chemin de fer du Nord, 1846–1937* (Paris, 1973), *passim;* M. Lévy-Leboyer, *St-Gobain, 1872–1912, op. cit.*; F. Crouzet, "Essor, déclin et renaissance de l'industrie française des locomotives, 1838–1914," in *Revue d'histoire économique et sociale*, 55e vol. (1977), n° 1–2, pp. 112-sqtes.

8. P. Lanthier, "Les dirigeants des grandes entreprises électriques en France, 1911–1973," in M. Lévy-Leboyer, ed., *Le patronat de la seconde industrialisation* (Paris, 1979), pp. 101–36. In the automobile industry, small teams of 3–5 fellow-workers helped Louis Renault, from the opening of the shop in 1899, André Citroën when he left the Mors company to start on his own, and Robert Peugeot, in 1922, when he modernized the Sochaux plants; cf. G. Hatry, *Louis Renault* (Université de Paris-I, unpubl. Ph. D. thesis, 1982), p. 120; J. L. Loubet, *Histoire d'une entreprise automobile, Citroën, 1919–1939* (Université de Paris-X Nanterre, unpubl. Ph. D. thesis, 1978); and Ph. Girardet, *Ceux que j'ai connus* (Paris, 1952), on the Peugeot company.

9. J. P. Daviet, *La direction de la Cie de St-Gobain, op. cit.*

10. M. Lévy-Leboyer, "Le patronat français a-t-il été malthusien?"

232 M. Lévy-Leboyer

*Le mouvement* social, n° 88 (1974), pp. 3–ff; G. Ahlström, *Engineers and Industrial Growth* (London, 1982), p. 38.

11.  M. Lévy-Leboyer, "Le patronat français, 1912–1973," in M. Lévy-Leboyer, *Le patronat, op. cit.*, p. 174; and P. Lanthier, *Le patronat électricien, art. cit.*

12.  Besides J. A. Roy, *Les Schneider, op. cit.*, cf. P. Fritsch, *Les Wendel, rois de l'acier* (Paris, 1952), and M. Lévy-Leboyer, *The Managerial Experience of St-Gobain, op. cit.*

13.  Pioneers of these policies were the managers of department stores in Paris, the Boucicaut (le Bon Marché) and the Congnacq-Jay (la Samaritaine); cf. M. B. Miller, *The Bon Marché. Bourgeois Culture and the Department Store, 1869–1920* (Princeton University Press, 1981). The same ideas, within the constraints of an entirely different environment, were applied in the automobile industry, in particular at Peugeot in the 1920s and the late 1930s, when seniority and fidelity bonuses were reenacted.

14.  Speaking of the Schneiders' works as they were in the 1930s, at a meeting of former students of the Ecoles des Arts et Métiers in October 1979, Pierre Chaffiotte, president of the Association, who had made his career with the firm, after his father, praised the company as "un magnifique instrument de promotion sociale, donnant à tous l'égalité des chances"; cf. Cl. Beaud, "Les ingénieurs du Creusot à travers quelques destins du milieu du 19e au milieu du 20e siècle," in *Ingénieurs et Société* (Colloque, le Creusot, October 1980), p. III-2.

15.  The Baron Pierre Hély d'Oiseel, who was elected president in 1936, was the fifth man in the family to hold either a seat on the board or the presidency (since 1830), and he succeeded to his father-in-law, president Roederer, himself of a family who had been for many generations on the board. P. Hély d'Oiseel came from the Ecole des Mines, while Alphonse Gérard, president of the company from 1917 to 1931, again the fourth member of the family on the company's board, was a Polytechnicien ingénieur du Corps des Mines.

16.  Peugeot's loss with its bankers, A. Oustric and Gualino, amounted to 61.4 million F, the equivalent of the cash balance they had left with them, their condition for issuing the last capital increase had been that the funds would be drawn monthly. The firm had to reduce their short-term commitments from 263 to 31 million F in 1936, forcing its agents to assume a more independent position and to find credits with local banks.

17.  E. Michelin had partly refunded the company's capital so that it had 350 million F of reserves and amortized capital and 700 million F of short-term net assets in 1928, 535 and 965 million in 1932.

18.  Out of 400 million F capital, 325 were cancelled and transfered as passive shares (parts de fondateurs) to the creditors for half their claim, the other half being covered, for the same nominal amount, by new bonds at 3.25% interest. And 135 million F of new shares were issued, making in all (with the 75 million F left to the older shareholders) a new capital of 210 million F; J. L. Loubet, *L'entreprise Citroën*, pp. 143–46.

19.  *Automobiles Peugeot. Rapport aux actionnaires*, 18 March 1937; J. L. Loubet, *op. cit.*, pp. 166–68.

20.  The very large firms—St-Gobain, with 3.7 billion F market value in 1929, and Citroën, then with 1.9 billion market value—realized $50–75 million annual turnover, i.e. only a fraction of 3–5% of the large American oil and automobile companies, 12–15% of the leaders in electrical industries.

# COMMENTS

Makoto Seoka
*Kyoto Gakuen University*

The main points of issue in Lévy-Leboyer's essay can be summed up and commented on as follows.

1. He emphasizes the diversity of family firms in France. He points out that family firms, in the degree of their "financial autonomy and secure basis," might vary with the timing when they were initiated. Therefore, he distinguishes "the older group, dating back for many of its members from Napoleon's days" from "the more recent ones, having often started their operations at the turn of the century." On the other hand, as regards the latter, he points out "the paradox of French family firms, in the early part of the 20th century," that is to say, "the great majority were considered as having had long years of experience and capital accumulation," but "only a limited number," as he shows, "had reached a position of financial autonomy and a secure basis."

This suggests that we should take account of the difference in the timing of the commencement between family firms in relation to the economic conditions under which they have been placed, as well as the difference in their size, in order to analyze their ownership and management. Of course, we also know that family firms do not exist independently of the economic conditions, and that the degree of the potential entrepreneurial ability to change the economic conditions at any particular time and place must be taken into account, because the economic conditions themselves are also sociological phenomena. For example, as David S. Landes has suggested, "the influence of French entrepreneurial psychology on her economic structure has been and is extremely important."

2. "Major increases in business' annual turnover" after the beginning of the 20th century brought about "a shortage of liquid

funds," that is, "imbalance between cash funds and the flow of current operations." In order to meet with this situation, bankers were appointed on the board and a lot of new shares were issued. (We know that the important work of Lévy-Leboyer, published in 1964, presents a favorable view of French bankers.) As a result, "the threat of a separation between ownership and management had become an actual issue." Then family firms devised three pragmatic ways to "strengthen the authority of managers having to supervise the activities and coordinate the resources of what had become, probably in too short a time, large-scale organizations." They were the adoption of a holding company organization, the formation of family trusts and the issue of preference shares. But these ways were only "temporary devices that could not stop the slow erosion of families' influence over business activity." The family firm had to "transform itself into a loose federation of semi-independent units with a holding organization at the top," in order to maintain family influence and survive in the world of "large-scale production and mass markets," in the direction of which the social inheritance had operated against organizing economic pressures. (At any rate, we are confident that with Lévy-Leboyer's work supplementing Bertrand Gille's study of the Rothschilds and Jean Bouvier's of Crédit Lyonnais, we have a fair body of evidence.)

3. Lévy-Leboyer points out the importance of their hierarchical structures as one of the features of internal business organization. These hierarchies were "made up of two different sets of personnel and objectives, one for general management and external relations, and one for more routine and concrete duties." Moreover, all large-scale enterprises in the 20th century came to have "the board of directors" and "central executive offices." Lévy-Leboyer, to explain their relation, uses the expression that these two sets of authority were "working in a highly cohesive way." But it seems that he should explain this relation more concretely and more exactly.

4. Lévy-Leboyer points out that family firms laid stress on "the problem of training their work-force," and managed to fix it through "highly paternalistic measures." But whether or not this tendency could be observed only in the family firms in France should be

clarified, in view of the opinion of Rondo Cameron that the French system's high quality of technical education was a great advantage for supplying the necessary skilled "work-force."

    5.    At any rate, Lévy-Leboyer seems to give us the family character of French business and its self-imposed goal of financial self-sufficiency.

# Family Enterprise and the Rise of Large-Scale Enterprise in Germany [1871–1914] —Ownership and Management—

Jürgen Brockstedt
*Freie Universität Berlin*

The genesis of large-scale enterprises is closely connected with the economic rise of the German Empire.[1] For this reason, the period from 1871 until World War I is to be dealt with here. After the so-called "Gründerjahre" (1871–1873), development at first began with a long crisis which led to relative stagnation. Not until the mid-1890s did a period of comparatively rapid and steady growth follow, which lasted until 1914 and was only interrupted in 1900–1902 and 1907–1909.[2] The German economy, which had been relatively backward in comparison with England and other industrialized countries of Western Europe, reached their level and even assumed a leading position in a few areas such as the production of pig-iron and steel and the electrical and the chemical industries.[3] This growth was associated with considerable changes in the enterprise sector.

Some of these changes—those which took place in the area of ownership and management—are to be investigated here. In order to clarify the background to the following questions, the genesis of large-scale enterprises will be dealt with first. Then we shall examine the transition from owner-enterprise and family enterprise to manager-enterprise, the separation of capital ownership from disposition or control of capital, that is, the shift of entrepreneurial decision making processes, and the question of whether, with the rise of large enterprises, the influence of entrepreneurial families declined in the period from 1871 until World War I. The third part of this study is concerned with the differences between the

237

legal form and the actual exercise of management in family enterprises as large-scale enterprises. And finally, management in family
enterprises and non-family enterprises will be compared.

In order to present a more complete picture of the position and
development of family enterprises up to 1914, attention will also be
given to medium-sized and small enterprises, since the greater part
of family enterprises were undoubtedly of this kind.

The study of these topics is problematic for different reasons.
Above all, scholarly historical research in the area of family enterprises is still rather undeveloped, a state of affairs which has rightly
been deplored by a number of authors.[4]

## I.

The rise of large-scale enterprises had already started before 1871,
although the tendency to enlarge was not yet as  developed as it
became after the founding of the Empire. As already stated, smaller
and medium-sized firms in the form of sole proprietorships or personal
partnerships predominated. Large-scale enterprises existed above all
in branches with a high capital requirement such as railway companies and banks. In these areas, some of which were entirely new,
the form of the joint-stock company (Aktiengesellschaft, AG), which
was to play an important part in the development of large enterprises, was used right from the start.

The structures of enterprises changed considerably in the "Gründerjahre." Above all, the number of newly formed joint-stock  companies rose sharply: while 295 companies with capital amounting to
2,404 million marks were formed in the period from 1851 until 1870
(1st half-year), the period from July 1870 until 1874 saw the addition of 857 joint-stock companies with total capital of 3,306 million
marks.[5] This boom was made possible by the liberalization of the
joint-stock company law in 1870, which also facilitated enterprise
growth.[6]

The crisis which set in after 1873 had various effects: Numerous
newly formed enterprises, not least joint-stock companies, went
bankrupt. The remainder were faced with stiff national and international competition and had to adjust to the difficult conditions.

In spite of, or indeed because of this, long-term development was one of concentration and expansion, that is, the number of large-scale enterprises rose.[7] This development became still more pronounced after the economic boom from the mid 1890s onwards and continued until 1914. Since large-scale enterprises were preponderantly share companies, the numerical development may serve to clarify this process: in 1886/87 2,143 joint-stock companies existed, with capital amounting to 4,876 million marks. In 1909 there were 5,222 joint-stock companies with total capital of 14,723 million marks.[8] From 1873 until 1913, the joint-stock companies' capital rose roughly tenfold.[9] For the year 1914, Tilly has ascertained the existence of 548 large-scale enterprises with 1,000 or more workers each, that is, about one-eighth of those employed in industry.[10]

Various authors agree that the rise of large-scale enterprises proceeded at a remarkable rate, that this rise influenced the growth of the economy, and vice versa.[11] The causes of this intensive development were manifold. Thus the general situation of the market, with (at least from the 1890s onwards) demand rising by leaps and bounds, led to a form of automatic expansion, for large new markets provided a motive for mass production and enterprise expansion.[12] The prolonged crisis situation after 1873 necessitated not only organization and rationalization in the technological and commercial areas of the enterprises, but also led to the concentration and expansion of enterprises as well as to cartellization as a means of securing larger shares of the market.[13] Employing many qualified experts as well as modern technology, the enterprises, with large capital requirements, sought to lessen entrepreneurial risks through growth, that is, through incorporating further stages of production and marketing.[14] Technological change (railways, telegraph) also made enterprise growth possible by widening the markets.[15] Tilly gives particular emphasis to the influence of the banks, the state, the bureaucracy and science of the genesis of large-scale enterprises.[16] Finally, the comparative backwardness of the German economy is stressed as a particularly significant cause, since it provided a motive for many entrepreneurs to adopt the advanced technology and more modern organizational forms of the Western industrial nations (above all

England and the U.S.A.) in order to be able to compete in Germany and on the world market.[17] These are some important causes of the rapid growth of large-scale enterprises; a number of them will be discussed in greater detail below.

The essential investment decisions which influenced the genesis of large-scale enterprises could lead to differing growth strategies.[18] Expansion could be achieved through internal and external enlargement (through founding new enterprises or changing the legal form of existing ones, or through fusion or expansion); according to Chandler and Daems this was usually accompanied by functional integration and product diversification.[19]

Integration was a form of expansion which was increasingly used in many branches of industry. Thus the raw material industry and further stages of production, as well as marketing, were integrated into the iron and steel industry. Unlike their English counterparts, German industrialists were particularly interested in marketing, because in Germany independent wholesale trade in industrial products was not so well developed.[20] This was particularly evident in the electrical and the chemical industries as well as in the production of sewing machines and bicycles.[21] In branches which were more labor-intensive, such as engineering, there was less integration.

Product diversification was another means through which large-scale enterprises developed.[22] Here too, individual branches such as the electrical industry and the chemical industry were more strongly represented, while others, such as textiles, leather goods and ceramics were less diversified.[23]

The degree to which integration and diversification were used as growth strategies differed not only from one branch of industry to another but also between the industrialized nations.[24] In this connection, Chandler and Daems assume that, in America, integration preceded diversification and that both took place earlier there than in England.[25] Siegrist has demonstrated what Kocka had already surmised—that in Germany it was not uncommon for diversification and integration to take place simultaneously; diversification and integration did not take place any later in Germany than in the U.S.A., but were used as entrepreneurial strategy simultaneously or even, in some cases, earlier. This is particularly true of diversification, which was already being used in Germany before 1900, whereas it was not generally employed in the U.S.A. until after 1920.[26] The causes of these different developments are to be seen in the utterly different market structures facing large-scale enterprises, in the fear of national and international competition and in Germany's comparative economic backwardness.[27] Developments similar to those in Germany also took place in France and Japan.[28]

The relatively strong influence of the banks is seen as being not the least of the factors which affected the growth of large-scale enterprises.[29] Large share banks had played an important part in financing the expanding industries in the 1850s as well as in the "Gründerjahre" after 1870.[30] Comparative backwardness led not only to the more frequent appearance of joint-stock companies, but also to the more frequent founding of investment banks and to the greater influence of these banks.[31] In Kocka's view, the significance of the banks was not equally strong in all respects.[32] According to him, their direct influence on large-scale enterprises was transformed in the 1890s and after the crisis of 1900–1902 into a more indirect influence which was exercised by the bank directors in the supervisory boards (Aufsichtsräte) of the enterprises. That large family enterprises such as Krupp, Thyssen or Siemens vigorously resisted the influence of the banks is well-known. We can also speak of a similar attitude in well-known salaried entrepreneurs such as Emil Kirdorf (Gelsenkirchener Bergwerks-AG), Emil Rathenau (AEG) or Nikolaus Eich (Mannesmann-Werke), even if the struggle for independence within managerial enterprises was not so easily won.[33] In general, it can be stated that the banks' controlling influence on large-scale enterprises was greater in times of crisis than in economically favorable situations.

Taken as a whole, the formation of widely diversified and integrated large-scale enterprises in Germany had made considerable progress by 1914[34]: in order to belong to the hundred largest industrial enterprises, capital amounting to at least 3.8 million marks was necessary in 1887, and in 1907, capital amounting to at least 10 million marks was  necessary; this group of 100 large-scale enterprises was headed in 1887 by the Dortmunder Union AG (iron and steel industry) with 40 million marks share capital and in 1907 by the Friedrich Krupp AG with 180 million marks. The legal form of the share company certainly facilitated enterprise expansion; nevertheless, until the 1920s there were no very large enterprise units comparable with trusts in the U.S.A., because appropriate preconditions such as large markets did not exist and because it was possible to reach the same end (control of the market) with the help of cartels and syndicates.[35] In comparing the development in Germany to that in the U.S.A., we must thus not only modify Chandler's thesis on the role played by integration and diversification on the growth of the enterprises, we must also note certain differences relating to the maximum size of enterprises, without as yet being in a position to quantify these differences.

## II.

It is assumed that close and mutual relationships existed between enterprise growth on the one hand and the transition from owner or family enterprises to managerial enterprises on the other.[36] We shall now examine this transition more closely, whereby we are above all interested in the question whether the influence of entrepreneurial families on central entrepreneurial decisions was lessened during this transformation period or merely assumed a different form.[37]

Changes in the area of ownership and of disposition and control in the area of entrepreneurial decisions and the legal form of enterprises represent a long-term process which is not over even today. According to Chandler, the transition to managerial enterprises in a somewhat modified form may be divided into three stages, a procedure which is useful for the purposes of historical research:[38] in the owner-managed enterprise, long-term strategic decisions and tactical management decisions are taken by the owners (personal enterprise); in the intermediate stage (entrepreneurial enterprise), the tactical management decisions are taken by managers while entrepreneurial decisions on financial policy, the use of resources or the appointment of senior executives are taken by the founder or his family, that is, by the owners; the third and last stage is represented by the managerial enterprise, in which the capital is relatively widely distributed and salaried entrepreneurs with no significant ownership in the enterprise make the long-term as well as tactical decisions.

If Chandler's thesis to the effect that the rise of managerial capitalism was due to enterprise growth is to be applied to Germany, the causes of the transition from personal to managerial enterprise must first be presented.[39] These causes must have been fundamental, for during the Industrial Revolution the influence of the family had been absolutely dominant.[40]

A precondition of the transition to managerial enterprise was the enterprise form of the joint-stock company. Over and above this, the transition was in part connected with the rise of large-scale enterprises. For the growth of such enterprises, on the one hand a great deal of capital and, on the other hand, new, modern organizational and management structures were required. Both of these could be more easily achieved with joint-stock companies than with the help of sole proprietorships or personal partnerships.[41] The latter were not necessarily willing to take the risk of expansion to large-scale enterprises, that is, a legal form with risk distribution like that of the joint-stock companies had to be used. Owner-entrepreneurs were frequently not prepared to accept the rules of the joint-stock company such as the limit on disposal over capital, because they would thus have lost their independence ("Herr-im-Haus" point of view). From time to time, succession within the entrepreneurial family had to be secured by transforming the enterprise into a joint-stock company, as in the case of Krupp in 1902, or an entrepreneurial family was no longer capable of running the enterprise, as in the case of Mannesmann.[42]

In this connection the so-called "Buddenbrook-effect" is more frequently mentioned as the reason for assuming the legal form of the joint-stock company.[43] By this is meant that for a number of reasons such as extravagance, disinterest or lack of progeny entrepreneurs of the third generation were no longer in a position to continue running the family enterprise. But the reduction and spreading of risk is also named as a motive, for an entrepreneurial

TABLE 1  The 100 Largest Industrial Enterprises in Germany; Legal Form at Foundation, in 1887 and 1907.

| Legal form at foundation | gp | gp | gp | gp | cb co | lp | sp | state | js co | cb co | sp |
|---|---|---|---|---|---|---|---|---|---|---|---|
| 1887 | gp | co. ltd. | cb co | js co | js co | js co | js co | js co | js co | cb co | sp |
| Mining | 1 | | 1 | 1 | 5 | | | 1 | 12 | 3 | |
| Building | 2 | | | | | | | | | | |
| Iron and metal | 8 | | | 11 | 1 | | | | 10 | | |
| Engineering | 3 | | | 7 | | | | | 2 | | |
| Electrical ind. | 1 | | | | | | | | 1 | | |
| Chemical ind. | | | | 7 | | | | | 3 | | |
| Textiles | | | | 1 | | | | 1 | 1 | | |
| Rubber | | | | 1 | | 1 | | | | | |
| Wood | | | | | | 1 | | | | | |
| Food | | | | 3 | 1 | | 1 | | 1 | | |
| Unknown 7 | | | | | | | | | | | |
| Total | 15 | | 1 | 31 | 7 | 2 | 1 | 2 | 30 | 4 | |
| **1907** | | | | | | | | | | | |
| Mining | 3 | | | | 3 | | | | 8 | 8 | |
| Building | 2 | | | | 1 | | | | 1 | | |
| Iron and metal | 2 | | | 12 | | | | | 11 | 2 | |
| Engineering | 2 | | | 8 | | | | | 1 | | |
| Electrical ind. | 2 | | | 3 | | | | | 1 | | |
| Chemical ind. | 1 | | | 11 | | | | | 4 | | |
| Textiles | 1 | | | | | | | | 1 | | |
| Paper | 1 | | | | | | | | | | 1 |
| Food | 4 | | | | | | | | 1 | | |

| Unknown | 1 | | | | | | | |
| --- | --- | --- | --- | --- | --- | --- | --- | --- |
| Total | 7 | 5 | 41 | 5 | 2 | 27 | 10 | 1 |

Source: Kocka and Siegrist, op. cit., pp. 98–112.

gp=general partnership; cb co=cost-book company; lp=limited partnership; sp=share partnership; co. ltd.=limited liability company; js co=joint-stock company.

TABLE 2   German Shipbuilding Enterprises 1911/1913 (1000 or more employees).

| Name of firm headquarters | Actual legal form | Since | Year of foundation | Legal form at foundation | Preceeding firm since | Nominal capital in million marks (1911) | Employees (w=workers) (1913) |
|---|---|---|---|---|---|---|---|
| Atlas-Werke, Bremen | js co | 1902 | 1902 | js co | — | | 2,000 w |
| Blohm & Voß, Hamburg | sp | 1891 | 1877 | gp | — | 12.0 | 10,000 |
| Germania-Werft (Krupp), Kiel | js co | 1865 | 1882 | js co | 1865 | | 7,000 |
| Howaltswerke, Kiel | js co | 1889 | 1876 | spr | — | 7.75 | 3,500 |
| Neptun, Rostock | js co | 1890 | 1881 | gp | 1850 | 2.2 | 1,970 |
| Actien-Gesellschaft Reiherstieg-Schiffswerft und Maschinenfabrik, Hamburg | js co | 1879 | 1706 | spr | — | 5.0 | 2,800 |
| Schichau Werft, Danzig, Pillau, Elbing | spr | 1852 | 1852 | spr | — | | 9,000 |
| Flensburger Schiffbau-Gesellschaft, Flensburg | js co | 1872 | 1872 | js co | — | 3.3 | 2,800 |
| G. Seebeck, Geestemünde, Bremerhaven | js co | 1895 | 1876 | spr | — | 3.5 | 1,100 |
| J. C. Tecklenborg, Bremerhaven, Geestemünde | js co | 1897 | 1879 | spr | — | 4.0 | 3,000 |
| Bremer Vulkan, Bremen | js co | 1893 | 1893 | spr | 1805 | 10.0 | 3,500 |

| Hamburger Vulkan, Hamburg | js co | 1907 | 1907 | js co | | 15.0 | 7,600 w |
|---|---|---|---|---|---|---|---|
| Stettiner Vulkan, Stettin | js co | 1857 | 1857 | js co | 1851 | — | 7,440 w |
| A.-G. Weser, Bremen | js co | 1872 | 1872 | js co | 1848 | 7.336 | 6,000 |

spr=sole proprietorship; gp=general partnership; js co=joint-stock company; sp=share partnership.

family can, by transforming the enterprise into a joint-stock company, limit entrepreneurial risk and acquire capital with which it can gain an interest in other firms.[44]

This raises the question: to what extent did the change to the enterprise form of the joint-stock company, that is, the transition to the managerial enterprise, take place? Regrettably, the present state of research does not permit of any exact statements in this respect; however, Kocka and Siegrist have published some findings which represent considerable progress in this area.[45] In their study of the hundred largest industrial and mining enterprises they have arrived at new conclusions for the period from 1887 until 1907 (Table 1). Of the firms investigated in their first survey (1887), less than one fifth (15) had retained the legal form of the personal partnership or the sole proprietorship. Among these, however, were very large firms such as Krupp, Siemens, Borsig, Schichau-Werft, Stinnes and Stumm, and also a large number of iron, coal and steel enterprises in Upper Silesia, whose owners were great landowners. The proportion of enterprises which had been converted into capital companies such as joint-stock companies and the like, was more than twice as high (31). In the field of mining there were a few (7) cases of conversion from cost-book companies (bergrechtliche Gewerkschaft) to joint-stock companies, and almost one-third (30) of the large-scale enterprises were founded with share company status.

If we compare these results with those of 1907, we can see a striking reduction of over 50% in the number of enterprises whose legal form as sole proprietorships or personal partnerships had not been altered since their foundation, the great majority of which were owned by Silesian magnates. The tendency for enterprises to be converted into capital companies was considerably greater than in the earlier period (c. 50% of the 100 enterprises). In this connection, mention must also be made of the appearance of a new legal form, the "company with limited liability" (Gesellschaft mit beschränkter Haftung—GmbH). Among the enterprises, which were founded as capital companies, two points may be noted: first, the number of joint-stock companies has become smaller and secondly, cost-book companies represent a higher proportion (10) of the total. We can assume that a considerable number of the enterprises which were transformed into capital and cost-book companies may be regarded as entrepreneurial enterprises. The proportion of joint-stock companies which were managerial enterprises can only be determined with difficulty, but was certainly larger than in 1887.

The development of managerial enterprises is not equally marked in all branches of industry (Table 1). In the mining industry, for example, essential elements of the managerial enterprise were realized relatively early; however, the mining companies were mostly still entrepreneurial enterprises.[46] In the iron and steel industry there was a high proportion of joint-stock companies; nevertheless, entrepreneurial families still retained a very strong influence. The entrepreneurial element also remained in engineering.[47] In new capital-intensive branches such as the chemical and electrical industries, entrepreneurial enterprises predominated; however, managerial enterprises gained in relative importance. In the textile industry there was only a slight degree of integration and diversification and the enterprise form of the joint-stock company was used relatively late; of the large-scale enterprises in the textile industry, only a few firms are represented as joint-stock companies.[48] The same is true for the remaining branches of industry, such as food, paper and building.

These results are supplemented by the conclusions of a specialized investigation of the shipbuilding industry in Germany (Table 2).[49] Of the 13 large-scale enterprises existing in 1913, only one, the Schichau-Werft in Danzig, which was one of the largest, remained a single proprietorship and family enterprise until 1929. Against this, there were at least seven joint-stock companies such as the Atlas-Werke, Neptun-Werft, Reiherstieg-Werft, Flensburger Schiffbau-Gesellschaft, Bremer Vulkan, Hamburger-Stettiner Vulcan and AG Weser, which were run as managerial enterprises. A characteristic of these joint-stock companies was that the shares were distributed among a limited circle of merchants, ship owners, industrialists (above all, owners of iron foundries and engineering works) and bankers. Five of these shipyards developed out of family enterprises or partnerships, while two were founded as joint-stock companies. The remaining shipyards may be described as family enterprises with entrepreneurial management. In the case of the Howaldt-Werft, a new family took over the enterprise, and the Germania-Werft became a family enterprise belonging to Krupp in 1902.

Entrepreneurial families lost a considerable amount of influence in the shipbuilding industry. Nevertheless, of the large shipyards existing in 1913, four important and two smaller enterprises were still run as family enterprises. Taken as a whole, these findings do not seem to differ greatly from generalized statements and suppositions on how the influence of entrepreneurial families in German industry developed.

Even if the sources do not permit of a classification according to the three enterprise types in every case, we may nevertheless assume that, in general, the rise of large-scale enterprises (mostly joint-stock companies) led to a reduction in the number of family enterprises among the large-scale enterprises,[50] a trend which was intensified in the 1920s.[51] If we look at the development of family influence in a less restricted sense, with influence defined more through disposal of and control over capital than through formal ownership in an enterprise, we must come to a different judgement.[52] Thus, a number of large-scale enterprises such as Siemens, Krupp, Gutehoffnungshütte, Hörder Verein, Eisen-und Stahlwerke Hoesch, Deutscher Kaiser (Thyssen), Rheinische Stahlwerke (Otto Wolff) and Stollwerk were controlled by families, although their outward appearance was that of capital companies. Further studies of individual firms would also reveal further cases of control by entrepreneurial families. These "hidden" family enterprises continued to exist as entrepreneurial enterprises, although the number of managerial enterprises has increased more rapidly since World War II. In 1960, one large-scale enterprise in six was controlled by an entrepreneurial family.[53]

So far, the problem of the declining influence of entrepreneurial families has been treated in relation to those families which had ownership in the firm. However, recent research has shown that a number of families of salaried entrepreneurs also deserve attention, above all families of director generals such as Baare (Bochumer Verein) or Lueg (Gutehoffnungshütte/Haniel), which dominated large-scale enterprises for two or even three generations, even when they possessed no significant share in their firms.[54] Personality, professional ability, and business and social contacts of the salaried entrepreneur and director-general were the decisive factors here, which enabled him to determine the long-term policy of the enterprise against the interest of the shareholders or the supervisory board. There was a tendency in managerial enterprises—particularly in economically favorable periods—to let one manager direct the enterprise for as long as possible, and a few top managers tended to appoint their sons as their successors. Thus, in such cases, we can also speak of the influence of entrepreneurial families.[55]

Despite the reservations expressed above, Chandler's thesis that there was a gradual transition from personal to entrepreneurial to managerial enterprise is confirmed by research on the development in Germany.[56] The entrepreneurial enterprise was the dominant type among large-scale enterprises, the sole proprietorship was less common and the managerial enterprise increased in relative importance up to 1907 without, however, being represented in great numbers.[57] Yet the extent of transition to the managerial enterprise should not be overestimated, as the research carried out by Kocka and Siegrist has shown. L. Hannah recently reached similar conclusions.[58] Furthermore, the changes in enterprise structure varied greatly from one branch to another; due to greater concentration, capital requirements and greater intensity of research, the managerial enterprise was more strongly represented in certain branches of industry such as mining, iron and steel, the electrical and chemical industries and, above all, in the field of railway and insurance companies than in other branches.[59]

Even if the development of the integrated, diversified, large managerial enterprise was probably a general tendency in advanced industrialized nations at the beginning of the twentieth century, a comparison of individual countries nevertheless reveals some differences. Thus, in Germany, and also in France, Italy and Switzerland, the personal and entrepreneurial enterprises existed longer than in the U.S.A., where the managerial enterprise spread sooner and faster.[60]

## III.

If the differences between the legal form and the actual exercise of management in family enterprises are examined—we are here dealing chiefly with large-scale family enterprises—it may be asserted that the family enterprise existed in all legal forms. The extent to which this was the case and the relationship between the formal legal framework and the actual management of the enterprises will now be briefly discussed with respect to the various enterprise forms.

In the sole proprietorship the owner runs the enterprise and makes the short-term as well as the essential medium-term and long-term decisions. Most small and also many medium-sized enterprises belong to this category, especially in less capital-intensive branches. Large-scale enterprises, on the other hand, are seldom represented in this area. The following statistics also illustrate this:[61] according to estimates, there were about 150 large-scale enterprises with 1,000 or more employees each in 1882; by 1895 the figure was twice as high; only a very few of these large-scale enterprises were sole proprietorships; in 1907 almost two-thirds (65%) of all those in employment were employed by sole proprietors, 13% worked in joint-stock companies and the rest in personal partnerships or in a limited liability company (GmbH). As a large-scale and at the same time a personal enterprise, the sole proprietorship had few chances because the demands made on management and the capital requirements were too high. Krupp belonged to this category until the 1860s, since Alfred Krupp exercised all the essential entrepreneurial functions himself until then. Thereafter, although the enterprise form remained unchanged, the style of leadership altered from personal to entrepreneurial management, since Krupp appointed a board of directors, while he himself and also his son Friedrich retained the power of making the long-term entrepreneurial decisions.[62] In their early stages the firms Robert Bosch (electrical industry), Borsig (engineering) and the Schichau-Werft (shipbuilding) may also be regarded as belonging to this small group of large-scale enterprises.

Personal partnerships such as the general partnership (Offene Handelsgesellschaft, OHG) or the limited partnership (Kommanditgesellschaft, KG), are characterized by the principle of co-ownership, whereby the owners (two or more) make the day-to-day as well as the long-term management decisions. In the case of the limited partnership, it is not uncommon for the special partner (Kommanditist) to play no part in the decision-making processes, because he is liable only to the extent of his share (original investment). These two enterprise forms, above all the general partnership, were represented in large numbers in trade and also, before 1871, in industry. As industrialization and the growth of enterprises increased from the 1870s onwards, this enterprise form was replaced in the field of industry by others, such as the joint-stock company or the limited liability company. In a few large-scale industrial enterprises such as Henschel & Sohn, Opel (KG) or Henckel & Cie., the proprietors did not wish to admit any outside influence, and so the form of the personal partnership was retained, as the following statistics show[63]: of the 100 largest industrial enterprises, about fifteen were still personal partnerships in 1887, while in 1907 only about eight still had this form. Remarkably, the number of personal partnerships in the capital-intensive metal industry was relatively large. As a rule, these were family enterprises in which the entrepreneurial family attempted to preserve its influence with the help of such legal forms. In another branch, the textile industry, such enterprise forms were used still longer. Thus, a study of the textile industry in Westphalia has established that, in 1913, 69% of the enterprises investigated were personal partnerships, 17% were sole proprietorships and only 10% were joint-stock companies.[64] The type of management in personal partnerships probably depended chiefly on the size of the enterprise. The medium-sized enterprises were mostly personal enterprises, while large-scale enterprises must be classified as entrepreneurial enterprises, and this becomes increasingly true the closer we draw in time to World War I.

The limited liability company (GmbH) stands, so far as its legal form is concerned, between the joint-stock company and the personal partnership. After over two decades of experience with the joint-stock company, it was decided in 1892 to introduce the limited liability company for medium-sized and large-scale enterprises.[65] This accommodated the enterprises' and not least the entrepreneurial families' wish to avoid the publicity obligations of the joint-stock company and to gain new capital without enlarging the circle of partners too greatly.[66] Often, relatives or acquaintances were invited to become partners with limited liability. Furthermore, in conflicts over the family estate, the limited liability company was a form suitable for preserving the enterprise and its capital on the one hand and, on the other, for reducing the heir's risks as partner as far as possible. At any rate, the risks for the family enterprise and the extent of outside influence could be kept within limits with this form. For these reasons, although the limited liability company proved its strength in the medium-sized enterprises above all, large-scale enterprises also existed as limited liability companies, as the study carried out by Kocka and Siegrist has shown: they established the existence of five limited liability companies among the 100 largest enterprises in 1907.[67] More or less independent of the size of the enterprise, the limited liability company can be designated as an entrepreneurial enterprise, since the proprietors appointed management; its functions, however, were in many cases exercised by one or more of the proprietors. Thus, the limited liability company also has some of the characteristics of a personal enterprise, since the proprietors make the long-term decisions and to some extent the day-to-day managerial decisions.

The share partnership (Kommanditgesellschaft auf Aktien, KGaA) represents a special form of the joint-stock company and was used for similar reasons as the limited liability company. Here, too, relatives or acquaintances were often approached to meet the capital requirements. Among large-scale enterprises, the share partnership was virtually insignificant, since only the shipbuilding enterprise of Blohm & Voss in Hamburg assumed this form.[68] Since nearly all the shares were still held by Blohm, the transformation resulted from the need which arose from time to time to acquire capital for expansion as well as the need for standing credit.[69] The style of leadership corresponded to that of the entrepreneurial enterprise.

Another special form of the capital company is the cost-book company, which was chiefly represented in the mining industry. The cost-book companies were certainly able to compete with the joint-stock company, for their number rose from 6 in 1887 to 10 in 1907.[70] The reason for their relative popularity lay partly in the fact that they were not required to publish annual reports, partly in the obligation to make further contributions (selection of the readiness to take risks) and partly in the fact that such companies were easy to control and influence, for, as in the case of the limited liability company and the share partnership, the number of shareholders was limited. The majority of cost-book companies may be designated as entrepreneurial enterprises.

The legal form of the joint-stock company was particularly important for enterprise growth in Imperial Germany. Various arguments may be adduced in support of this. First, attention is again drawn to the large increase in the number of joint-stock companies.[71] Due to the emergence of the limited liability company and the fact that the personal partnership was able to assert itself among the large-scale enterprises, Siegrist regards it as probable "that the institution of the joint-stock company and the like was in many cases and increasingly so, an important but in the last resort not an absolutely necessary condition for the founding of large-scale enterprises."[72] Despite the apparent reservation expressed here, we may agree with the general observation that, from the point of view of the legal technicalities involved, the joint-stock company had advantages as against the sole proprietorship and the personal partnership.[73] This is particularly true in respect to raising capital for large and risky investments, including the development of large-scale enterprises by means of horizontal and vertical concentration.[74] A regional study on heavy industry in Westphalia has established that the joint-stock company was best able to assert itself there, for it was the less successful and smaller enterprises which made use of traditional legal forms.[75] A final judgement on the joint-stock company as a legal form and the consequences arising from this form for the exercise of management is not yet possible.

The law dating from 1870 lays down the institutions and competencies of the joint-stock company.[76] Thus, the board of directors (Vorstand) is responsible for the day-to-day decisions, whereby the members of the board are allocated various functions. Through the chairman (director general) the board also usually participated in the long-term entrepreneurial decision-making process, while the supervisory board (Aufsichtsrat) was concerned with control of the enterprise and with its long-term goals. The actual character of the joint-stock company, by which we mean the factual exercise of management, took two forms, namely, the joint-stock company as managerial enterprise and as entrepreneurial enterprise. In the first case, salaried entrepreneurs make the long-term decisions. In the second case, top executives make the tactical decisions and the proprietor or his family makes the strategic decisions. In this case, the joint-stock company is a family enterprise and the form of the joint-stock company is used to increase capital and thus, to expand the enterprise; however, the entrepreneurial family has a considerable share in the capital and occupies the leading position on the board of directors or the supervisory board. How large the shares of the entrepreneurial families were in each case cannot and need not be discussed here. In general, a great effort was made to secure as large a share as possible.[77]

A few examples of large family enterprises which existed in the form of joint-stock companies can serve to clarify the stage of transition from sole proprietorship to managerial enterprise, which was typical for the period from 1871–1914. Of these, the firm of Krupp has often been cited and is the most interesting example because it was run in the form of a large sole proprietorship, first as a personal enterprise, and, from the 1870s on, as an entrepreneurial enterprise. In 1903 the enterprise was transformed into a joint-stock company but retained the status of entrepreneurial enterprise. The reason for this change lay, first, in the will of the founder, Alfred Krupp, which provided that the entire enterprise should only be inherited by the respective eldest descendant.[78] Then, his son Friedrich had no male heirs at the time when he drew up his will, but only two daughters below the age of majority, of whom the elder, Bertha, was to become the sole heir of the entail (Gesamteigentum).[79] In this situation a means has to be found of preserving the enterprise according to the founder's wishes of appointing a collective leadership for the large-scale enterprise and of gaining access to the capital market. These goals could best be achieved through converting the enterprise into a joint-stock company. The Krupp family owned almost all the shares in the new company and, after a transitional period, continued to exercise a decisive influence on the development of the enterprise through its chairmanship of the supervisory board.[80]

In other enterprises, too, the transition to the joint-stock company could be problematic. When W. v. Siemens retired from the management of the business at the end of 1889, the general partnership Siemens & Halske was converted into a limited liability company.[81] Shortly before his death in 1892, Siemens was urged by the banks to convert the firm into a joint-stock company so that it could expand and thus hold its own against the stiff competition it was facing from AEG.[82] This step was prevented by his death.[83] Another attempt made by an entrepreneurial family to maintain its influence in a joint-stock company was without success. Between 1885 and 1890, the Mannesmann brothers founded and built up several companies which produced pipes. They wished to expand these companies further, and since they lacked the necessary capital, business ability and organizational talent, they approached the well-known industrialist Eugen Langen (Cologne) and the Siemens brothers, with the result that the Mannesmann Walzwerke AG was wound up and reestablished under the direction of the Deutche Bank with the collaboration of Siemens and Langen.[84] The Mannesmann brothers were not successful businessmen and in 1893 they were forced by Siemens and the Deutsche Bank to withdraw from the enterprise entirely. From then on, one can designate the Mannesmann firm as a managerial enterprise, since it was no longer influenced by controlling shareholders.[85]

In other enterprises, the transition to the joint-stock company was usually less problematic. Thus, for example, the iron and steel works founded as a general partnership in 1873 by several members of the Hoesch family was converted into a joint-stock company in the same year because of capital requirements; the post of director-general and the chairmanship of the supervisory board in the new company were both occupied by members of the family.[86] In the "Gutehoffnungshütte" (iron and steel production), the entrepreneurial family Haniel exercised considerable influence through the supervisory board from 1873 on.[87] The normal state of affairs is probably reflected in such conditions rather than in the changes which took place in enterprises like Siemens or Krupp. Nevertheless, we may assume that most of the conversions to joint-stock companies which took place with increasing frequency among large-scale and medium-sized enterprises from the 1880s onwards were not absolutely voluntary. Market conditions, the competitive situation and the influence of the banks were among the decisive factors.

Our statements on legal forms and management must still be regarded as provisional. Nevertheless, it may be agreed that not every form of management could be employed in each of the various legal forms discussed above. The sole proprietorship had to depend largely on the style of personal enterprise, although that of entrepreneurial enterprise could also be found. Equally, both types of management were possible and usual in personal partnerships. In both legal forms, the size of the enterprise was the essential factor determining the style of management. And, finally, in capital companies, managerial leadership appeared alongside entrepreneurial, whereby the latter still clearly predominated. Entrepreneurial families favored legal forms which allowed them as much influence and control as possible. They still adhered to the "Herr-im-Haus" point of view. This need was best met by sole proprietorships and personal partnerships. Enterprises continued to grow until World War I and this forced entrepreneurs to have recourse to the capital market. Nevertheless, they wanted to limit the influence of the banks and other investors as far as possible. In order to achieve both aims, it was necessary to find a compromise: the legal forms of the capital companies were adopted but, at the same time, the entrepreneurial families attempted to secure their own influence through large capital ownership and through occupying important positions in the governing bodies. The forms of the limited liability company, the share partnership or the cost-book company were more suitable to these purposes than the joint-stock company. But compromise solutions were also possible with joint-stock companies, since these could equally be run as entrepreneurial enterprises in which the entrepreneurial family had a decisive influence. Until 1914 this was the dominant style of management in joint-stock companies. The number of joint-stock companies which were run as managerial enterprises also increased; however, these did not become more significant until the 1920s.

## IV.

As the final problem to be discussed in this paper, we shall now compare management in family enterprises with management in non-family enterprises and, here again, we are treading uncertain ground.[88] This comparison concerns aims, attitudes and behavior in the context of entrepreneurial decisions made by entrepreneurial families and sole proprietors on the one hand and salaried entrepreneurs on the other. This problem will be discussed against the background of the transition from the sole proprietorship to the managerial enterprise and the rise of large-scale enterprises. For a long time it was assumed that entrepreneurs were differently motivated:[89] the owner and capitalist were allegedly interested in large profits, the salaried entrepreneur in high income and low dividend payments. This view, which we present here in a simplified form, has to some extent been corrected by recent research in the U.S.A.[90] But it is still not clear whether there were not any significant differences between the actions and attitudes of the two entrepreneurial types. This assumption was also long held in Germany.

During the Industrial Revolution, the vast majority of enterprises were small and medium-sized and the style of leadership was personal, that is, liberal entrepreneurs managed without hard and fast rules and relied on their efficiency, intuition and experience, and on their own willingness to work hard and to take personal financial risks.[91] After 1873, management was affected by far-reaching changes. Extensive new demands of a quite different nature were made on enterprise management by the economic crisis and still more by enterprise growth.[92] Not only was technology becoming more and more complicated, expansion, cartellization and the influence of the banks also forced enterprise managements to direct more attention to problems of information, coordination, organization and planning. It became increasingly necessary to abandon the old, liberal, individual forms of behavior and adopt systematic management methods. But this process was a gradual one, for there was no small degree of resistance from individual entrepreneurs who clung to the old style. For a long time, improvisation and systematic methods existed side by side.[93] Science only made a slow advance into the field of management.[94] This was allegedly easier in the area of technology than in business administration.[95]

At all events, the basic aims such as profit, expansion and maintaining the enterprise were the same.[96] Probably on the basis of a comparison between Siemens and AEG, Kocka assumes that, so far as investment decisions are concerned, family enterprises were more likely to be wary of resolute expansion so as to remain independent for as long as possible.[97] Not uncommonly, however, the competitive situation forced family enterprises to adopt comparable investment strategies. In the case of medium-sized and small enterprises, it can certainly be assumed that they were more reserved in all matters relating to investments and were more concerned with maintaining and securing their position than corresponding non-family enterprises.[98] A few research results seem to indicate that the organizational structures in family enterprises were less dynamic than those in non-family enterprises, which tended more to plan and make specific organizational improvements and to rely less on spontaneous regulations.[99]

Perhaps the attitude of the entrepreneur is more a problem of the size of the enterprise than a question of whether it was or was not a family enterprise. The development in a large-scale enterprise such as Krupp can be seen as an indication that this is the case. At the beginning of the 1870s, Krupp had already begun to organize his enterprise efficiently and to run it according to the very exact methods and rules appropriate to the needs of a large-scale enterprise.[100] Thus, the individualistic, improvising, inspired style of leadership of earlier times was superseded. So far as investment decisions were concerned, the differences were at most gradual, in that Krupp, for example, avoided bank loans whenever possible and instead tried to finance the expansion of his enterprise through government funds or self-financing.

The research which has been done in this area does not yet permit us to prove or disprove the hypothesis on differences in attitudes and actions with finality; at most we can speak of tendencies such as those described above.[101] Such a tendency is expressed in the statement that salaried entrepreneurs inclined more than owner entrepreneurs to rational, objective and systematic behavior; it must be added, however, that the owners of large family enterprises behaved similarly.[102]

## V. Summary

It is clear that the number of large-scale enterprises rose in the period from 1871–1914. While the number of these enterprises remained small in comparison with the many medium-sized and small enterprises, their increasing significance for the national economy cannot be overlooked.[103]

The development of large-scale enterprises in Germany confirms Chandler's thesis on the transition from the sole proprietorship and family enterprise to the managerial enterprise via the intermediate stage of the entrepreneurial enterprise. However, the managerial enterprise was still an exception, while the entrepreneurial enterprise was dominant. In certain branches, such as railway and insurance companies and banks, and in enterprises which were founded as joint-stock companies, the managerial enterprise was more common than elsewhere.

Differences with respect to the legal form and the actual exercise of management in large family enterprises appeared in the capital companies, above all in joint-stock companies. In general, family enterprises favored legal forms such as the sole proprietorship or the personal partnership, in which the individual entrepreneur and his family could assert their influence without formal legal limitations. But if they were forced through market conditions and the competitive situation to adopt the form of the joint-stock company in order to acquire capital for investments, they attempted with a fair degree of success to secure influence through owning as much of the capital as possible and through occupying important positions in the enterprise.

So far as the problem of a comparison of management in family enterprises and management in non-family enterprises is concerned, the present state of research does not permit a clear answer. In general, salaried entrepreneurs appear to have inclined more than family and owner entrepreneurs to objective, rational and systematic behavior, but we should not overlook the fact that entrepreneurs in large family enterprises behaved comparably. The size of the enterprise and the market situation prompted them to adopt similar attitudes and forms of behavior.

The results of the investigations under discussion indicate that the role of the family enterprise did not change fundamentally in the process of enterprise growth until 1914. Family enterprises were largely able to adjust to necessary changes in the market, the size of the enterprise, organization, management and legal forms without the entrepreneurial families losing influence to a very great extent. But we cannot deny that in the long run the influence of the business families diminished.

Finally, a small group with considerable influence came into being during these changes—the families of leading salaried entrepreneurs. They were able to free themselves of outside influence such as that of the banks and to run the large-scale enterprises entrusted to them with sovereign command. Further research must be devoted to them as well as to the owner entrepreneurs if we are to arrive at a more definite solution of the problems dealt with here.

## Notes

1. J. Kocka, *Unternehmer in der deutschen Industrialisierung* (Göttingen, 1975), p. 88; Richard Tilly, "Das Wachstum der Großunternehmen in Deutschland seit der Mitte des 19. Jahrhunderts," in Richard Tilly, *Kapital, Staat und sozialer Protest in der deutschen Industrialisierung. Gesammelte Aufsätze* (Göttingen, 1980), p. 97.
2. Kocka, *Unternehmer*, pp. 88–89.
3. Ibid., p. 88.
4. H. Pohl, "Unternehmensgeschichte in der Bundesrepublik Deutschland. Stand der Forschung und Forschungsaufgaben für die Zukunft," *Zeitschrift für Unternehmensgeschichte*, Vol. 22 (1977), No. 1, pp. 26–44; Kocka, *Unternehmer*, pp. 1–11; Wolfram Fischer, "Some Recent Developments in the Study of Economic and Business History in Western Germany," in R. E. Gallman (ed.), *Research in Economic History* (Greenwich, Con., 1977), pp. 247–85.
5. Werner Sombart, *Die deutsche Volkswirtschaft im 19. Jahrhundert und im Anfang des 20. Jahrhunderts* (Berlin, 1921), p. 86.

6. Tilly, *op. cit.*, p. 98.
7. Ibid., p. 97.
8. E. Moll, "Statistik der Aktiengesellschaften in Deutschland," *Handwörterbuch der Staatswissenschaften*, Vol. 1 (1923), 4. ed., pp. 141–60.
9. Kocka, *Unternehmer*, p. 101.
10. Tilly, *op. cit.*, p. 95.
11. Ibid., p. 95; Kocka, *Unternehmer*, pp. 88–89; W. Feldenkirchen, *Die Eisen- und Stahlindustrie des Ruhrgebiets 1879–1914. Wachstum, Finanzierung und Unternehmensstruktur ihrer Großunternehmen* (Wiesbaden, 1982), pp. 42–43.
12. Kocka, *Unternehmer*, p. 92; Tilly, *op. cit.*, p. 95.
13. Ibid., p. 98; Alfred D. Chandler and Herman Daems, "Introduction —The Rise of Managerial Capitalism and its Impact on Investment Strategy in the Western World and Japan," in H. Daems and H. van der Wee (eds.), *The Rise of Managerial Capitalism* (Louvain, The Hague, 1974), p. 1; Kocka, *Unternehmer*, pp. 92, 94.
14. Ibid., p. 92; Chandler and Daems, *op. cit.*, pp. 16–20.
15. Ibid., pp. 1, 16.
16. Tilly, *op. cit.*, p. 96.
17. J. Kocka and H. Siegrist, "Die hundert größten deutschen Industrieunternehmen im späten 19. und frühen 20. Jahrhundert. Expansion, Diversifikation und Integration im internationalen Vergleich," in N. Horn and J. Kocka (eds.), *Recht und Entwicklung der Großunternehmen im 19. und frühen 20. Jahrhundert* (Göttingen, 1979), p. 94.
18. Chandler and Daems, *op. cit.*, pp. 15–16.
19. Ibid., p. 15; J. Kocka, "Expansion—Integration—Diversifikation. Wachstumsstrategien industrieller Großunternehmen in Deutschland vor 1914," H. Winkel (ed.), *Vom Kleingewerbe zur Großindustrie* (Berlin, 1975), pp. 204–206; Kocka, *Unternehmer*, p. 101.
20. Ibid., p. 95.
21. Kocka, *Expansion*, p. 212.
22. Kocka, *Unternehmer*, pp. 93–96; H. Siegrist, "Deutsche Großunternehmen vom späten 19. Jahrhundert bis zur Weimarer Republik. Integration, Diversifikation und Organisation bei den 100 größten deutschen Industrieunternehmen (1887–1927) in international vergleichender Perspektive," *Geschichte und Gesellschaft*, Vol. 6 (1980), p. 82.
23. Kocka, *Expansion*, pp. 209–10.
24. Kocka, *Unternehmer*, p. 96; Chandler and Daems, *op. cit.*, p. 16.

25. Siegrist, *Großunternehmen*, pp. 79–83.
26. Ibid., p. 82.
27. Kocka, *Expansion*, p. 216.
28. Chandler and Daems, *op. cit.*, p. 16.
29. Ibid., p. 9; Tilly, *op. cit.*, pp. 106–107; Kocka, *Unternehmer*, p. 100.
30. Ibid., p. 100.
31. Kocka, *Expansion*, p. 217.
32. Kocka, *Unternehmer*, pp. 101–104.
33. Ibid., p. 116; H. Pogge von Strandmann, *Unternehmenspolitik und Unternehmensführung. Der Dialog zwischen Aufsichtsrat und Vorstand bei Mannesmann 1900 bis 1919* (Düsseldorf, Wien 1978), p. 27; Helmut Böhme, "Emil Kirchdorf. Überlegungen einer Unternehmerbiographie," *Tradition*, Vol. 13 (1968), p. 286.
34. Kocka and Siegrist, *op. cit.*, pp. 79–82.
35. Norbert Horn, "Aktienrechtliche Unternehmensorganisation in der Hochindustrialisierung (1860–1920). Deutschland, England, Frankreich und die USA im Vergleich," in N. Horn and J. Kocka (eds.), *Recht und Entwicklung von Großunternehmen im 19. und frühen 20. Jahrhundert* (Göttingen, 1979), p. 178.
36. Kocka and Siegrist, *op. cit.*, p. 58.
37. Hartmut Kaelble, "From the Family Enterprise to the Professional Manager: The German Case," in L. Hannah (ed.), *From Familiy Firm to Professional Management: Structures and Performance of Business Enterprise* (Budapest, 1982), p. 50 (Eighth International Economic History Congress).
38. Chandler and Daems, *op. cit.*, pp. 5–7; Kocka and Siegrist, *op. cit.*, pp. 58, 63.
39. Kocka, *Expansion*, pp. 207–208.
40. J. Kocka, "Familie, Unternehmer und Kapitalismus. An Beispielen aus der frühen deutschen Industrialisierung," *Zeitschrift für Unternehmensgeschichte*, Vol. 24 (1979), p. 100; L. Hannah, "Introduction," in L. Hannah (ed.), *From Family Firm to Professional Management: Structure and Performance of Business Enterprise* (Budapest, 1982), p. 4.
41. Kocka, *Unternehmer*, p. 101.
42. Hannah, *op. cit.*, p. 5; Kocka, *Familie*, pp. 134–35.
43. Ibid., pp. 134–35.
44. Hannah, *op. cit.*, p. 6.
45. Kocka and Siegrist, *op. cit.*, pp. 59–81; Siegrist, *Großunternehmen*, pp. 76–88.
46. Kocka and Siegrist, *op. cit.*, pp. 65, 67.

47. Ibid., p. 73.

48. H.-J. Teuteberg, *Westfälische Textilunternehmer in der Industrialisierung* (Dortmund, 1980), pp, 41, 43; Hisashi Watanabe, "Die Industrielle Revolution in Japan und Deutschland. Ein Vergleich," in J. Schneider (ed.), *Wirtschaftskräfte und Wirtschaftszweige, Festschrift für H. Kellenbenz*, Vol. 5 (Stuttgart, 1981), p. 385.

49. These are results of my own ongoing research.

50. Kocka and Siegrist, *op. cit.*, p. 79.

51. Siegrist, Großunternehmen, pp. 67–88.

52. Kaelble, *op. cit.*, 51.

53. Ibid., p. 52.

54. Ibid., p. 52; Feldenkirchen, *op. cit.*, p. 313; Tilly, *op. cit.*, pp. 166, 277; G. Adelmann, "Führende Unternehmer im Rheinland und in Westfalen 1850–1914," *Rheinische Vierteljahrsblätter*, Vol. 35 (1971), p. 341.

55. Feldenkirchen, *op. cit.*, p. 313; Tilly, *op. cit.*, p. 106; H. Siegrist, *Vom Familienbetrieb zum Managerunternehmen. Angestellte und industrielle Organisation am Beispiel der Georg Fischer AG in Schaffhausen 1797–1930* (Göttingen, 1981), p. 55.

56. Siegrist, *Großunternehmen*, p. 88.

57. Ibid., p. 88.

58. Hannah, *op. cit.*, p. 4.

59. Ibid., p. 2; Kocka, *Expansion*, pp. 218–19.

60. Chandler and Daems, *op. cit.*, p. 9; Hannah, *op cit.*, p. 2; Siegrist, *Familienbetrieb*, p. 55.

61. Kocka and Siegrist, *op. cit.*, pp. 98–112; H. Pross, *Manager und Aktionäre in Deutschland. Untersuchungen zum Verhältnis von Eigentum und Verfügungsmacht* (Frankfurt, 1965), pp. 47, 49.

62. O. Neuloh, *Die deutsche Betriebsverfassung und ihre Sozialreformen bis zur Mitbestimmung* (Tübingen, 1956), pp. 151–52.

63. Kocka and Siegrist, *op. cit.*, pp. 80–81.

64. Teuteberg, *op. cit.*, p. 41.

65. Horn, *op cit.*, p. 126.

66. Ibid., pp. 126, 136.

67. Kocka and Siegrist, *op. cit.*, pp. 81–82.

68. H. G. Prager, Blohm & Voss, *Schiffe und Maschinen für die Welt* (Herford, 1977), p. 39.

69. Ibid., p. 39.

70. Kocka and Siegrist, *op. cit.*, pp. 80–81.

71. See Chap. 1.

72. Siegrist, *Großunternehmen*, p. 86.

73. Horn, *op. cit.*, pp. 133–34.

74. Ibid., p. 178; N. Reich, "Auswirkungen der deutschen Aktienrechtsform von 1884 auf die Konzentration der deutschen Wirtschaft," in N. Horn and J. Kocka (eds.), *Recht und Entwicklung der Großunternehmen im 19. und frühen 20. Jahrhundert* (Göttingen, 1979), p. 255.

75. T. Pierenkemper, *Die westfälischen Schwerindustriellen 1852–1913* (Göttingen, 1979), pp. 149–51.

76. Horn, *op. cit.*, p. 128; Kocka, *Unternehmer*, pp. 123–24.

77. Prager, *op. cit.*, p. 39; W. Treue and H. Uebbing, *Die Feuer verlöschen nie. August Thyssen-Hütte 1890–1926* (Düsseldorf, 1966), pp. 24–28.

78. W. Berdrow and F. G. Kraft, *Alfred Krupp und sein Geschlecht* (Berlin, 1943), p. 196.

79. E. Schröder, *Krupp, Geschichte einer Unternehmerfamilie* (Göttingen, 1968), pp. 93–94.

80. W. Boelcke (ed.), *Krupp und die Hohenzollern. Aus der Korrespondenz der Familie Krupp 1850–1916* (Berlin, 1956), pp. 109–11.

81. S. v. Weiher, *Werner von Siemens. Ein Leben für die Wissenschaft, Technik und Wirtschaft* (Göttingen, 1980), p. 85.

82. Kocka, *Unternehmer*, p. 91.

83. Weiher, *op. cit.*, p. 83.

84. Strandmann, *op. cit.*, pp. 15–27; H. Koch, *75 Jahre Mannesmann. Geschichte einer Erfindung und eines Unternehmens, 1890–1965* (Berlin, 1965), pp. 28–67.

85. Strandmann, *op. cit.*, p. 26.

86. *80 Jahre Eisen- und Stahlwerk Hoesch, 1871–1951* (Heidelberg, Duisburg, 1951), pp. 13, 16.

87. F. Büchner, *125 Jahre Geschichte der GHH* (Oberhausen, 1935).

88. J. Kocka, "Management und Angestellte im Unternehmen der Industriellen Revolution," in R. Braun et al (eds.), *Gesellschaft in der Industriellen Revolution* (Köln, 1973), p. 162.

89. Chandler and Daems, pp. 28–29.

90. Ibid., pp. 30–32.

91. Kocka, *Management*, pp. 162–63.

92. Pierenkemper, *op. cit.*, pp. 122, 133; Kocka, *Unternehmer*, pp. 101–10.

93. Ibid., pp. 111–13.

94. J. Kocka, "Industrielles Management: Konzeptionen und Modelle

in Deutschland vor 1914," *Vierteljahrschrift für Sozial- und Wirtschafts-geschichte*, Vol. 56 (1969), pp. 354–55.

95. Ibid., pp. 356–57; Kocka, *Unternehmer*, p. 111.
96. Ibid., pp. 117–18.
97. Kocka, *Expansion*, pp. 224–25.
98. Chandler and Daems, *op. cit.*, p. 31; Teuteberg, *op. cit.*, p. 14; Hannah, *op. cit.*, pp. 3–4; Kocka, *Unternehmer*, p. 119.
99. Ibid., pp. 126–27; Feldenkirchen, *op. cit.*, p. 310.
100. Neuloh, *op. cit.*, pp. 151–53; *General-Regulativ für die Firma Fried. Krupp in Essen a. d. Ruhr* (1872), (Krupp-Archiv).
101. Chandler and Daems, p. 31.
102. Kocka, *Unternehmer*, pp. 122–23; H. Siegrist, "Vom Familienbetrieb zum Managerunternehmen," in *Schweizer Gesellschaft für Wirtschafts- und Sozialgeschichte* (ed.), Die Unternehmer, Jahreskongreß 27.11. 1981, Vol. 1 (1982), p. 57.
103. H. Pohl, "Zur Geschichte von Organisation und Leitung deutscher Großunternehmen seit dem 19. Jahrhundert," *Zeitschrift für Unter-nehmensgeschichte*, 26 (1981), pp. 145–46.

# COMMENTS

Takeshi Yuzawa
*Gakushuin University*

Family firms in the form of sole proprietorships or partnerships played an important role in the early stage of industrialization, because those company forms made it easy to raise funds and acquire reliable personnel on a small scale. The family firm was quite suited to cope with the changing business circumstances of that period. But after the middle of the nineteenth century, family firms had to confront different business conditions which were caused by the introduction of the "share company" and the appearance of new industries stimulated by the development of new technologies. As a result, there occurred large-scale companies with much capital and effective organizations. The main points I would like to discuss relate to the fact that there are lots of famous, big businesses in Germany originating from family firms, such as Siemens, Thyssen, Mannesman and Krupp, and various processes were used by traditional families to maintain control over their companies.

Indeed, some family firms succeeded in maintaining their businesses by changing their management structures and recruiting professional managers, but others could not adapt themselves to changing business circumstances. According to Dr. Brockstedt, less than one-fifth of all firms in 1887 had retained the legal form of the personal partnership or the sole proprietorship and in general, the rise of largescale enterprises (mostly share companies) led to a reduction in the number of family enterprises among the large-scale enterprises, a trend which was intensified in the 1920s. This tendency was promoted in Germany especially by banks.

Accordingly, several problems arise when comparing family businesses in Germany with those in other countries. My first question relates to the characteristics of the family in Germany, that is to say, the main motives to control the family firm so tightly and continue the cooperation among family members for several generations. In Japan, successful family firms often maintained a family code or set of principles to maintain its organization and assets, which were very effective in controlling the business even if the company form was changed and professional managers were allowed to make strategic decisions. I wonder if there are examples in Germany of enforcing family ties over successive generations, besides that of Alfred Krupp, who willed that his assets be inherited solely by his eldest son. There may be several ways to preserve family ties. Is it possible that the same or similar family code mechanism was in operation when Walter Rathenau succeeded as chairman of AEG after his father's death? And also it would be interesting to receive an explanation on the relation of Werner Siemens in Germany with his brother William in England. What made the family members cooperate with each other? In any case, it is necessary to elucidate the meaning of "collective leadership" and its practical accomplishments.

Dr. Brockstedt stresses that diversification and integration did take place earlier in Germany than in the U.S.A., which was caused by their "utterly different market structures" and that "developments similar to those in Germany also took place in France and in Japan." But in Japan, some family firms organized holding companies, adopting share partnerships or limited partnerships, and developed huge zaibatsu concerns. They controlled big companies in the major industries, unrelated to their original business in trading, banking, shipping, mining, iron works, machinery and so on. This process is similar to, for instance, that of Rockfeller, whose business originated in the oil industry but extended to many major industries. Were there any cases in Germany where family firms became holding companies and diversified not only their products, integrating related industries, but also expanded their businesses beyond the related goods or services? Of course it is well known that banks in Germany had powerful control over industrial companies by using Kontokorrentgeshäft (overdrawn account system) and organizing Konzern (concerns). But there were big family firms like Krupp, Siemens, Thyssen which were comparatively independent of banking control.

Why did these strong family firms not enter other fields unrelated
to their main business and organize comprehensive concerns by
establishing holding companies?

Lastly, it is necessary to discuss the emergence of professional
managers and their role or function in these companies. According
to Chandler's scheme, the role of managers in entrepreneurial enterprises will be different from those in managerial enterprises. In
either case, professional managers become necessary as firms grow in
size and complexity. But presumably, in Germany there were special
conditions to be considered. As J. Kocka points out, "The bankers
representatives in the supervisory boards of industrial corporations
were themselves salaried managers, since the large investment banks
were managerial enterprises" (Chandler and Daems, *Managerial
Hierarchies*, p. 112 n. 14). Were there any differences in managerial
attitudes toward decision making between professional managers
trained in their company and those sent from banks?

# Family Business in Nineteenth-Century America: Ownership and Management Patterns in the Textile Industry

Barbara M. Tucker
*Rutgers University*

Within the past twenty years, American businessmen have felt the effects of stiff competition especially from the Japanese and the Germans. Economists and historians alike have tried to analyze why American industry is lagging behind other nations. Many have argued that concern for short-term gains has worked to the detriment of American firms. A glance at the Japanese industrial system reveals a commitment to stability, to long-term development, and to collective behavior. In Japan the family firm served as a foundation stone for economic development. In the United States the family firm also has an important position in the economy. Du Pont, H. J. Heinz, Firestone, and Levi Strauss come immediately to mind. Today approximately one-fifth of *Fortune*'s list of 500 manufacturing firms show evidence of familial control or involvement.[1]

Despite the endurance of the family firm and the spectacular contribution made by leading family enterprises to administrative patterns and procedures, this business form has been maligned. Charges of mismanagement, nepotism, poor profit discipline, immobile marketing because of product-family identification have been made against them. Such criticism is not recent, for the pros and cons of familial ownership and management have been debated for over a century. Writing in 1832, Samuel Slater, an early factory master, offered advice to would-be manufacturers warning them that a business failed when its owners "who themselves engaged in other pursuits, have invested the net profits of their business in manufacturing and left the latter to the superintendence of others," for

271

"It is in this triple capacity of money lender, employer, and laborer that our most successful manufacturers have succeeded."[2] Economic historians have questioned Slater's advice since then and have labelled his enterprise and early familial capitalism generally as conservative.[3] The public corporation with its complement of salaried managers has become the symbol of American big business.

While individual entrepreneurs have been the focus of considerable historical attention, little research has been devoted to the contributions made by the family firm to American business organization and industrial development. Although a detailed overview of the family firm is beyond the scope of this paper, a case study of the textile industry from 1790 to the late nineteenth century will highlight several of the weaknesses and strengths of both family firms and public corporations. The textile industry is an especially appropriate area of research. The first to adopt the factory system, early factory masters experimented widely with various management, ownership, and labor forms. Two distinct approaches emerged, one associated with small-scale, family-dominated enterprises and the other with corporate ownership and professional management. Patterned after the Arkwright-Strutt system in England, and known subsequently as the Slater system, the former plan was characterized by the partnership form of ownership, personal management, and the family system of labor. Small in scale, confined initially to the single process of spinning, and employing water as the motive power, these firms often were often owned and operated by kinship units. Samuel Slater introduced and developed this system in the United States. Concerned with longterm growth, identified personally with the manufacture of fine quality cotton and woolen goods, and determined to maintain that reputation, Slater and later his sons spent their time, energy, and capital building up the family business. While innovations were introduced slowly and after considerable thought, the firm nevertheless pursued a policy of continuous, regular change including developments in cost accounting, integration, product diversification, and the use of brand names to meet the demands of new and rapidly expanding markets. Traditional and tied initially to an eighteenth century philosophy which stressed patriarchalism, the Slaters prospered. The mercantile agency, R. G. Dun and Company, gave them high marks. In their 1889 credit report they recorded that this was a "Close Corporation owned by Slater family. Goods sold through their own commission house of S. Slater and Son of New York . . . . H. N. Slater Jr. the head of the concern lives here, and manages the business. They do a large business and their credit stands first class with the Banks and trade."[4]

Introduced by Francis Cabot Lowell, a Boston merchant, the second industrial pattern to develop in the textile industry was characterized by innovative technology, the integration of spinning and weaving, corporate ownership, professional management, and the use of a female labor force. Successful and especially profitable, this system achieved world-wide recognition for its imaginative and novel approach to industrialization. Historians have claimed that this model, known subsequently as the Lowell system, "was the most important thing which could have happened to the cotton industry," for it was "taken up by men with the best business imagination in the land, unhampered by its traditions, concerned with making fortunes and building states, not with manufacturing cotton cloth."[5] Initially more spectacular than the Slater approach, the Lowell firms encountered serious difficulties within a generation of their establishment. As ownership became more diverse, and as management was left to hired men, there was a tendency to emphasize immediate gains and to maximize profits, often at the expense of the introduction of new technology or product diversification. For stockholders and directors, the firm represented primarily a source of income.

Although faced with numerous problems, the Lowell firms gained and retained a national reputation in the industry. They were the darlings of the Industrial Revolution and considered the legitimate precursors of American big business. This acclaim can be explained partly because the Lowell firms, more than the Slater enterprises, reflected the wider social and cultural currents in American society—the movement toward individualism. The order of society was changing. The astute critic of ante-bellum society, Alexis De Tocqueville, observed that "Individualism is a calm and considered feeling which disposes each citizen to isolate himself from the mass of his fellows . . . ."[6] Each person became responsible for ordering and defining his own economic, social, political, and religious role. Social organization no longer revolved around the family, the church, or the community.[7] Business organization came to reflect this new trend in society.

## I.

Samuel Slater established the first successful spinning mill in the United States. In 1789 Samuel Slater, a British-born mechanic trained under Jedediah Strutt of Derby, entered into a partnership with William Almy and Smith Brown, members of a well-known Providence mercantile family. Under the contract, Slater agreed to construct a purpose-built yarn spinning mill at Pawtucket, Rhode Island, to build machinery based on the Arkwright model, and to hire and supervise workers to operate the equipment. His partners financed the venture and assumed responsibility for purchasing all supplies and for vending yarn. For a decade Slater managed day-to-day operations at Pawtucket, and despite serious problems which divided the partners and caused considerable stress to all, the business flourished.[8]

From Pawtucket the factory system spread throughout New England, Pennsylvania, and New York. Initial growth was slow. It has been estimated that by 1808, only fifteen spinning mills were operating in the United States and that fully one-half of them belonged either to Samuel Slater, to one of his Pawtucket partners, or to one of his former employees.[9] Although few in number, some manufacturers and their associates feared that the local market could not absorb even this modest increase in yarn. Writing to his children in 1810, Moses Brown urged caution in the expansion of the business:

> Our people have "cotton mill fever" as it is called. Every place almost occupied with cotton mills; many villages built up within 16 miles of town and spinning yarn and making cloth is become our greatest business. We were first to get into it. Samuel Slater has sold out one half of one mill and I should be pleased my children could do, with their four, in part as he has done.[10]

As the comments by Brown indicated, Slater had followed an

independent course of action. He first broke with Almy and Brown in 1799 when he joined with his kinsmen to construct a small mill across the river in Rehoboth, Massachusetts. This was the first of many ventures. For almost four decades, Slater invested heavily in manufacturing and business concerns, and at his death in 1835, he owned outright or held a major interest in approximately eight textile factories, a wholesale and commission firm, and a textile machine firm.

Slater's earliest factories were water-driven spinning mills located in upstate Rhode Island, Connecticut, and southern Massachusetts. In these firms, ownership and management went hand in hand. Adopted first at Pawtucket, the partnership form of ownership was retained, notwithstanding the attractiveness and the advantages of incorporation. During the War of 1812, incorporation had become popular, and by the war's end, seventy-five textile firms had received charters; yet Slater was not among them.[11] He was not persuaded to adopt this form of ownership, preferring instead traditional partnership agreements or single proprietorships. For his small scale spinning enterprises, large amounts of capital were not required; one or two partners easily supplied the funds necessary to construct a factory and to operate from four to five thousand spindles. Furthermore, partnerships had the advantage that a simple line of organization could be adopted to manage the firms: proprietors not only owned the concern but usually managed it, often working alongside laborers on the factory floor. Slater distrusted outsiders and preferred to superintend the factories himself or to entrust the task to one of his partners.[12]

The selection of suitable partners was crucial and only kin, close family friends or business associates—all considered trustworthy individuals—proved acceptable. The Slatersville property was a case in point and represented the type of arrangement Slater preferred. In 1806 Samuel Slater and his brother, John Slater, joined forces with Almy and Brown to develop a factory site on the Mohegan River in upstate Rhode Island. While the three Pawtucket partners financed the venture, John Slater managed the factory and the industrial community of Slatersville which developed around it. The partners continued to invest heavily in land, to expand factory operations, and to construct additional dwellings and facilities for the families who migrated there for work. Over the years, ownership changed hands several times and Samuel Slater and his brother eventually purchased for $160,000 the interest of the other partners. In 1832 the firm was renamed S. & J. Slater.[13] By this time they owned 1200 acres in the region, operated almost 10,000 spindles, and employed over 300 people.[14]

While Slatersville proved profitable and successful, Samuel Slater nevertheless wanted to strike off on his own, and the acquisition of land and water privileges in an area of south central Massachusetts known as Oxford South Gore (later renamed Webster) afforded him that opportunity. Interest in the region began in 1811 when he entered into a partnership with Bella Tiffany, a family friend, to construct a cotton factory. Through reinvestment of profits, the business grew, and within the decade a woolen factory, a saw and grist mill, workers' housing, and other facilities were constructed. Expansion continued. By 1832 Slater valued the real estate, machinery, and stock on hand at Webster at over $300,000.[15] By then he had acquired ownership of all factories and real estate. The Webster factories and the industrial community which emerged there represented the full development of the Slater system, one which incorporated a traditional way of life within the context of the factory system and the wage economy.

In the design of his factory towns, Slater adopted the traditional open-field village pattern associated with rural New England community life. At the center of the village stood a church surrounded by single family dwellings constructed by Slater for the use of his labor force. Shops soon emerged to compete with the factory store for the custom of employees. Around this central village, Slater purchased hundreds of acres of land and divided them into company farms and tenant holdings. The factories were not found in the village area but were built a short distance away, thus maintaining a separation between industrial and community life.[16]

The system of labor employed, the type of jobs allocated to individuals, and the form of discipline adopted all mirrored customary values and practices. In all of his factories Slater employed family labor. Under the family system of labor, a division of work based on age, gender, and marital status emerged. In assigning jobs, formulating discipline and designing his community, Slater sought to preserve patriarchal authority, to safeguard his own prerogatives and those of the householders he employed. Male householders were not expected to enter the factory but were given traditional, socially acceptable, task-oriented jobs such as farm labor, construction work, carting, and painting. The few who entered the factory filled only supervisory positions such as overseers, clerks or second hands, or occupied skilled positions such as mule spinner. Married women also remained within their customary sphere, the home. They cared for their families, tended family garden plots provided by the firm, and when piece work was available, they took in weaving or picked cotton clean of stones and other matter. But parents seldom worked in the factory tending machines alongside their sons and daughters. Children, adolescents, and unmarried women comprised the factory labor force. And Slater tried to incorporate traditional values and practices associated with a New England way of life within the factory itself. To discipline his labor force and inculcate obedience, punctuality, attention to duty, the values thought necessary for a docile, efficient labor force, Slater relied upon traditional institutions. Values taught in the home and the church were transferred to the factory, and internal self-discipline rather than an elaborate system of rewards and punishments characterized the discipline evident there.[17]

The system established by Samuel Slater at Webster required close attention, but Slater's investments were widespread, and he could not devote his time exclusively to this chore. Slater faced a serious managerial problem, and he tried to induce his sons to take an active interest in the supervision of the concern. In 1818 he recruited his eldest son, Samuel, to help him. But the boy was frail, and he died. He then turned to his second son, John II, recently turned sixteen: "You will have to make your appearance at Oxford [Webster] or here in one of the stores as per conversation with you some time past. It is highly important that one or more of my sons was learning the business so as to in some measure relieve me from the close attention which I have to attend to."[18] The boy was withdrawn from school and sent to the factory. Yet Slater did not transfer full operational authority to him. John Slater II served a long appren-

ticeship under his father. Although fifty-three years of age now and
suffering from rheumatism, Samuel Slater did not allow his son
appreciable discretion in the actual operation of the factory. Through
correspondence and frequent visits to the factory site, Slater monitored his son closely.[19]

Although detailed supervision of his son absorbed valuable time,
Slater preferred to entrust partial management to this young, in-
experienced boy rather than to hire an outsider. Kinship ties, more
than proven skill or competence, dictated his choice of managers.
This decision insured that the business would be run according to
his wishes, that he would save the expense of paying high salaries to
men who might prove dishonest, inefficient or lazy, and that his son
would thoroughly learn the family business. Besides John Slater II,
his other sons, George Basset Slater and Horatio Nelson Slater, served
long apprenticeships under him. They did not exercise real authority
until 1829 when Samuel Slater formed a family partnership, Samuel
Slater and Sons, to supervise the Webster property. And Slater only
relinquished authority reluctantly. By 1829 he was old, crippled
by rheumatism, and convinced that new ideas were needed if his vast
business network was to survive and prosper. Rather than reorganize
the business himself and abandon the programs of ownership and
management that had served him well for decades, he went into
semi-retirement and left the business to his sons.

What prompted Slater to adopt this type of system? Despite his
voluminous business correspondence, his public addresses and publications, and the numerous books and articles published about him,
Samuel Slater remains an enigmatic figure. Certainly he was ambi-
tious, determined to succeed, hardworking, and frugal, but such
motivation explains only partly the man's complex nature.

Scholars have attributed many of his business decisions to "entrepreneurial conservatism," to economic dislocations in the industry,
or to a desire to preserve his reputation for producing high-quality
products.[20] Yet these reasons alone do not explain adequately his
actions. To understand his system, his attitudes toward patriarchy
should be understood. Although one of the most successful businessmen in America, Slater was bound by a traditional world view which
influenced his actions and decisions.

Slater was no cost-benefit capitalist; he thought of the world on different terms than those of industrial capitalism. He believed that the father was head of the household, that economic decisions and responsibilities rested with him, that wife, children and servants occupied a subordinate position in the unit. Rights however were coupled with responsibilities, and he had a duty to feed, clothe, shelter, guide, protect, and educate all who came under his authority.

Throughout his long career, Slater adhered to patriarchal notions of authority and responsibility. His business organization reflected his beliefs. The partnership form of ownership allowed him to retain primary authority and control. This permitted him to move quickly to institute new policies or to alter old ones. No prior authorization from a board or directors or from investors was necessary; no valuable time was lost through negotiation or through the procrastination of others; no one questioned his decisions or interfered with their implementation. Divided authority among owners caused problems and between owners and managers brought disaster.

Patriarchal notions also allowed Slater to influence the behavior of those around him. If they wanted to share in the inheritance, to become independent economically, his sons had to obey his orders and wishes. This allowed him to determine their education, marriage, and career choices. None of the Slater children attended university, and no one entered a career outside of business. Devotion to kinship and family predominated. Slater demanded and received the loyalty, cooperation, and service of his sons. The latter function was important. He believed successful manufacturers "employed their families in the labors of the business, and to the extent of this savings of the wages of superintendence and labor, realized the gross profits of manufacture."[21] For George, John II, and Horatio Nelson Slater, intellectual and economic independence came only with the death of their father.

Slater's attitude toward the family and paternal authority extended to the recruitment, management, and discipline of his labor force. In his factory communities, he assumed responsibility for providing hands with an acceptable form of work, shelter, food, education, and religious instruction: the customary duties of a master. Through personal contact with workers, through the exercise of a mild authority, by recognizing the rights of householders and by assuming the traditional obligations of a master to a servant or a father to a child, Slater sought to cement a bond between labor and management and to secure their support and devotion. He succeeded. While strikes and labor militancy plagued other factory masters in the 1820s and 1830s, the Slater mills were free from strife.[22]

## II.

When Samuel Slater died in 1835, his sons reorganized his vast enterprise. Confident, competent businessmen, George, John II, and Horatio Nelson Slater were willing to break with tradition, to remove what they believed to be unnecessary impediments to the smooth, efficient and profitable operation of the Slater firms, and to move them into the mainstream of nineteenth-century American industrial development.

Several years before his death, Samuel Slater recognized that his values and his way of doing business were out of step with those around him. The Panic of 1829 had highlighted those differences. During the 1820s the textile industry had boomed. "THE COTTON MANUFACTURE is increasing at a wonderful rate in the United States," boasted the *Niles Weekly Register* in 1828. "Many of the old mills are worked to their utmost production, and new ones are building or projected, in all parts of our country. The more the better."[23] But their optimism was premature. Many of these new firms were poorly equipped and improperly managed. When an economic downturn occurred in 1829, some of these manufacturers went under while others were forced to temporarily suspend operations. Banks closed, money was in short supply, and credit dried up. A spate of bankruptcies ensued.[24] Even the well-managed and more profitable firms such as those owned by Samuel Slater were not immune. In January 1829 Slater acknowledged that "It is rather a pinching time here for money; . . . I have a very heavy load on my back, &c. It is true, I am on two neighbours' paper, but am partially secure, and hope in a day or two, to be fully secured against an eventual loss, . . ."[25] The expected upturn did not come, however, and by the early summer recovery appeared remote. Slater found himself stretched to the limit. Unable to raise the funds immediately, he was forced to issue thirty notes against his vast business interests, including claims against his factories.[26]

Financial losses, however, were less important than the loss of self-respect he suffered. His friend and biographer, George White, noted significant changes in the man; unaccustomed to failure, "he never before knew what it was to be unable to meet every demand, and could generally anticipate calls. He said to me 'I felt the more, because I had never been used to it.' He felt his dignity as a business-man hurt, . . ."[27] But more was lost than this. Slater realized that his world had vanished, that the ideals and the values which had guided his personal conduct and business decisions belonged to the past, and that he was out of touch with contemporary events. Competition had replaced cooperation.

In 1829 the economy bore scant resemblance to the one he had entered in 1789. It was now characterized by the growth of the market economy and the shift away from local self-sufficiency in food, clothing, and other goods. Slater thought of the world and his relationship with fellow businessmen and laborers on different terms than those demanded by the growing market economy. Pecuniary interests alone did not dictate his actions. Yet economic survival in Jacksonian America required adjustments. Costs had to be calculated and reduced. If Samuel Slater would not institute cost-saving measures, his sons would. When his sons gained control of the family business, they directed it along a new path.

Commitments to traditional concepts of patriarchalism gave way to competitive capitalism. The Slater brothers chose to respond more to present economic conditions than to past ideals. Under their direction the ownership, the management, the channels used to purchase supplies and to sell goods, and the labor policies employed previously by their father came under immediate and thorough review. The youngest of the three partners, Horatio Nelson Slater, advocated a complete overhaul of the family business, and he became the chief architect of the reorganization that followed. Under his guidance, which lasted for four decades, the firm prospered and became one of the leading manufacturing companies in the United States.

In the reorganization of the business, the brothers had one goal: cut costs. First they rationalized their holdings by selling some factories and consolidating or enlarging others. Within a decade of their father's death, they sold the Providence Iron Foundry, the Providence Machine Shop, the Slater and Wardwell store, the Steam Cotton Manufacturing Company, and in 1848, the Slatersville property.[28] Interest focused on the Webster holdings, and they attempted to streamline operations there. The three woolen factories were reorganized as the Webster Woolen Company in 1847, and three years later, the four cotton mills were reorganized as Union Mills. In 1850 the Phoenix Thread Mill was merged with Union Mills. These factories were enlarged in 1853, 1861, and 1865. Both the Webster Woolen Company and Union Mills were owned exclusively by Samuel Slater and Sons.[29]

Ownership policies also came under review. The year following Samuel Slater's death, the three brothers broke with long-standing family tradition when George Slater, George Wardwell, and Benjamin Hoppin petitioned the state legislature for a charter of incorporation for the Sutton Manufacturing Company. Capitalized at $60,000, this new firm issued 120 shares of stock worth $500 each. Although legally a corporation, stock was never widely dispersed, no new shares were issued nor were any of the original shares traded. Of the stock issued, two-thirds was held by the Slater family and the rest circulated privately among close family friends or long-time business associates. Between 1836 and 1860, approximately forty shares of stock passed back and forth among the Hoppin brothers, George Wardwell, George Blackburn, and Ezra Fletcher, who were merchants, a trader, a commission agent, and the clerk of Samuel Slater and Sons.[30]

Effective control of the company, however, remained with Horatio Nelson Slater who assumed the presidency of the corporation early in the 1840s and remained in that position throughout the antebellum period. Under his direction the company pursued a deliberate expansion program, and he added 600 to 700 additional spindles and began construction of a new building. While investment lagged during the depression years, H. N. Slater plowed back all profits in 1849, and this practice continued for another decade. During the

1850s no dividends were issued, and all profits were reinvested in the construction of buildings and tenements, the purchase of new equipment including a steam boiler, and the acquisition of additional real estate in Sutton township. When the company resumed dividend payments in 1860, it was small: $3,600 or 6 per cent of the par value of each share of stock. Irregular thereafter, the company issued dividends which fluctuated widely from one year to the next.[31] For tax purposes, Horatio Slater submitted the following account of his company to the Tax Commissioner at Providence, Rhode Island in 1872. This was the first time information on the market value of the stock appeared in company records:

| Sutton Manufacturing Company | 1872 |
|---|---|
| Capital stock | $60,000.00 |
| Par Value per Share | 500.00 |
| Market Value per Share | 650.00 |
| Value of Real Estate | 51,000.00 |
| Value of Machinery | 23,000.00 |

Source: Sutton Manufacturing Company, vol. 45, 1818–1899, Administrative Sales, H. N. Slater to Tax Commissioner, Providence, Rhode Island, May 1872

Although the Sutton Manufacturing Corporation proved successful and the company prospered, the Slater family did not immediately move to incorporate the Webster holdings. Until 1865 it remained an unincorporated partnership.[32]

Management procedures were reexamined as well, and a new scheme was adopted to supervise the remaining firms. The brothers established Providence as the permanent headquarters for Samuel Slater and Sons, and while John Slater II managed the office, Horatio Slater supervised operations at Webster, and George Slater set up residence at Wilkinsonville. When important decisions were required, "a general Family interview" was convened in Providence.[33] But John Slater's health was poor, and while on vacation at St. Croix in 1838, he died. Another reorganization took place. The supervision of the Providence office passed to Horatio Slater. To assist him, he hired Ezra Fletcher, a former partner in the Slater and Wardwell firm. As company clerk, Fletcher handled all cor-

respondence with cotton factors, retailers, commission agents, manufacturers, and factory agents.[34] Periodically, he visited the various
mills, inspected the factories, quizzed the agents and suggested ways
to increase output, improve the quality of the yarn and cloth, and
most importantly, increase efficiency and eliminate waste.[35]

Throughout the ante-bellum period, the working relationship
between Slater and Fletcher was cordial. In 1843 Fletcher even
acquired $10,000 worth of stock in the Sutton Manufacturing
Company.[36] But Fletcher's role was clearly that of secretary and
advisor: on his own initiative, he could not authorize funds or make
consignments. Horatio Slater personally signed all bank drafts, set
prices for goods and terms for sale, and approved all consignment
orders. Repeatedly, Fletcher had to apologize to commission agents:
"Our Mr. H. N. Slater is not about and we are holding our goods
until his return," or "wishing to consult our Mr. H. N. Slater on the
subject is our reason for not answering before."[37] But Fletcher was
not the only nor the most important agent employed by Samuel
Slater and Sons. Horatio Nelson Slater placed the actual operation
of the factory under specially trained, skilled factory agents, a program initiated in 1829 before the death of his father. Over the years
he ceded more and more responsibility to these men.[38]

To manage the mills, the Slater family hired men who possessed a
detailed knowledge of textile production but who nevertheless lacked
either the capital, the skill, or the incentive to construct and to
operate their own factories. The Slaters cautioned their agents to
restrict their attention to the production of cloth and not be drawn
into other affairs, because the factory would undoubtedly suffer and
"fall short of its proper perfection so long as it has not the undivided
care of the superintendant."[39] In specific terms, their duties included
blending raw cotton for the picking and the carding room, packaging
and shipping goods, maintaining accurate records, and recruiting
and paying hands—all activities Alfred Chandler labels operational
functions. The factory agent was a technician who worked under
the strict direction of the Slater family.[40]

To monitor their activities, the Slater brothers developed a sophisticated form of cost accounting. This was introduced during the
depression years and represented a major advance over the double-

entry bookkeeping employed by both Slater's competitors and those who adopted the Lowell system. It appears that other firms did not introduce a comparable accounting system until the 1850s.[41]

By the 1830s the first step had been taken in separating entrepreneurial functions from operating functions. Never again would the Slaters participate personally in the day-to-day operations of the factories: such work was left completely to paid, professional factory managers. Within a decade, traditional ideas and practices had been replaced by new forms of management designed specifically to meet the demands of an expanding factory system. Not only did the Slater brothers examine the internal management of their firm, but also they reviewed the sales mechanism employed by their father. Like most New England manufacturers in the 1820s, Samuel Slater had consigned his goods to specialized selling houses located in the major commercial centers of Boston, New York, Philadelphia, Baltimore, and Charleston. Although he worked through middlemen, Slater had tried to prevent large amounts of cloth and other goods from falling into the hands of a single dealer. In the Philadelphia market, for example, he employed a minimum of seven different agents. Although an agent might charge that "if several houses have them here they will get the price down as a matter of course," Slater ignored the complaint.[42]

The fees paid to middlemen plus the high cost of production threatened to price Slater goods out of the market, and to remedy this, the Slater brothers devised a number of schemes. In the mid-1830s, they designed a stamp to be placed on their manufactured goods. Although Samuel Slater and Sons did not pioneer the use of brand names, it realized early the advantages and the attractions which its name held with the public. One of its most successful stamps was entitled the "Triumph of American Manufacturers." Capitalizing on the patriotism engendered by the Mexican War, Horatio Slater was able to advertise successfully and to market his goods under the Triumph ticket. For several years his agents could not stock enough of the Triumph cloth to meet demand.[43] Underhill and Company implored Slater:

March 20 begins our order (given last fall) for unknown's to be

stamped "Triumph of American Manufacturers" as agreed upon
then, and I hope you will not forget it, as we expect to make a great
display with goods from the "Sons of the first manufacturer in the
United States."[44]

A more serious attempt to not only meet competition, but also to
lower prices occurred in 1845 and again in 1849 when Horatio
Slater abandoned consignment sales altogether and tried to sell his
goods directly to agents, jobbers, merchants, shopkeepers, and
manufacturers. Commission agents were informed "that we do not
now have any cotton goods to consign as we are selling them at the
mill as fast as made."[45] Agents who wished to carry Slater goods had
to buy them outright. To former commission agent, George Blackburn and Company, he wrote: "As we do not wish to consign any
of our first quality shirtings we propose to sell you as many as you
want at 8 cents less 10 per cent for cash delivered at the Depot here,
which will give you a larger commission than I would to occur . . .
in consignment."[46] But Slater's optimism faded in July when trade
declined, and he again had to return to the consignment system.
Another attempt to sell goods directly from the factory occurred four
years later, but within a year it too was abandoned, and Slater once
again returned to traditional outlets.[47] Slater nevertheless continued
to flirt with this idea, and he succeeded in bypassing middlemen in
1866 when he opened a warehouse in New York and sold goods
directly to wholesalers and retailers.[48]

In the purchase of cotton, the Slater family was able to bypass earlier commission agents and thus save money. Initially Samuel Slater
and Sons ordered Sea Island and the finest grades of upland cotton
through a number of commission agents located in Charleston,
Mobile, and New York. Because the Slaters failed to receive sufficient
supplies from these agents, and because they wished to avoid the
commission house fee, they sought to establish an alternate method
of procuring cotton. To accomplish this they employed itinerant
peddlers who attended sales meetings and auctions in communities
throughout the South and purchased cotton on their account.
Charles Rogers of Mobile was one of these agents. In 1834 he attended sales meetings in Columbus, Georgia, and Apalachicola,
Florida. In the latter town he found that the excellent staple and

silky quality of the cotton there rivalled that of the finest New Orleans product. It was purchased and shipped directly to Samuel Slater and Sons.[49] By employing such men, the firm cut costs considerably and pioneered an alterate method of cotton procurement. Following the Civil War, peddlers became prominent figures at cotton sales, and many northern factory masters turned to them for their supplies.

The Slater brothers reassessment of ownership, management, sales, and purchasing procedures reduced costs somewhat but not enough to lower prices appreciably. To compete successfully against foreign importers and domestic manufacturers, one expense remained to be reviewed: labor costs. The death of Samuel Slater gave his sons the opportunity, the increased competition evident in the industry gave them the excuse, and the cost accounting system provided them with the information thought necessary to institute wide-ranging changes in the system of labor employed. The family system of labor was submitted to close scrutiny and was found wanting: it appeared an expensive and inefficient use of manpower resources. First of all, not everyone employed by the firm contributed directly to the production of yarn, cloth, and thread. Farm hands, day laborers, carpenters, and masons—the fathers of Slater factory workers—represented an increasingly unjustified drain on already short resources. Why should the firm continue to pay men whose contribution to factory production was negligible? By the 1840s itinerant, adolescent hands, many of them Irish or French-Canadian, could be hired to perform specific tasks and for low wages. They represented an inexpensive alternative to family labor, and in the 1850s, Slater began to replace Yankee family labor with Irish and French-Canadian hands.

The reorganization of Samuel Slater and Sons was completed by 1870, and little change took place thereafter. This firm was an especially profitable one. The economic success of the family can be gauged partly from the estimates of their wealth made by R. G. Dun. Guesses at best, the credit agency believed the family worth approximately $500,000 in 1856 and twice that much two decades later. But in 1876 it had to confess that while "They are currently quoted with over a million dollars . . . no one outside the family can furnish a definite estimate."[50] By all accounts such estimates fell short of real worth. In 1899 the heirs of Horatio Nelson Slater shared over nine million dollars in stocks, bonds, real estate, and other investments.[51] While the Slater firm was an especially successful and well-managed firm, it was not considered an innovative leader in the industry. The public corporation established by Lowell held that distinction.

## III.

Francis Cabot Lowell made a dramatic impact upon the American textile industry when, with eleven associates, he formed the Boston Manufacturing Company in 1813 and constructed a large-scale, fully integrated spinning and weaving factory at Waltham, Massachusetts. This was an incorporated venture where ownership and management, technically at least, were divided. Young girls and women drawn from the surrounding area composed the labor force introduced to operate the new equipment developed by Lowell. From Waltham the new system spread throughout northern New England. When operations began, a new phase in American textile production was launched.

The factory system introduced at Waltham broke with tradition; it represented a new way of viewing not only factory organization and operations but also society in general. It stood out in bold contrast to the system Slater introduced earlier. A brief examination of the Lowell system will highlight the innovative aspects of this factory form and the implications it held for society. If Slater represented a seventeenth-century traditional world view centered on the household and kin, Lowell indicated a new direction for society.

Unlike Samuel Slater, Lowell's earliest experience was not in the factory but in the counting house. As a supercargo aboard his uncle's ship, Lowell learned firsthand the problems associated with the import-export business. This venture did not command his complete attention, however, and he began to speculate in bulk commodities and to invest part of his capital in manufacturing and real estate. In the years preceding the War of 1812, he made inquiries into textile manufacturing. He learned about it initially from his uncles and then on a visit to England in 1811, he observed new weaving machines. Upon his return to the United States, he described the loom to a local mechanic who constructed a crude wooden device for him. Run by water, this machine produced a sturdy cut of cloth suitable for the growing Western trade. The decision then became whether to spin yarn himself or to purchase it from other manufacturers. Lowell opted for the first plan. At Waltham he constructed a purpose-built factory and combined the two processes of spinning and weaving in the same factory, the first step toward vertical integration. The adoption of the loom necessitated the development of other equipment, and within a decade beginning in February 1813, winders, dressers, speeders, and filling frames were introduced, and most of the technological inventions associated with the Waltham system were set in place.[52]

Innovations continued. Young, unmarried women recruited from rural communities throughout New England were hired to operate the new equipment. To attract and retain this form of labor, Lowell paid cash wages and designed a community to meet the needs and demands of this novel labor force. The history of the Lowell women workers is well known and does not need to be repeated here.[53]

Lowell not only introduced new forms of technology, factory organization and labor, but also he diverted from traditional practices as well in the areas of ownership and management. Lowell's first project required about $300,000, more capital than he could raise. To solve this problem, he applied for and received a charter of incorporation from the Commonwealth of Massachusetts and sold shares in the new business to Boston associates, friends, and relations. Patrick Jackson, his brother-in-law and a major subscriber together with Paul Moody, a mechanic, had charge of operations. Although Lowell and his associates adopted the corporate form of ownership and divided ownership from management, in practical terms, the firm continued to be managed like a traditional mercantile firm. The number of initial subscribers was small, and they kept in constant touch with Lowell, Jackson, and Moody. Owners, in essence, actively participated in management. Collectively, these men made most decisions even those concerned with day-to-day operations.[54]

The experiment at Waltham proved successful. As Nathan Appleton, one of the initial subscribers to the scheme noted: "From the first starting of the first power loom there was no hesitation or doubt about the success of this manufacture."[55] Sales rose from $23,628 in 1817 to over $260,000 four years later.[56] Lowell began to diversify. He set up a machine shop and offered to sell Waltham equipment to other manufacturers. Clients, however, had to purchase an entire set of machines, and on the sales, the corporation earned approximately 25 percent profit. Dividends climbed as the return on invested capital rose to 17 percent in 1817.[57]

With such obvious financial rewards in view, the stockholders devised plans to reap the maximum benefit from the business, and with the death of Francis Cabot Lowell in 1817, no one served to restrain them. Charges for Waltham equipment were doubled; the associates declared a special stock dividend of $50,000 in 1820 and decided to finance expansion through the issue of new shares of stock rather than to pay for it from existing profits. Furthermore, the Directors ordered in 1820 that proceeds from this new issue "shall belong to the present company & be divided among them as part of their profits."[58] After all calculations were made, the Waltham subscribers shared $50,000 in special dividends, another fifty shares of stock valued at $57,500 plus $32,500 in profits realized from the sale of 150 new shares of Boston Manufacturing Company stock to new proprietors. In 1822 sales from machinery together with the subsequent sale of the machine shop itself brought in another $152,000. Of this amount, $100,000 was designated as income by the Directors and distributed to the shareholders. Profits continued to climb and this was reflected in the dividend issues: 25 per cent in 1823, 25 per cent in 1824 and 35 per cent the following year. From the Waltham experiment, stockholders realized that the industry offered rewards beyond the profits derived from manufacturing cloth. Equipment sales could be lucrative and considerable profits could be gained from stock manipulation.[59]

Several proprietors decided to build upon the success of the parent company, and they started another concern further north in Chelmsford, Massachusetts. In 1821 Nathan Appleton, Paul Moody, Patrick Jackson, and the Boott brothers formed an association, the Merrimack Company, to purchase land and water rights in the area and to construct a new factory based on the Waltham model. Capitalized at $600,000, the original 600 shares of stock were held by five investors. Each stockholder then approached friends, associates and kin to take additional shares. Within four months, the number of shareholders climbed to 47, with each investor subscribing to approximately $12,500 worth of stock.[60] In 1824 the Merrimack Directors voted to establish second corporation, the Hamilton Company, but before plans could be concluded, a new program was advanced. Directors of the Merrimack concern decided to concentrate on manufacturing and to divest themselves of land, water privileges, and a machine shop recently acquired from the Boston Manufacturing Company. They resurrected the former Proprietors of the Locks and Canals on Merrimack River, a firm formed originally in 1792, and turned over assets and rights to the organization. This firm subsequently became the architect of a new industrial community, Lowell. It distributed water rights, sold mill sites, and constructed equipment for new firms who chose to operate in Lowell.[61] Still, the number of investors in these firms remained small and confined largely to those who had participated earlier in the Boston Manufacturing Company. A balance sheet for Francis Cabot Lowell II, dated December 31, 1828, listed shares in the Merrimack Company, the Hamilton Company, the Locks and Canals Company, and the Boston Manufacturing Company together with two small ventures, the Amesbury and the Newton mills, for a total of $57,000.[62]

This began to change, however, as new factories were constructed in Lowell. Amos and Abbott Lawrence, owners of a large commission house in Boston, entered the community organizing the Tremont Mills, the Suffolk Manufacturing Company, and the Lawrence Manufacturing Company in the 1830s. Capitalized at between $600,000 and $1,200,000 each, the Lawrence brothers had to cast widely for investment capital. Approximately 128 people, for example, subscribed to stock in the Lawrence Manufacturing Company alone, and many of them had little previous experience in the textile industry. Merchants, traders, and professional men began to divert capital from other sectors to this highly profitable industry. By the 1830s manufacturing had become a safe, secure avenue for surplus capital.[63]

Proprietors in these mills and two subsequent ventures, the Boott

Cotton Mills, established in 1835, and the Massachusetts Cotton Mills, completed four years later, had to purchase mill sites, property, equipment, and water privileges from the Locks and Canals Company. Costs for equipment alone ran between $20.00 and $22.00 per spindle. Compared to prices paid by manufacturers elsewhere, this was exorbitant. In July 1836, the Amoskeag Manufacturing Company paid $14.00 per spindle for its machinery, approximately one-third less than Lowell equipment.[64] Nevertheless, investors scrambled to secure shares in the new corporations. Amos Lawrence, for example, thought the Boott Cotton mills a "good concern" and purchased shares for himself and his sons.[65] Lawrence had a right to be optimistic. In 1832 the Appleton, Merrimack, and the Hamilton companies manufactured 4,275,849, 6,460,000 and 3,650,000 yards of cloth, respectively. At the Lawrence factories, output was equally impressive. Even during periods of economic dislocation or labor unrest, production schedules were maintained. For the six months ending January 1837, John Aiken, agent for the Tremont and Lawrence mills, reported that 3,407,731 and 4,919,923 yards of cloth had been manufactured and that quality "has been good in the main, *very good.*"[66]

Returns on capital at Lowell were high. At the Suffolk Mill profits for the period from 1831 to 1839 averaged over 17 percent annually. The Merrimack Company averaged 14 percent of net worth between 1828 and 1835. Virtually all earnings were paid out in dividends, and whenever additional capital was required for expansion or renovation, new stock issues were launched.[67]

With the success of these firms, further factory sites were developed at Taunton, Three Rivers, Nashua, Saco, Canton, and Manchester, and men of the stature of John Cushing, a retired China trader, competed with the Lawrence, Appleton, and Thorndike families for new stock issues. While new investors found this industry an attractive outlet for their capital, most of them avoided active participation in the management of the concern. In fact, many like Cushing removed themselves completely from involvement in the business by hiring firms such as Bryant and Sturgis to act on their behalf.[68]

Administration fell to a small group of stockholders. A three tier system of management, first evident at Waltham, continued to be employed to operate the new firms. At the top stood the Board of Directors comprised largely of major stockholders. One of their most important duties was the selection of a capable and efficient treasurer and a skilled factory agent: the two most important positions in the business. As Nathan Appleton explained:

> The principle on which these corporations have been established, has always been, the filling of these important offices with men of the highest character and talent which could be obtained. It has been thought, and has been found to be, the best economy, to pay such salaries as will command the entire services of such men.[69]

Usually a stockholder, the treasurer operated out of Boston or a major commercial center, and men such as Kirk Boott, Patrick Jackson, John A. Lowell, and Francis Cabot Lowell II served in these positions. Through personal visits and correspondence, they closely supervised the factory agent—a technician responsible for actually operating the factory and overseeing various services connected with it.[70]

The position of treasurer was an especially sensitive one. Until the 1830s each man defined the position in his own terms, with some devoting more time and energy to the position than others. This became an issue, and stockholders tried to define the duties, responsibilities, and remuneration attached to the office. This was especially evident at the Merrimack Company in 1837 when Kirk Boott, who had held the position of Treasurer for decades, died and was replaced by Francis Cabot Lowell II. When this was announced, investors and other interested parties sought to regularize the line of authority between the Directors, the treasurer, and the agent. Edward Brooks, who was related to the Boott family by marriage, was concerned that Lowell would not devote enough attention to factory matters. Writing to Lowell in 1837, he suggested that "it should be distinctly understood that the whole time of the agent was to be devoted to the Business of the Company to the exclusion of any other occupation," and he was concerned that Lowell had too many outside commitments.

> In your case, I presume from the conversation we have had together, and from your well known scrupulousness in the performance of

whatever you undertake that there will be no difficulty on this score.
I have understood that you intend to resign immediately the employment you now hold under the city of Water Commissioner, and for
myself I should be perfectly willing to leave it to your own sense of
duty to decide how far you were justified in taking upon yourself
responsibilities of any kind.[71]

Brooks suggested that the duties and the responsibilities be spelled
out clearly so that all parties would know what was expected. For
a short period, Lowell held the position of treasurer and then
resigned.[72]

Brooks and others believed that birthright should not qualify a
person for such an important position. The sons of Lowell, Appleton,
and Lawrence should not expect to assume the position and the
responsibilities in the industry held by their fathers. Competence,
diligence, accountability were more important than family in the
selection of treasurer and other managers. Still problems continued.
Although Lowell was replaced, those who followed him failed to
earn the respect of stockholders.

For decades thereafter, the duties and the responsibilities of the
treasurer and other officers continued to be a point of debate among
the investors until it reached a critical point during the Civil War.
Frustrated with the existing managerial arrangements at several of
the Lowell firms, J. C. Ayer, a medical doctor and a stockholder,
launched an attack upon the administrators. In a pamphlet entitled
*Some of the Usages and Abuses in the Management of Our Manufacturing
Corporations*, published in 1863, he levelled charges of incompetence,
deceit, favoritism, and obstruction against current managers. With
"widely-scattered ownership has come this combination of officers,
skilled by long practice to wrest from the owners all access to,
influence upon or voice in the management of their interest," wrote
Ayer. He believed that the offices of the company were rarely filled
by competent men. Instead "they are more generally occupied by
men who have failed to be very valuable in any other pursuit. . . ."[73]

He also questioned the continued employment of middlemen to
sell factory products, especially the monopoly allowed A. & A.
Lawrence & Co., and J. W. Paige & Co. "Through their monopoly

of this business, they not only exclude other commission merchants from a participation in it but they also shut out the benefit which would accrue to the companies from the natural competition for it. This monopoly could not be retained by fair means, while it is known that the work can be better done for less than half the money."[74]

Other problems plagued these early mills. The Lowell firms faced serious and repeated difficulties with their labor force of young women. Workers struck first in 1834 then again in 1836; labor strife continued into the following decade. Labor and management relations remained strained, and the New England women were replaced in the 1840s and 1850s by Irish and French-Canadian family labor.[75]

By the 1860s, when the administration of the Lowell firms had passed to a new generation of managers, serious questions had emerged concerning the operation of the business. Yet these firms were slow to alter the policies that had served them well for years. Slow to innovate, wracked by charges of incompetence and torn by divisions between labor and management, the Lowell firms nevertheless dominated the industry and set the pattern for American business development. The Slater system and family business generally was out of step with the wider vision of American society which stressed individualism over familial values. Laborers, managers and investors each sought personal gains. Maximization of income, not mutual cooperation and respect, not long-term development, not stability, characterized the emerging industrial sector.

## NOTES

1. Robert G. Donnelley, "The Family Business," *Harvard Business Review* 42 (July-August 1964), p. 96.
2. Louis McLane, *Documents Relative to the Manufactures in the United States*, 2 vols. (Washington, D.C., 1833), 1: 928–29.
3. Alfred D. Chandler, *The Visible Hand: The Managerial Revolution in American Business* (Cambridge, 1977), pp. 9–14. Caroline F. Ware,

*Early New England Cotton Manufacture: A Study in Industrial Beginnings* (Boston, 1931), p. 60, and Peter J. Coleman, "Rhode Island Cotton Manufacturing: A Study in Economic Conservatism," *Rhode Island History* 23 (July 1964), pp. 65–80.

4.  Massachusetts vol. 100, p. 540 September 4, 1889, R. G. Dun & Co. Collection, Baker Library, Harvard University Graduate School of Business Administration, Cambridge Massachusetts. (Hereafter cited as R. G. Dun & Co. MSS).

5.  Ware, *Early New England Cotton Manufacture*, pp. 61–62.

6.  Alexis de Tocqueville, *Democracy in America*, ed. J. P. Mayer and Max Lerner (London, 1966), p. 506.

7.  Ian Watt, *The Rise of the Novel* (Berkeley, 1957), p. 61.

8.  Barbara M. Tucker, "The Merchant, the Manufacturer, and the Factory Manager: The Case of Samuel Slater," *Business History Review* LV (Autumn 1981), pp. 300–301.

9.  *American State Papers, Finance*, 2: 427; Ware, *Early New England Cotton Manufacture*, pp. 30, 128, 301–302 and Peter J. Coleman, *The Transformation of Rhode Island, 1790–1860* (Providence, 1963), pp. viii, 130–31.

10. Moses Brown to T. Rogerson, Providence, 11 November, 1810; Almy and Brown Papers. Samuel Slater Production Reports and Correspondence, Rhode Island Historical Society, Province, Rhode Island (Hereafter cited as Almy and Brown MSS).

11. Massachusetts, *Revised Statutes of the Commonwealth of Massachusetts* (1836), Chapter 14, sec. 1; William C. Kessler, "Incorporation in New England: A Statistical Study, 1800–1875," *Journal of Economic History* VIII (May 1948), p. 43; Coleman, *Transformation of Rhode Island*, p. 115; Ware, *Early New England Cotton Manufacture*, pp. 145, 148.

12. Tucker, "The Merchant, the Manufacturer, and the Factory Manager," pp. 301–306.

13. William R. Bagnall, *Textile Industries of the United States, 1639–1810* (Cambridge, 1893), pp. 399–400.

14. George S. White, *Memoir of Samuel Slater, the Father of American Manufacturers Connected with a History of the Rise and Progress of the Cotton Manufacture in England and America with Remarks on the Moral Influence of Manufactories in the United States* (Philadelphia, 1836), pp. 215, 259; *McLane Report*, 1:970–71; Bagnall, *Textile Industries of the United Stetes*, pp. 397–400, Frederick L. Lewton, "Samuel Slater and the Oldest Cotton Machinery in America," *Annual Report of the Board of*

*Regents of the Smithsonian Institution Showing the Operations, Expenditures, and Condition of the Institution for the Year Ending June 20, 1926* (Washington: 1927), p. 507.

15. *McLane Report*, 1: 576–77.
16. Barbara M. Tucker, "The Family and Industrial Discipline in Antebellum New England," *Labor History* 21 (Winter 1979–1980), pp. 57–58.
17. Ibid., 60–65.
18. Samuel Slater to John Slater, North Providence, March 30, 1821, Samuel Slater and Sons, vol. 235. Samuel Slater Collection. Baker Library. Harvard University, Cambridge, Massachusetts (Hereafter cited as Slater MSS).
19. Slater MSS, Smuel Slater and Sons, vol. 235, Samuel Slater to John Slater, North Providence, 5 March, 1826; ibid., 27 March 1826, ibid., 4 May 1826; ibid., 23 February 1826; ibid., 16 November 1828; ibid., 12 March 1828; ibid., 15 March 1828.
20. Alfred D. Chandler, "Samuel Slater, Francis Cabot Lowell and the Beginnings of the Factory System in the United States" (unpublished paper, Harvard Business School, 1977), p. 22; Coleman, "Rhode Island Cotton Manufacturing," p. 66; Bagnall, *Textile Industries of the United States*, p. 399 and Ware, *Early New England Cotton Manufacture*, p. 76.
21. *McLane Report*, 1: 928–29.
22. Massachusetts, *Report on Statistics of Labor* (1880), Part 1, "Strikes in Massachusetts," pp. 9–14.
23. *Niles Weekly Register*, 28 June 1828.
24. Brendan F. Gilbane, "A Social History of Samuel Slater's Pawtucket, 1790–1830" (Ph. D. dissertation: Boston University Graduate School, 1969), p. 492.
25. Samuel Slater to Moses Brown, Cyrus Butler, Brown & Ives, North Providence, January 7, 1829, quoted in White, *Memoir of Samuel Slater*, p. 247.
26. Ibid., pp. 244–48; "A Financier of the Old School," *Proceedings of the Worcester Society of Antiquity*, 5 (1879): pp. 9–10; see also *Niles Weekly Register*, June 28, 1828 and July 4, 1829.
27. White, *Memoir of Samuel Slater*, p. 245.
28. Slater MSS, Introduction and Arrangement of the Slater Collection; Coleman, *Transformation of Rhode Island*, p. 131; Bagnall, *Textile Industries of the United States*, pp. 399–401.
29. "200 Years of Progress," *Webster Times*, 1939, pp. 8–9.

30. Slater MSS, Sutton Manufacturing Company, vol. 1, Company Minutes, 1836–1860. ibid., vol. 3, Transfers of Stock, 1837–1860.
31. Slater MSS, Sutton Manufacturing Company, vol. 1, Company Minutes, 1836–1897; ibid., vol. 45, Administrative Sales, Memo of Dividends, 1818–1899.
32. "200 Years of Progress," pp. 8–9.
33. Slater MSS, Samuel Slater and Sons, vol. 235, Samuel Slater to John Slater, 22 April, 1831.
34. Ibid., S. &. J. Slater vol. 15, Fletcher to John Wright, Providence, March 1838; Samuel Slater and Sons, *Slater Mills at Webster* (Worcester, n.d.), p. 10.
35. Slater MSS Phoenix Thread Mill, Fletcher to Storrs, Providence, 4 August 1847; ibid., Union Mills, vol. 187, Fletcher to Storrs, Providence, 9 May, 1850; ibid., vol. 190, Fletcher to Storrs, Providence, 15 January 1853; ibid., vol. 189, Fletcher to Storrs, Providence, 9 March 1854.
36. Ibid., Sutton Manufacturing Company, vol. 3, Transfer of Stock, 4 September, 1843.
37. Ibid., Steam Cotton Manufacturing Company, vol.14, Fletcher to Hallock, Providence, 27 April, 1833; ibid., Samuel Slater and Sons, vol. 203, Fletcher to Samuel Slater and Sons, Providence 13 January 1846; ibid., 1 March 1847; ibid., 10 September 1845; ibid., 29 April 1846.
38. Tucker, "The Merchant, the Manufacturer and the Factory Manager," pp. 306–13.
39. Slater MSS, General Box 1, Samuel Slater and Sons to D. W. Jones, Providence, 26 September, 1835.
40. Tucker, "The Merchant, the Manufacturer and the Factory Manager," pp. 306–13.
41. Ibid., p. 308–309.
42. Slater MSS, Samuel Slater and Sons, vol. 210, Hunt Brothers to Samuel Slater and Sons, New York, 10 September, 1839; ibid., 21 September, 1839.
43. Ibid., Union Mills, vol. 185, Waite to Samuel Slater and Sons, Webster, 3 August, 1836; ibid., C. Howe to George A. Kimball, Webster, 28 February, 1834; ibid., Samuel Slater and Sons, vol. 210, Hunt Brothers to Samuel Slater and Sons, New York, 22 August, 1836; ibid., vol. 212, Thomas Remington Samuel Slater and Sons, 7 May, 1836.
44. Ibid., Samuel Slater and Sons, vol. 210, Underhill and Company to Samuel Slater and Sons, New York, 17 March, 1846.

45. Ibid., Samuel Salter and Sons, vol. 117, Samuel Slater and Sons to R. & D. M. Stebbins, Webster, 28 February, 1845. It appears that Slater might have tried this scheme earlier in 1840 as well. See Slater MSS, Union Mills, vol. 114, Samuel Slater and Sons to Jacob Price Company, Webster, 24 November, 1840.

46. Ibid., Samuel Slater and Sons, vol. 117, Samuel Slater and Sons to G. Blackburn & Co., Webster, 13 February, 1845.

47. Ibid., Samuel Slater and Sons, vol. 190, Caufield to Storrs, New York, 26 October, 1849.

48. Ibid., vol. 198, Mills and Co., to Samuel Slater and Sons, Chicago, 21 August, 1850; ibid., H. Low to Samuel Slater and Sons, Paterson, 9 February, 1852.

49. Ibid., Samuel Slater and Sons, vol. 205, Joseph Rogers to Samuel Slater Apalachicola, 8 December, 1834; ibid., Macon, 21 November, 1838.

50. R. G. Dun & Co., MSS, Rhode Island vol. 9, January 1856; bidid., Massachusetts, vol. 97, 1 April, 1876.

51. Slater MSS, Estate of H. N. Slater, vol. 35, Commonwealth of Massachusetts Probate Court, Worcester, 31 January, 1900; ibid., Will, Horatio N. Slater Jr., July, 1891.

52. David J. Jeremy, *Transatlantic Industrial Revolution: The Diffusion of Textile Technologies between Britain and America, 1790–1830s* (Cambridge, 1981), pp. 180–203; see also Ware, *Early New England Textile Manufacture*, p. 63, Nathan Appleton, *Introduction of the Power Loom and Origin of Lowell* (Lowell, 1858), pp. 13–14 and Robert V. Spalding, "The Boston Mercantile Community and the Promotion of the Textile Industry in New England, 1813–1860" (Ph. D. dissertation, Yale University, 1963), pp. 11–13.

53. For an excellent discussion of the Lowell women, see Thomas Dublin, *Women at Work: The Transformation of Work and Community in Lowell, Massachusetts, 1826–1860* (New York, 1979).

54. Appleton, *Introduction of the Power Loom*, pp. 8, 24; see also, Paul F. McGouldrick, *New England Textiles in the Nineteenth Century* (Cambridge, 1968), p. 21.

55. Appleton, *Introduction of the Power Loom*, p. 10.

56. Ware, *Early New England Cotton Manufacture*, p. 70.

57. Spalding, "The Boston Mercantile Community and the Promotion of the Textile Industry in New England," pp. 22, 28.

58. Directors Records, Boston Manufacturing Company, 25 February, 1820 quoted in Spalding, "The Boston Mercantile Community and the Promotion of the Textile Industry in New England," p. 31.

59.  Spalding, a keen critic of the Boston Manufacturing Company
     wrote: "The sale of the shop appears to have been a carefully engi-
     neered transaction to drive up the price of Boston Manufacturing
     stock to enable the promoters to liquidate their holdings at a profit.
     James Jackson, Patrick Tracy Jackson and Israel Thorndike, the
     largest hareholders, all disposed of the major portion of their shares.
     After the transfer the value of Boston stock fell steadily, reaching a
     low of $600 during the 1829 recession. The company later devaluated
     its stock and its performance was undistinguished. See Spalding,
     "The Boston Mercantile Community and the Promotion of the
     Textile Industry in New England," p. 41.
60.  Ibid., pp. 31–36.
61.  Appleton, *Introduction of the Power Loom*, p. 28; George S. Gibb., *The
     Saco-Lowell Shops: Textile Machinery Building in New England, 1813–
     1949* (Cambridge, 1950), pp. 66–68.
62.  Schedule of Property of Francis Cabot Lowell II, Balance Sheet, 31
     December 1829. Francis Cabot Lowell II Papers, Massachusetts
     Historical Society, Boston, Massachusetts (Hereafter cited as F. C.
     Lowell II MSS).
63.  Lance E. Davis, "Stock Ownership in the Early New England Tex-
     tile Industry," *Business History Review*, 32 (1958), p. 208.
64.  F. C. Lowell II MSS, Permanent Investment of the Amoskeag
     Manufacturing Company, July 1, 1836.
65.  Amos Lawrence to William Lawrence, Boston, 29 April 1835. Amos
     Lawrence Papers, Massachusetts Historical Society, Boston Mas-
     sachusetts (Hereafter cited as Amos Lawrence MSS).
66.  *McLane Report*, 1: 340–341; Amos Lawrence MSS, John Aiken to A.
     Lawrence, Lowell, 13 February 1837 and ibid., 22 February 1837.
67.  McGouldrick, *New England Textiles in the Nineteenth Century*, pp. 121–
     38.
68.  Amos Lawrence MSS, Jackson Company, List of Stockholders, June
     23, 1838.
69.  Appleton, *Introduction of the Power Loom*, p. 29.
70.  For a discussion of the agents duties and responsibilities see Chandler,
     *Visible Hand*, pp. 68–72.
71.  F. C. Lowell II MSS, Edward Brooks to Francis Cabot Lowell,
     Boston, May 23, 1837.
72.  Appleton, *Introduction of the Power Loom*, p. 34.
73.  J. C. Ayer, *Some of the Usages and Abuses in the Management of Our*

*Manufacturing Corporations* (New York reprint, 1971 /1863/), pp. 21–22.

74. Ibid., p. 21.
75. Dublin, *Women at Work*, pp. 86–131.

# COMMENTS

Eisuke Daito
*University of Tokyo*

As is well known, two types of cotton manufacturers emerged during the industrial development of New England: one was the small-scale family business manufacturing yarn; the other was the large-scale, fully integrated corporation which mechanized the weaving and spinning processes. Many attempts have been made to examine the relative importance of their respective contributions to the industrial development of the United States. Professor Tucker confirms the common view that the "Lowell-type dominated the industry and set the pattern for American business development." Her focus of attention in this paper is on the relationship between ownership and control and closely related managerial problems. In the following, I want to ask some questions concerning Professor Tucker's presentation.

1. Sections I and II of her paper are devoted to a detailed case study of Slater's firm. Professor Tucker's most important conclusion here is that "to understand his system, his attitudes toward patriarchy should be understood." Since Slater thought that "divided authority among owners caused problems, and between owners and managers brought disaster," he made all important decisions himself. And his business decisions reflected his personal beliefs. In this sense, his firm may be properly termed a personal enterprise. Under such circumstances, it might be expected that when he died or retired, his system would be reorganized. And indeed, "when his sons gained control of the family business, they directed it on a new path." Professor Tucker analyzes the rationalization plan of the sons in detail and emphasizes that a substantial difference existed between the father and sons in terms of the ideals and values which guided their business decisions. It seems to me, however, that the changes in man-

agerial practices pointed out by Professor Tucker essentially show us the firm's process of growth from a sole proprietorship dominated by the founder to a family business with division of labor and cooperation among family members.

2.  Slater classified cotton mills in Rhode Island into three categories: those run by their owners, those run by skilled mechanics operating on borrowed capital, and those run by managers the owners hired to manage the mills for them. From Slater's point of view, the first category was the most promising one, and that's how he ran his firm. He thought that the third was the least likely to succeed. Since there were variations among Rhode Island mills, I would like to know to what extent conclusions derived from the analysis of Slater's firm apply to other cases.

3.  Professor Tucker writes as follows: "Although Lowell and his associates adopted the corporate form of ownership and divided ownership from management, in practical terms the firm continued to be managed like a traditional merchant firm." The number of initial subscribers was small and most of them actively participated in management. Judging from these facts, this is an accurate description of the situation in the Boston Manufacturing Company. But the Act of Incorporation of Massachusetts at the time did not confer limited liability, and one wonders, therefore, why the subscribers wanted to have a charter of incorporation instead of entering into a partnership contract.

4.  Lastly, I would like to ask Professor Tucker for comments concerning two points not covered in her paper. One is the role of family firms in the American business system in the last quarter of the 19th century and early years of the 20th century, when many big businesses emerged. The other concerns the Lowell-type mills. As Professor Tucker points out, they set the pattern for American business development, but they were not able to grow into true managerial enterprises in the 20th century. I want to ask why they could not.

# SUMMARY OF CONCLUDING DISCUSSION

Shigeaki Yasuoka

## I.

The organizing committee and several interested participants met on the evening of January 7, 1983, to consider the course of the concluding discussion planned for the following day. As an outcome of that meeting the following two items were agreed upon:

1. The *raison d'être* of family businesses should first be discussed.
2. A comparison of several distinguishing features of the ownership and management of family business should be undertaken. Several suggestions were made as to what these should be.

The following is a summary of the comments I made at the start of the concluding discussion.

"We learned from our experience last year that in the space of three hours it is possible to discuss only a few topics of concern. Therefore I would like to ask you to agree to limit discussion to just one or two points. To begin with I shall present a broad overview of what we have discussed during the last three days. Then I shall invite you to exchange views on the relative merits and demerits of family businesses. Finally I would like each of the participants to list the distinguishing features of family businesses in his country.

"At the Budapest Conference last year Professor Hannah, organizer of the family business section, while emphasizing that in regard to research in the history of management simple dichotomies are best avoided, pointed out that they may prove useful in certain contexts. Entering on the blackboard in one or two words the distinguishing features of family businesses in a certain country may

actually be more primitive than using simple dichotomies. I also
had some misgivings about this, but since it has become part of the
tradition of the Fuji Conference to summarize the discussion in this
manner, as a historian I feel bound to respect that tradition. I would
like to request the cooperation of participants in this regard.

"Next I will summarize the problems we have discussed. First,
there is the definition of family business. I shall adopt Professor
Miyamoto's definition, which is a comparatively flexible one. The
following types of firms are categorized as family businesses: 1)
firms in which the majority of capital is held by a single family or a
few families, but which is managed by non-family members; and
2) firms in which the share of capital held by a particular family
is minor, but which are controlled and managed by that family.
More generally, let us define family businesses as those which are
controlled, managed and/or majority-owned by a particular family.
(Here we must acknowledge the fact that as time progresses the
"majority" in majority ownership tends to diminish.)

"Secondly, from a historical point of view the formation of a family
business is in some way or other the outcome of blood ties. In particular, while an enterprise is still relatively small this is generally
the case. With the popularization of the company system and the
need to enter into contracts with others, it no longer remains necessary to depend on blood ties in the business world. As scale and
required capital increase, so too does the required level of technology, while generally the part played by the family begins to
decrease. As the scale of a family business expands, the familial
character of the business also diminishes.

"In very highly developed countries, such as the United Kingdom,
France, West Germany and the United States, by the end of the
1920s this had become the case. Japan also reached this stage in the
1930s. However, Professors Payne and Lévy-Leboyer both pointed
out that in all these countries there are also a multitude of middle-
sized family businesses. In the retailing and service industries the
number of family businesses is large, in all probability just because
the capital requirements are not great and the level of technology is
quite low. On the other hand, if one looks at the spinning industry
for example, in countries making continual progress, such as the

United Kingdom, family businesses are numerous, while in countries which from the outset utilized a high level of technology, such as Japan, public companies are the rule since initially a great deal of capital was required. Here it is important to recognize differences in the roles and situations of family businesses varying according to the conditions under which a country entered into industrialization. Between developed and developing countries these differences are particularly striking.

"As I have argued above, while in developed countries large family businesses have tended to disappear, in developing countries they continue to be common and to play an important part in the national economy. This is clear from the reports given by Messrs. Ito and Hattori. It was also true in prewar Japan. *Sekai no Zaibatsu Keiei* [The Management of Zaibatsu Worldwide] edited by Shin-ichi Yonekawa takes up the cases of zaibatsu in India, South Korea, the Philippines, Brazil and Argentina. The case of Thailand is taken up in *Hatten-tojōkoku no Zaibatsu* [Zaibatsu in Developing Countries] edited by Shoji Ito and published by the Institute of Developing Economies (1983). Professor Keiichiro Nakagawa has pointed out that when an underdeveloped country develops very rapidly, large family businesses with diversified management inevitably emerge (*Hikaku Keieishi Josetsu* [Comparative Studies in Business History], University of Tokyo Press, 1981). In such countries the continued existence of large family businesses (or zaibatsu) continues to be a very real problem. These companies, while being involved to a certain extent in abuses of power, help to encourage industrialization. During the period of Japan's industrialization, from the end of the nineteenth to the beginning of the twentieth century, many zaibatsu or large family businesses with diversified management emerged. (In contrast, large family businesses in developed countries by and large had been restricted to a single type of industry.)

"The somewhat paradoxical fact that the industrialization of Japan was the result of exclusive family investment has been a stimulus to research in the history of zaibatsu. It has also been a spur to attempts to understand zaibatsu from the point of view of ownership and management. Research into family businesses restricted to zaibatsu alone is inadequate. In future, research in Japan into the history of the management of family businesses must widen its field of interest. The papers presented by Professors Miyamoto and Asajima have made a start in that direction.

"With the above considerations as background, this conference took up the topic of international comparisons of family businesses. Consequently the focus of interest is different from that of the Budapest Conference.

"The reason I have emphasized the ownership of large family businesses is that the attitude of Japanese owners with regard to capital and management is distinctively different from that in Western society. To Western scholars my thesis may appear strange. However, this will not be so in the case of scholars from developing countries. I believe that this conference has advanced mutual understanding of research being conducted into the history of management of large family businesses in several countries."

## II.

After presenting the above précis, I called for a list of the virtues of family businesses. The following points of merit were suggested: (1) potentiality for simplified (or quick) decision-making; (2) fundraising, organ banks; (3) dividend policy, accumulation of capital; (4) employment system, employer-employee relations; (5) capacity for innovation.

## 1.

Although there are examples of public companies with strong leadership able to reach quick decisions, in general simplified decision-making depends on the existence of a small number of owners with identical interests. Even within a family decisions can be delayed when members fail to reach agreement (Payne). The holding company of the Mitsui zaibatsu was delayed in going public because the owning family and the executives were unable to reach agreement. However, it is generally said that family businesses are quicker at making decisions than businesses circumscribed by the opinions of many shareholders.

**2.**

As far as fund-raising goes, the owner of a family business, being unrestrained by the views of other investors, can determine the apportionment of profit-sharing and reinvestment. There are occasions when a family business can reinvest more positively and find funds with less difficulty than the typical public company. Zaibatsu-affiliated banks in Japan, for example, had pretty much the attributes of organ banks, and were major sources of funds for the zaibatsu companies, and during the Meiji Period there were many other organ banks as well, not affiliated with particular zaibatsu. One example of an affiliate bank was discussed in Professor Asajima's paper. Professor Lévy-Leboyer contended that organ banks are distinctively Japanese, while Messrs. Hattori and Ito described them as being universal in developing countries.

On the other hand, the owning family often seeks dividends as opposed to reinvestment. This is what happened in the case of the Mitsui family between 1877 and 1890.

**3.**

When determining dividend policy, family businesses are usually able to easily appraise the long-term growth in the business that can be expected from holding internal reserves (Lévy-Leboyer). Professor Miyamoto expressed the view that family businesses either hold large internal reserves or pay large devidends, but with corroborative evidence it may be necessary to take the scale of the business into consideration.

**4.**

The employment system was not discussed very much. It was generally thought that familistic labor relations were best, as for example in the cases of the management of Slater and Du Pont. It is arguable whether familism is the ideal or merely a means of personnel management, but we did not discuss this. It became clear that it was not possible to reach a simple conclusion as to the relative merits or demerits of family businesses in respect to the above items.

Manifestly, whether a certain item will function as a point of merit or demerit depends on the circumstances, so there is a need to collect and classify data for a number of representative cases.

**5.**

Although family businesses are very adaptable and adept at entering new fields they generally do not last more than three generations. As family businesses grow they provide vitality to the economy. Then they decay to make way for newer family businesses (Payne). Today, while large family businesses have lost their *raison d'être*, middle-sized manufacturing family enterprises survive many generations, and family businesses are a must in the service and transport industries (Lévy-Leboyer). During the first stages of industrialization in developing countries, family businesses took the initiative in many new fields and accelerated innovation. In South Korea and India the non-partition of business property is a crucial aspect of family businesses, while the retaining of salaried executives becomes necessary for the survival of large enterprises over the long term (Hattori).

## III. Framework of Comparison

The seven speakers were asked to fill in the table "Framework of Comparison" (see p. 314) for purposes of discussion. The main criteria of the framework were as follows: First, with respect to ownership: (1) What institutional form does ownership take? (2) What is the principle of ownership? (3) What legal form does it take? (4) How is inheritance bequeathed? Second, with respect to management: (5) Who is in possession of actual authority? (6) What is the scope of that authority? Does it include long-term decision-making as well? (7) What sort of training does the successor receive?

Obviously, the above criteria are not adequate for successfully comparing the characteristics of family businesses in different countries. However, I believe that they are a useful guide to some of the significant differences.

*Japan:* The capital of holding companies of large zaibatsu-like family businesses from the end of the nineteenth century until the

1920s was collectivistic. Moreover, as I have emphasized, it was essentially an indivisible asset or *Gesamteigentum*, even when legally it was the possession of an individual, especially in the Houses of Mitsui and Yasuda. Usually the holding company was either a partnership or a limited partnership which was later reorganized as a joint-stock company. Subsidiaries were joint-stock companies whose stock was entirely or in greater part the possession of the holding company. The holding company determined the management policy of each subsidiary.

Management, both day-to-day and long-term decision-making, was the responsibility of salaried executives. The owners voiced their views on matters of management policy, but in the final analysis they concurred with the opinions of the salaried executives. The owners received a college or university education and were attached to the holding company or some of its subsidiaries, but they did not function as prominent managers or directors. This was also true of many second- and third-generation owners of middle-sized family businesses.

*Korea:*   As Korea was under Japanese rule in the first half of the twentieth century, zaibatsu-like large family businesses did not appear until the 1950s. The founders of these companies are still in control, but the time is coming for them to make way for the next generation. Basically property is divided equally upon inheritance, and the right of ownership passes to inheriting individuals. However, attempts which have been made to set up foundations and give the shares to them may help to unite owning families. As a rule, enterprises are managed by their owners. In order to instill management abilities in their children, owner families often send them abroad for a university education. Since the tendency towards individualism is stronger in South Korea than in either Japan or India, it will be interesting to see what aspects of zaibatsu-affiliated industrial groups are preserved in the future.

*India:*   Circumstances in India during the period before Independence and since Independence differ markedly. The trend during the latter part of the nineteenth century towards large family businesses became active in the twentieth century. The system of ownership of property and inheritance was coparcenary and (after

the 1950s) individual. At first, the inheritance system based on sur-
vivorship existed; then the principle of succession was added to it.
Managing agencies and holding companies have been the means of
business management; since Independence holding companies have
become dominant. There has also been a shift away from partnerships towards private companies, and today the latter are common.
Moreover, since 1956 various legal restrictions have been placed on
the management agency system. In the views of Messrs. Ito and
Hattori, individual ownership of property is more common in South
Korea than in India. However, in both countries the owners are
involved in actual management, and the successor to the business
receives both on-the-job training and a school education. In both
cases the businesses involved are increasing in scale and their numbers are increasing, so it has become necessary to retain salaried
executives.

    *U.K.:*   In the U.K. individual ownership is the norm, and the
property of a business is inherited in accord with the will of the
founder. Usually several families provided the original capital, so
from 1870 until 1920 joint-stock private companies were the rule.
The investors themselves were devoted to management and actual
authority was assumed by the owner-manager (chairman of the
board of directors). The successor received on-the-job training
through the apprentice system and later on often went to university.

    *France:*   The system of individual ownership operates in France
just as in the U.K., except that since inheritance is usually divided
it is easier to break up capital ownership. The owner-manager ad-
ministers the business after on-the-job training and a college education. Joint-stock companies are the norm. Perhaps family trust ought
to have been added to the table for U.K. and France.

    *Germany:*   Individual ownership is the rule in West Germany but
partnerships or joint-stock companies are also established. The eldest son often inherits the business. Since sole proprietorships, partnerships or supervisory boards are adopted by the owners, perhaps these
ought to have been entered under "legal form" on the table. The
subsidiaries of holding companies are normally joint-stock companies.

    *U.S.A.:*   Individual ownership is the rule and businesses take the form of partnerships, trusts or holding companies, while institutions take the form of corporations. Perhaps it would have been better, for the purposes of comparison with other countries, to have entered partnership and corporation under "legal form" with trust and holding company under "institution." Actual authority, with respect to both short- and long-term policy making, resides with the kinship group or salaried managers. The successor receives both on-the-job training and a school education.

The Western scholars did not list "holding company" as one of the institutional forms of ownership for their respective countries; but, strictly speaking, perhaps they ought to have. In fact, a comparison of the distinguishing features of holding companies in different countries might well have been preferable. I had expected that "holding company" and "trust" would have been listed among the institutions in Western countries, and that in the case of West Germany *Fideikommisse* would have been listed because, as is well known, it was recognized for the estates of not only the aristocracy but also the bourgeoisie. Here one ought to recall that in 1943 under the Krupp Law the hereditament of the Krupp family estate was acknowledged.

In Japan, in order to adopt a modern legal system the hereditament of property was prohibited amongst the bourgeoisie (merchants and zaibatsu included). The hereditament of property amongst the aristocracy was provided for in the *Kazoku Seshu Zaisan-ho* (The Peerage Hereditament Property Law) of 1886, which was amended in 1914. Had we been able to discuss matters more fully, the various ways in which family businesses are preserved in Western countries might have become clearer, and this could have proved useful in comparing with the ways employed by family businesses in the various Asian countries. Perhaps on account of the inadequacy of my original proposals, our discussions did not extend to that level of sophistication.

Our conference might have been even more fruitful if it had been possible to debate the relations between owners and salaried managers in the light of a comparison of the way efforts were exerted by the owners to wield command.

TABLE 1   Framework of Comparison: Large Family Firms in Formative Period of Big Business

(1983. 1. 8)

| Period | Ownership | | | | Management | | |
|---|---|---|---|---|---|---|---|
| | Institution | Principle | Legal form | Inheritance system | Actual authority | Scope of authority | Successor's training system |
| Japan 1890–1940 | H.C. | (collective) indivisible | H.C. → Partnership Subsidiary → J.S. | Primogeniture | Salaried manager | L.T. Decision making | College, OJT |
| Korea 1950's–Present | Operating H.C. | Individual | J.S. | Divided | Owner manager | | College → Overseas, OJT |
| India 1850's–1950's | Managing Agent (H.C.) | Coparcenery (joint) | Partnership → P. Ltd. | By survivorship | Owner manager | | OJT |
| India 1950's–Present | Managing Agent → H.C. | Individual | P. Ltd. | By survivorship By succesion | Owner manager | | OJT/college |
| U.K. | | | | | | | |
| France | | | | | | | |
| Germany | | | | | | | |
| U.S.A. | | | | | | | |

Abbreviation:   H.C.=Holding Company, J.S.=Joint-Stock company, L.T.=Long-term, OJT=On the job training, Sb=Supervisory board, P.Ltd.=Private company, Ltd.

All the columns on the table were filled by seven speakers, some of whom were unwilling to publish it. Then only the columns of the countries reconfirmed by the project leader after the conference are entered here.

# INDEX

Ajinomoto, 37

Birla family: directors of, in group companies, 157, 158; group companies of, 149; management of, in group companies, 154; management training by, 161–162, 164
Bolton Committee Report, on British family firms, 174–175, 180, 194, 199 nn. 13, 14; *tables*, 174, 175, 194
Boston Manufacturing Company: and Francis Cabot Lowell, 288; shareholders of, 290
(*see also* Lowell, Francis Cabot)
Bridgestone, 37
Buddenbrook effect, 5, 189, 243

Chandler, Alfred D., *see* Chandler model
Chandler model, of family companies, 33–35, 184, 240, 242, 243
Channon, Derek F., research of, on British family companies, 177–178, 190
Citroën, André, 214, 228
Citroën, 213, 214, 229
Company system, *see* Family businesses, Japanese: and company system

Dae Woo, 128–130
Daems, Herman, *see* Chandler model
Doosan zaibatsu, 139–141
Du Pont, Eleuthère Irénée, 22–23
Du Pont de Nemours and Company, *see* Du Pont family: business of
Du Pont family: business of, 22–25; and capital ownership, 8

Echigoya, *see* Mitsui family: and Echigoya
Eighth International Economic History Conference (1982), family business

research presented at, 4–7
Erickson, Charlotte, research of, on British steel industry (1950s), 193–194

Family businesses: decision making of, 308–309; definition of, 39–40, 306; in developed countries, 306–307; in developing countries, 6–7, 307; dividend policy of, 309; employment system of, 309; fund raising of, 308–309; innovation within, 310
Family businesses, British, 171–197, 312; advantages of 196–197; age and ownership statistics of, 190–195; and Britain's economic development, 186–195, 196–197; and Company Acts, 171, 172, 191; distribution of, by degrees of diversification, 176–177; future of, 178–186; and joint-stock companies, 172–173, 192; ownership and control of, 4, 5, 172–174, 175, 178, 180–186, 205 n. 80; partnerships of, 172–173, 190; private companies of, 171, 173
Family businesses, French, 209–230, 312; in automobile industry, 213–214, 228–229; business turnover of, 212–214; dual management structure of, 217–222, 223–227; and employee benefits, 219–221; and employee training, 219–220; financial structure of, 214–215, 227–228; labor turnover within, 221–222; older group of, 210–212; preference shares of, 215–217; trusts of, 215
Family businesses, German: *see* German enterprises, large-scale
Family businesses, Indian, 147–165; characteristics of, 311–312; and family ownership, 151–154; and management, 158–162, 163; structure of, 149, 151

Family businesses, Japanese, 1–3, 7–20, 28–29, 39–88, 310–311; civil and commercial laws concerning (1868–1912), 10–11, 52, 53, 54, 56; and company system (1869–1939), 19, 54–66; distribution of (1931–1941), 71, 75, 77; industrial fields of (1931), 74; legal forms of (1931–1941), 75, 77; limited and unlimited partnerships of, 18, 55–57, 61, 63, 84; management of, 7–12, 36–37; compared with non-family businesses (1931–1941), 71, 74, 77–78 81, 84, 85, 88; ownership of, 7–12, 75, 77; survival rates of (1894–1930), 67–69; tax law definition of, 71 (*see also* Zaibatsu, Japanese; Joint-stock companies, Japanese)

Family businesses, Korean, 121–142; characteristics of, 311

Family businesses, U.S.: characteristics of 5, 312–313; 19th century, in textile industry, 271–295

Florence, P. Sargent, research of, on large British companies, 175, 182, 183

German enterprises, large-scale, 237–262, 315; cost-book companies (Bergrechtliche Gewerkschaft) of 248–249, 254–255, 258; general partnership of, 252–253, 257; growth strategies of, 240; limited liability companies of, 248, 253–254, 257–258; management of, 258–260, 261; personal partnerships of, 238, 243, 248–249, 252–253, 255, 258; rise of, 238–242, 250, 261; share partnerships of, 254, 255; sole proprietorships of, 238, 243, 248, 251–253, 255–256, 258–259, 261; transition from family-owner to managerial, 242–243, 248–251. (*see also* Joint-stock companies, German)

Habakkuk, Hrothger John, research of, on British family companies, 187, 188, 196

Hannah, Leslie, research of, on family businesses, 4, 5, 77, 173, 182

Hanjin, 127–128

Holding companies, Japanese: head offices (*honsha*) reorganized as (1920s), 64; increase of (1925–1935), 63–64; ownership of (c. 1935), 65; performance of (1925–1942), 84–85; tax advantages of (1920s), 64

Horai-sha, 46–48

Hyundai, 131

Iwasaki family, 16–17, 118–120 (*see also* Mitsubishi zaibatsu)

Joint-stock companies, German: management and legal forms of, 251–258, 261; rise of, 238, 239, 241, 255; transitional role of, 243, 247, 248–249, 256 (*see also* German enterprises, large-scale)

Joint-stock companies, Japanese: national banks (*kokuritsu ginkō*) of (1868–1912), 10, 49–50; and family companies (1868–1912), 10; growth of (1868–1912), 57, 59; industrial fields of (1603–1867, 1868–1893), 41, 50–52; performance of (1925–1942), 84; prototypes of (1868–1893), 45–46

Joint-stock companies, Scottish, survival rates of (1856–1865), 191–192

Kōnoike family: business of, 25–26, 241, 243, 256, 260; and inheritance

Krupp, Alfred F., 26, 252, 256

Krupp family, 25–26, 256

Kumho, 134–135

Lowell, Francis Cabot, 273, 288, 289, 290

Lowell, Massachusetts: factories in, 291–292; factory management in, 292–294, 295

Merchant houses, Japanese: *bantō* (head clerk) management of, 2, 9, 35–36, 44; bookkeeping of, 43; ownership-management relation in, 8–10, 40–45 (*see also* Mitsui family; Kōnoike family)

Merrimack Company: capital returns of, 292; control of, 290–291, 293

Michelin, Edouard, 214

Michelin: preference shares of, 216; stock